Another Reason

Another Reason

SCIENCE AND THE IMAGINATION
OF MODERN INDIA

GYAN PRAKASH

PRINCETON UNIVERSITY PRESS

PRINCETON, NEW JERSEY

Copyright © 1999 by Princeton University Press
Published by Princeton University Press, 41 William Street,
Princeton, New Jersey 08540
In the United Kingdom: Princeton University Press,
Chichester, West Sussex

Library of Congress Cataloging-in-Publication Data

Prakash, Gyan, 1952–
Another reason : science and the imagination of
modern India / Gyan Prakash.
p.   cm.
ISBN 0-691-00452-8 (cloth : alk. paper)
ISBN 0-691-00453-6 (pbk : alk. paper)
1. India—Politics and government—1765–1947. 2. India—
Civilization—1765–1947. 3. Science—India—History. I. Title.
DS463.P67 1999
954—dc21   99-17185

This book has been composed in Janson

The paper used in this publication meets
the minimum requirements of
ANSI/NISO Z39.48-1992 (R 1997)
(*Permanence of Paper*)

http://pup.princeton.edu

Printed in the United States of America

1   3   5   7   9   10   8   6   4   2
1   3   5   7   9   10   8   6   4   2
(Pbk.)

FOR ARUNA, AMIT, AND KUNAL

Contents

Acknowledgments

ONE OF THE PLEASURES in writing this book has been the opportunity to learn from several fields of specialized knowledge. I could not have accomplished this without the help and wisdom of a large number of friends and colleagues, and the generous assistance of many institutions. From the very beginning of this project, I have had the benefit of Homi Bhabha's friendship and intellect; his comments, made always with great affection and with a sense of deep engagement, pushed me to look beyond the usual and the predictable. I cannot say enough about how much I value Nick Dirks' friendship; he read and commented on innumerable drafts—mailed, faxed, and e-mailed without much notice—cheerfully and promptly, and gave constructive suggestions when most needed. My colleagues in Subaltern Studies—Shahid Amin, Dipesh Chakrabarty, Partha Chatterjee, David Hardiman, Gyan Pandey, Shail Mayaram, M. S. S. Pandian, Gayatri Chakravorty Spivak, and Susie Tharu—have supported my work in a number of ways. I am especially grateful to Partha, without whose own pathbreaking work on nationalism I could not have conceived mine, and who has helped me to think through complex conceptual matters in more ways than one can imagine. I am also thankful to Susie, who went through the entire manuscript and gave detailed comments.

I feel deeply honored and extraordinarily lucky to have received support from two individuals, Ranajit Guha and Edward Said, whose pioneering writings opened the field of knowledge in which my own work is located. Ranajit Guha's characteristically brilliant reading of the manuscript and Edward Said's words of enthusiasm for my work gave me confidence by reminding me how rare it is to have one's work enriched and affirmed by those whose lives and writings one deeply admires.

During this project's early stages, it was especially useful to meet with and discuss my ideas in Delhi with Ashis Nandy and Shiv Viswanathan, whose writings on the history and sociology of science in India have been of seminal influence. I found kindred souls in Dhruv Raina and Irfan Habib; I have learned a great deal from their researches in the history of science. Also in Delhi, I drew sustenance from the affectionate endorsement of my concerns by my old and dear friends—Anand Sahay, Kamal Chenoy, Anuradha Chenoy, and Harendra Singh. I am grateful also to Rajeev Bhargava and Tani Sandhu for providing endless hours of warmth and lively intellectual exchange over the last several years. In Calcutta, Siddharth Ghosh kindly shared his knowledge of the history of technology in Bengal. In London, I was fortunate to run into Ian Kerr, who generously shared his knowledge of the history of the railways in India. I was also able to learn from David Arnold's research on the history of medicine and Sudipta Kaviraj's reflections on Indian nationalism. I could always count on Mark Mazower to make my stay in London full of thoughtful discussions and fun; he also helped me to see how the book's arguments could be made more sharp, with less clutter. I am grateful to Claude Markovits and Jean-Claude Galey for taking interest in my project and for giving me the opportunity to present a series of seminars on my work in Paris.

I gave gained much from the generosity of my colleagues at Princeton. Working with Natalie Davis in the Shelby Cullom Davis Center on the theme of colonialism and its aftermath was crucial in getting my project going. Liz Lunbeck, Steve Kotkin, and Bob Tignor were always willing to read and comment on drafts; Bill Jordan's doors were always open for thinking things through aloud; and Dan Rodgers helped me to appreciate more fully the importance of keeping in mind the book's intended readers. My colleagues in the History of Science Program were an invaluable resource. I do not know what I would have done without Mike Mahoney's erudition, which was matched only by his magnanimity in sharing it with me. Gerry Geison guided me in the field of the history of medicine, and Angela Creager was kind enough to go over my chapter on that subject. Norton Wise's patient hearing of my half-formed ideas on the history of science and his enthusiasm for the project gave me confidence.

Among other friends and colleagues, I must mention Aamir
Mufti, with whom I spent many hours on the phone discussing
the nature, limitations, and possibilities of Indian modernity;
Pratap Mehta, who helped me to think afresh the relationship
between religion and nationalism; and Sheldon Pollock, who
guided me through Sanskrit materials. Thanks are due also to
Lila Abu-Lughod, Benedict Anderson, Itty Abraham, Kumkum
Chatterjee, Steve Cross, Val Daniel, Jane Dietrich, Madhavi
Kale, Ivan Karp, David Ludden, Timothy Mitchell, Joan Scott,
Romila Thapar, Jyotsna Uppal, Peter van der Veer, and Milind
Wakankar. At Princeton University Press, I was fortunate in having Mary Murrell as my editor and friend; she was unfailingly
helpful and her judgments on issues ranging from the content of
the book to its design were always on the mark. The criticism and
suggestions from the two readers for the Press were unusually
smart and useful. And I could not have asked for a more attentive
and accomplished copy editor than Carolyn Bond.

Several institutions gave me generous assistance. A grant from
the Joint Committee on South Asia of the Social Science Research Council and the American Council of Learned Societies in
1990 supported the initial archival research on this project in
London. A fellowship from the American Philosophical Society
helped me to follow up on this research in London in 1991. Several grants from the University Committee on Research in the
Humanities and Social Sciences, Princeton University from 1990
to 1992 permitted me to make short research trips to Britain.
Senior short-term fellowships from the American Institute of Indian Studies during 1991–92, 1992–93, and 1996–97 supported
archival and library research in India. A fellowship from the National Science Foundation in 1997–98 relieved me from my
teaching duties for that year, enabled the concluding archival
work in Britain and India, and supported the completion of the
book manuscript. The Philip and Beluah Rollins Bicentennial
Preceptorship from Princeton University supported my leave in
1992–93, and the History Department was generous in giving me
sabbaticals during the spring semester 1991, and the academic

years 1992–93 and 1997–98. I am grateful to all these institutions for giving me more support than I perhaps deserved.

I am grateful to the staff of the following institutions where the research for this book was carried out: India Office Library and Records, and School of Oriental and African Studies, London; Nagari Pracharini Sabha Library, Varanasi; National Archives of India and Nehru Memorial Museum and Library, Delhi; National Library and St. Xavier's College Library, Calcutta; Sinha Library, Patna; Theosophical Society Library, Madras; Vigyan Parishad, Allahabad; and Firestone Library, Princeton University.

The arguments of this book were first presented at various lectures and conferences at universities and academic institutions in the United States, Britain, France, Germany, the Netherlands, Australia, and India. For these opportunities to present and discuss my work, I am immensely grateful to my hosts and audiences.

Thanks are due also to the publishers of following journals for allowing me to include in this book revised versions of previously published articles: "Science 'Gone Native' in Colonial India," *Representations* 40 (Fall 1992), 153–78; and "The Modern Nation as the Return of the Archaic," *Critical Inquiry* 32:3 (Spring 1997), 536–56. I am also thankful to Oxford University Press for allowing me to include "Science between the Lines," in Shahid Amin and Dipesh Chakrabarty, ed., *Subaltern Studies IX* (Delhi: Oxford University Press, 1996), 59–82. Acknowledgements are due to the British Library for permission to reproduce photographs from its collection.

As before, my extended family in the United States, Britain, and India has nourished my work in ways that only those near and dear can. I owe a heartfelt sense of gratitude to my sister Seema Di, whose house in Delhi has been a home away from home for many years. Aruna not only read and commented on every draft of everything I wrote, except these Acknowledgments, but, more importantly, she has shared living through the anxieties of thinking and writing. Working on this project meant prolonged periods of separation from her and from my children, Amit and Kunal, all of whom gave me more understanding and affection than I deserve. This book can never substitute for the time I was away from them, and I dedicate it to them as an acknowledgement of my awareness of the time lost.

Princeton, 1998

Another Reason

CHAPTER ONE

The Sign of Science

Life is like a stream. One bank is the Vedas and the other
bank is the contemporary world, which includes science and
technology. If both banks are not firm, the water will scatter.
If both banks are firm, the river will run its course.[1]

T HE EMERGENCE and existence of India is inseparable from the
authority of science and its functioning as the name for freedom
and enlightenment, power and progress. Standing as a metaphor
for the triumph of universal reason over enchanting myths, science appears pivotal in the imagination and institution of India, a
defining part of its history as a British colony and its emergence
as an independent nation. To speak of India is to call attention to
the structures in which the lives of its people are enmeshed—
railroads, steel plants, mining, irrigation, hydroelectric projects,
chemical and petroleum factories, public health organizations
and regulations, the bureaucracy and its developmentalist routines, educational and technical institutions, political parties, media and telecommunications, and now, the bomb. Together they
constitute a grid, a coherent strategy of power and identity underpinned by an ideology of modernity that is legitimated in the last
instance by science.

The beginnings of science's cultural authority in India lie in
the "civilizing mission" introduced by the British in the early
nineteenth century. It was then that colonial rule began to manifest a distinct shift from its late-eighteenth-century modality. As
the East India Company consolidated its territorial control, it
slowly shed its character as a body of traders whose eyes were on
quick and ill-gotten profits, and settled down to fashion a despotism aimed at developing and exploiting the territory's resources
efficiently and systematically. Signaling the new language of
knowledge and rule, the Company turned away from Orientalist

3

classicism and set about establishing a system of Western education designed to train Indians to serve as subordinate functionar-
ies in the colonial bureaucracy. The administration became regularized and extended its reach farther down into the colonized
society in its effort to generate new forms of knowledge about the
territory and the population. As the British produced detailed and
encyclopedic histories, surveys, studies, and censuses, and classified the conquered land and people, they furnished a body of
empirical knowledge with which they could represent and rule
India as a distinct and unified space. Constituting India through
empirical sciences went hand in hand with the establishment of a
grid of modern infrastructures and economic linkages that drew
the unified territory into the global capitalist economy.

After the suppression of the 1857 Mutiny, the pace of change
quickened and became more extensive. The lesson that the British drew from the Mutiny was that, if anything, colonial despotism had to tighten, not loosen, its noose; Indians were not to be
appeased but rather should be ruled with an iron hand and provided with good government. The replacement of Company government with Crown rule strengthened the impulse to develop
India into a secure and modern colony. Military engineers built
walls along rivers to tame their force and channel the water to
irrigate lands; the grid of railways and telegraphs expanded rapidly, making the vast space of India manageable and open to capital; medical doctors and scientists followed the railroads out into
the territory in an effort to isolate diseases, control epidemics,
and nurture bodies into healthy productivity. As the "long nineteenth century" wore on, bit by bit a new structure of governance
crystallized, and India emerged as a space assembled by modern
institutions, infrastructures, knowledges, and practices.

Underlying the configuration of India according to the new
structure of rule and knowledge was the authority and application
of science as universal reason.[2] The British saw empirical sciences
as universal knowledge, free from prejudice and passion and
charged with the mission to disenchant the world of the "superstitious" natives, dissolving and secularizing their religious world

views and rationalizing their society. "The conquest of the earth," Joseph Conrad wrote, "not a pretty thing when you look into it too much," was redeemed by "an idea at the back of it; not a sentimental pretence but an idea; and unselfish belief in the idea—something you can set up, and bow down before, and offer a sacrifice to."[3] The idea was to enlighten the natives, to extinguish their mythical thought with the power of reason. But the disenchantment of the world, as Theodor Adorno and Max Horkheimer observed, also served as a tool for setting up the mastery of those who possessed an instrumentalist knowledge of nature over those who did not. "What men want to learn from nature," they wrote, "is how to use it in order wholly to dominate it and other men."[4] Rudyard Kipling's short story "The Bridge-Builders" registers the intimate connection between control over nature and the exercise of domination over people who see nature in mythical terms. A paean to the heroic spirit of British engineers who successfully construct a railway bridge over the Ganges River against all odds, Kipling depicts the bridge as representing not only the domestication of nature but also the containment of the civilizational energy and fury of the river goddess. She becomes "Mother Gunga—in irons," symbolizing the triumph of British engineers over Indians and their culture.[5] For Kipling, this was a triumph not of gross imperial ambition but of the lofty will to free the natives from their own civilizational shackles.

To dominate in order to liberate was a profoundly contradictory enterprise. Conrad's acute observation—the necessity of "the conquest of earth" in pursuit of an "unselfish belief" in the idea of enlightening the natives—neatly captures how colonialism was caught up in an unavoidable split. European ideologues of colonialism were conscious of the paradox of practicing despotism in order to project the ideals of freedom, but there was nothing they could do to close the deep internal rift in their discourses. Compelled to use universal reason as a particular means of rule, the British positioned modernity in colonial India as an uncanny double, not a copy, of the European original—it was almost the same, but not quite. In the colonial context the

5

universal claims of science always had to be represented, imposed, and translated into other terms. This was not because Western culture was difficult to reproduce, but because it was dislocated by its functioning as a form of alien power and thus was forced to adopt other guises and languages. Science had to be tropicalized, brought down to the level of the natives and even forced upon them, so the argument went, if Britain was to do its work in India. The British were all too aware that the subcontinent was no tabula rasa, but rather was an ensemble of discrepant traditions and religions, different territories, languages, and loyalties, and numerous authoritative texts and social memories. It also contained live traditions of diverse and sophisticated philosophies and discourses of knowledge, the claims of which could not be put aside easily by Western science. To appropriate and forge all these into modern India entailed more than inventing a common name, more than replaying on the Indian stage the European drama of modernity. It meant the dislocation of that modernity to another context and its translation into the idioms of those it sought to transform and appropriate.

Translation in the colonial context meant trafficking between the alien and the indigenous, forcing negotiations between modernity and tradition, and rearranging power relations between the colonizer and the colonized. This is precisely what the Western-educated indigenous elite attempted as they sought to make their own what was associated with colonial rulers. Enchanted by science, they saw reason as a syntax of reform, a map for the rearrangement of culture, a vision for producing Indians as a people with scientific traditions of their own. The elite produced biting critiques of "irrational" religious and social practices, and acted with an acute sense of the novelty of their mission. Though rational criticism had been practiced in India long before the British set foot there, the Western-educated intelligentsia felt impelled to reinterpret classical texts and cast them in the language of the Western discourse. This produced the identification of a body of indigenous scientific traditions consistent with Western science. Nationalism arose by laying its claim on revived traditions, by appropriating classical texts and traditions of science as the heritage of the nation. To be a nation was to be endowed with science, which had become the touchstone of rationality. The representation of a people meant claiming that the nation possessed a body of universal thought for the rational organization of society. The idea of India as a nation, then, meant not a negation of the colonial configuration of the territory and its people but their reinscription under the authority of science. With great ideological imagination and dexterity the nationalists argued that Indian modernity must be irreducibly different, that the modern configuration of its territory must reflect India's unique and universal scientific and technological heritage. Thus, the Indian nation-state that came into being in 1947 was deeply connected to science's work as a metaphor, to its functioning beyond the boundaries of the laboratory as a grammar of modern power.

What follows tells this story of science's history as a sign of Indian modernity. The history of different scientific disciplines, while relevant, is not my central concern; the main object of my interest is science's cultural authority as the legitimating sign of rationality and progress. As such science means not only what scientists did but also what science stood for, the dazzling range of meanings and functions it represented. The rich and pervasive influence of science was rooted in its ambiguity as a sign—its ability to spill beyond its definition as a body of methods, practices, and experimental knowledge produced in the laboratory and confined only to the understanding of nature. As a multivalent sign, science traversed a vast arena, encompassing fields from literature to religion, economy to philosophy, and categories from elite to popular. Such divisions overlook and conceal how politics and religion, science and the state run into each other, how it is precisely through spillovers and transgressions that modernity penetrates the fabric of social life. Breaching conventions that separate and organize discrepant fields and disciplines—religion, anthropology, politics, science—I track a discourse of science that traverses little-known pamphlets and canonical writings, and figures minor and monumental. This approach casts into relief the

immense power of science, at once pervasive and hidden, instantiated in knowledges and identities but also constituted by them.

The chapters that follow are united by the concern to identify
science's functioning as culture and power. In this respect, what
appears central is science's association with the state—a relationship that both enabled the very formation of modern civil society
in India and overshadowed its functioning as an arena of public
discourse. The first part of the book turns to this historical feature of science's career in British India, describing how its close
relationship with the state conditioned its authority in the realm
of civil society. The British, deeply aware of their limited command over the territory and the people, set up modern institutions to develop a scientific knowledge of India and enlist Indians
in the ideology and practice of "improvement." The establishment of museums and exhibitions in the nineteenth century was
part of this effort. These institutions staged science as an aspect of
colonial power, and sought from Indians the recognition of
Western knowledge's authority. This required the displacement
of the colonizer/colonized binary and the undoing of the science/
magic opposition. Indians had to be conceded the capacity for
understanding if they were to be made into modern subjects, and
science had to be performed as magic if it was to establish its
authority. The irruption of this dislocation unleashed another,
uncertain dynamic of translation, making possible both the indigenization of science and the formation of the Western-educated
elite at the borderlines between cultures. Educated in Western-
style institutions and employed in colonial administration and
modern professions, this elite stood on the interstices of Western
science and Indian traditions, embodying and undertaking the
reformulation of culture in their reach for hegemony.

A central object of the elite's project of reformulating culture
was religion. For Hindu intellectuals, this quickly became a
search for an archaic science, for it was in the representation of a
scientific past that they sought to locate a Hindu universality in
Hinduism. Making a claim not unlike Hegel's claim for Germany, they asserted that the particular history of scientific Hin-

duism contained the source of universal history. This search for a universality was not reducible to nationalism, for it occurred under religious and philosophical impulses that were not always motivated by the idea of the nation. But the nation came to over-shadow the horizon of Hindu universality because it provided the dominant basis for a modern identity. As practicing scientists and Hindu religious reformers read ancient texts and interpreted tra-ditions to identify an original "Hindu science" upon which an Indian universality could stand, this also became the symbol for the modern nation. One gets an acute sense of nationalism's reach as one sees how it appropriated the past, the popular and elite traditions, and a range of intellectual contexts to bring them under the authority of the nation. Its lasting consequence was the identification of Hinduism as the cultural texture of the nation, as a national religion. This was not because of fundamentalist and sectarian urges, but rather was a product of the historical impera-tive that positioned the nation as the dominant framework for pressing India's claim to cultural universality. To assert that Hindu culture was equal to Western culture was to also claim that it was the heritage of all Indians. If this produced an authoritarian representation, the authority of the majoritarian image of the na-tion was composed on its margins. As in the case of colonialism, the nationalist project was unable to escape from the implications of the fact that the nation was a configuration of power and that the definition of India as an embodiment of Hindu science re-quired its signification in other signs. To signify the nation in the austerity of Vedic science, for example, meant policing the boundaries separating it from the seduction of the poetry and myths of the Puranas. But to use the latter's sensual playfulness to represent the cold rationality of the nation's essence was to also permit it to haunt the modern life of the Vedas.

The nationalist predicament dramatizes the functioning of the language of reason as an idiom of power in colonial India. Failing to achieve hegemony in civil society because of its elitism, this idiom could reach its fullest expression only in the state. At the level of the state, which, according to Ranajit Guha, was "an *absolute externality*" in colonial India, science was not encumbered with the task of constructing hegemony.[6] Thus, it could be used as an aspect of what Michel Foucault calls "governmentality." Foucault writes: "To govern a state will therefore mean to apply economy, to set up economy at the level of the entire state, which means exercising towards its inhabitants, and the wealth and behavior of all, a form of surveillance and control as attentive as that of the head of the family over his household and his goods."[7] Governmentality means a "pastoral form of power," and its chief concern is the population, which becomes available as a category understood through census classifications, famine mortality, epidemiological surveys and regulations, and statistics. The purpose of this form of power, as Foucault says, is to apply economy and maintain a healthy and productive population. The state is governmentalized.

The second part of the book is concerned with the governmentalization of the state, with the developmentalist impulse under which India was to be nurtured and exploited as a productive colony. Colonial governmentality operated as the knowledge and discipline of the other; it was positioned as a body of practices to be applied upon an alien territory and population. But here too, colonial conditions compelled the art of governance to operate as a mode of translation. This becomes evident in the realm of modern medicine, which was introduced in response to the outbreak of epidemics. The establishment of new forms and institutions of medical scrutiny, population statistics, sanitation campaigns, and vaccination drives brought a medicalized body into view. These institutions and tactics, however, were predicated on the recognition that the body, in this case, was irreducibly Indian. If this was so, why should Western therapeutics and the colonial state govern its conduct? Thus, medicalized bodies became objects of struggle as the nationalists mounted a campaign to seize the body from its colonial disciplines. Not only did the Indian nationalists strive to identify a national medicine, they (most notably Gandhi) also elaborated a highly regulated and gendered sexual discipline for the body. Participating in the field opened by colonial governmentality, the nationalists intervened to deflect governance in a different direction and mount a challenge to British power.

A similar strategy of nationalist inscription was also set to work in the realm of the relationship between technics and the state, that is in the constitution of the state itself as a configuration of technical routines, knowledges, practices, and instruments. The colonial effort to configure India and Indians as resources forged this relationship, manifested in the state's central role in establishing a network of railroads, irrigation, mining, industries, and scientific and technical agencies of administration. India as a territory, that is, as a geographical entity, had become organized as a space constituted by technics. As the nationalists reinscribed this technological order as the space of the nation, they also staked their claim on the state, which had become an embodiment of technics. The nationalists argued that colonial rule had impoverished this space, throttled its industries, and exploited its resources for Britain's benefit. The demand for the national development of the territory quickly and imperceptibly became the demand for state power, which was seen as nothing but an extension of the space constituted by technics. This analysis casts a different light on nationalist politics, illuminating how its fight to institute a nation-state was an attempt to seize the functions of governmentality from British rule, to bring the people within the hegemony of the nation. Thus, for all their differences over the value of modern science and technology, Mahatma Gandhi and Jawaharlal Nehru collaborated in the struggle for a nation-state, sharing the belief that the territory configured by modern technics was a national space that demanded an independent political order of its own. It was this struggle to seize control of the governmental power over the people that fueled pathological energies and carved up British India into the nation-states of India and Pakistan.

Perhaps nothing is more distinctive about Indian modernity than the intense, highly charged relationship it embodies between science and politics. Of course, modern science has always and everywhere existed cheek by jowl with power. In fact, as

11

Bruno Latour argues forcefully, Western modernity's character-istic separation of epistemology and social order serves only to license their hybridization; the distinction made between nature and society permits the translation of one into the other—the social construction of nature and the ordering of society as na-ture.[8] From this point of view, the intermixture of science and politics in India is not unusual. Yet their combination in India shows something extraordinarily urgent, an intimacy that is as intense as it is fragile. Introduced as a code of alien power and domesticated as an element of elite nationalism, science has al-ways been asked to accomplish a great deal—to authorize an enormous leap into modernity, and anchor the entire edifice of modern culture, identity, politics, and economy. The very exis-tence of India appears crucially dependent upon the stability of the apparatuses and practices it designates as rational—law, civil society, the nation-state, democratic institutions, capitalist econ-omy, modern medicine, and scientific and technological projects to control and exploit human and nonhuman resources. The in-telligibility of the dominant political discourses rests upon this architecture of Indian modernity; anything outside and beyond it is an unthinkable regression into the abyss of backwardness, anar-chy, and loss of identity.

Nowhere else was so much attempted with so little. Consider, as a contrasting example, the formation of Western modernity, for which the benefit of empire was crucial; its identity and au-thority were forged on the stage of colonial and imperial domina-tion. This is a hard lesson to learn for Western intellectuals. Even as trenchant a critic of positivist science as Latour fails to take into account empire's constitutive role in the formation of the West and assumes that it had forged its characteristic commit-ment to modernity *before* overseas domination. Thus, he suggests that imperialism's great divide between "us" and "them" was the exportation of the division between humans and nonhumans that Europe instituted within its borders.[9] But is it possible to deny the *simultaneity* of the formation of Western scientific disciplines and modern imperialism? One thinks, for example, of connections between the West's global expansion and the formation of the disciplines of ethnology, political economy, botany, medicine, geology, and meteorology. The Portuguese reflected on the constellations as they navigated around the globe; the Spaniards developed concepts of comparative ethnology as they encountered and conquered the peoples of the New World; the British classified plants and isolated germs as they established and ruled over their imperial possessions. The disciplines did not simply depend upon Europe's prior self-generated cultural and political resources; rather, their development in the course of trade, exploration, conquest, and domination instantiated Western modernity. As Edward Said remarks, empire constituted the social and physical space of Europe's cultural imagination; "the geographical notation, the theoretical mapping and charting of territory," he points out, "underlies Western fiction, historical writing, and philosophical discourses of the time."[10] The territories "out there" provided the foundation for the comfort and poise of "home"; the concept of "savage natives" helped European elites discipline their own working classes and peasants into modern subjects.

The colonies, on the other hand, were underfunded and overextended laboratories of modernity. There, science's authority as a sign of modernity was instituted with a minimum of expense and maximum of ambition. Army barracks existed side by side with, and dwarfed, hospitals; vaccinations were carried out with the drive of military campaigns; railroads transported troops and carried commodities for colonial exports and imports; and rational routines of governance doubled as alien despotism. Such estrangements of the welfare of the population in acts of imperial government undermined the very civilized/savage opposition that sustained the European claim to rule, forcing it to rework its founding assumptions and re-situate the operation of knowledge and power. It is in this context that Indian modernity emerges as undeniably different. For what stands out in the Indian case is how modern power has historically sought to overcome the limits imposed by its association with alien dominance, how the territory forged by colonial technics became the space of the Indian nation.

India was born in violence. Not only was it brought into existence and christened under the shadow of the conqueror's sword, India acquired its identity by a violent separation from the subcontinent's traditions and histories, which were reordered and pressed into service as its past, as the prehistory of its modern self. Navigating between the bank of the Vedas and the bank of modern science and technology, but holding neither one nor the other fixed, India appears simultaneously as something altogether new and unmistakably old, at once undoubtedly modern and irreducibly Indian. Therein lies Indian modernity's pervasive presence and precarious existence.

PART ONE

SCIENCE AND THE
RELOCATION OF CULTURE

Staging Science

Despotism is a legitimate mode of government in dealing
with barbarians, provided the end be their improvement,
and the means justified by actually effecting that end.
John Stuart Mill[1]

RUDYARD KIPLING'S NOVEL *Kim* (1901) opens with young Kim
O'Hara "astride the gun Zam-Zammah, on her brick platform
opposite the old Ajaib-Gher—the Wonder House, as the natives
call the Lahore Museum."[2] The Zam-Zammah, an eighteenth-
century cannon, once deployed to great effect by the Afghan ruler
Ahmad Shah Durrani in his military campaigns, had lost its military use by this time, but not its symbolic value: "Who hold Zam-
Zammah, that 'fire-breathing dragon,' hold the Punjab; for the
great green-bronze piece is always first of the conqueror's loot."
As Kim sat atop the cannon, kicking an Indian boy off it, he did
so as a conqueror for, as Kipling writes, "the English held Punjab
and Kim was English." But how is Kim's identity established?
Kipling tells us that Kim's mother, whose racial identity remains
unmarked, had been a nursemaid in a colonel's family and had
died of cholera when Kim was three, leaving him in the care of his
father, Kimball O'Hara. A sergeant in the Irish regiment of the
British army in India, the father took to drinking, drifted into
friendship with a "half-caste woman" from whom he learned the
joys of smoking opium, and "died as poor whites do in India." It
was from this half-caste woman who raised him that Kim discovered that he was English, as she, confusedly remembering the
sergeant's prophecies in his "glorious opium hours," told Kim
that everything would come out all right for him: "there will
come for you a great Red Bull on a green field, and the Colonel
riding on his tall horse, yes, and—'dropping into English'—nine
hundred devils."

17

Such was the fabulous tale of Kim's origins and the indeterminate process by which an English identity came to determine him. Kipling at once avows and disavows these ambivalent and hybrid sources of identity and authority when he asserts: "Though he was burned black as any native; though he spoke the vernacular by preference, and his mother-tongue in a clipped uncertain sing-song; though he consorted on terms of perfect equality with small boys of the bazaar; Kim was white." Obvious and easy though it is to see how *Kim* asserts racial polarities, we should not lose sight of the shadowy background against which they come into view. Kim's whiteness, for example, does not stand separate from his blackness but is bleached from his "burned black" skin. So immersed is the formation of Kim's racial identity and authority in difference—whiteness formed on the borderlines of black and white, fact and fable, English and the vernacular—that liminality becomes the fertile ground for the production of a powerful colonizer/colonized hierarchy. If the colonial hierarchy draws force from the rearrangement of cultural difference into cultural opposition, it also opens itself up to the effects of its uncertain construction; the specter of ambivalence and loss provokes the assertion of racial mastery and haunts its existence.[3] White dominance does not diminish but acquires a different balance when its authority is forged from imbrication with the black. Kipling's avowal of racial polarity takes on a different meaning when he produces the white from the black; the relationship between black and white is reshuffled as he displaces their statuses as self-contained, originary identities.

It is telling that Kipling chose a museum as the opening setting for his tangled drama of imperial identity and power. By the end of the nineteenth century, the collection and display of artifacts and human specimens in museums and exhibitions had become the most visible modes of marking Western dominance of the world. Beginning with the Great Exhibition at the Crystal Palace in London in 1851, imperial nation-states in Europe and North America engaged in intense competition to flaunt their possessions, to inscribe their respective signatures on objects and humans across the globe.[4] They classified, named, mapped, and ordered non-Western peoples and things to realize their desires for domination. In this project, no less important than establishing standards of art, aesthetics, history, and identity was the staging of Western science as universal knowledge. This was all the more prominent within colonial territories, where museums and exhibitions functioned as instruments of the nineteenth-century "civilizing mission." These not only defined what constituted art, culture, and history, but also showcased scientific knowledge and instruments as technologies of governance and improvement. As Britain's largest and most important colonial possession, India felt the full force of such a project. Collecting, cataloging, classifying, and displaying objects, these institutions sought to establish the universality of their classificatory enterprise and to position science as a sign of modernity and a means of colonial rule.[5]

The identification of colonial power in the functioning of museums and exhibitions should cause no surprise; the staging of Western science in the interests of Western dominance, after all, is a recognizably familiar story. What escapes the attention of this often-told tale of Western power, however, is the distorted life of the dominant discourse. So pervasive and enduring is colonialism's triumphant self-description of its own career that we frequently fail to identify the subterfuges, paradoxes, distortions, and failures that punctuated its exercise of power. At issue here is the history of those practices that arose in the field of colonial power but also reordered its terms, that anchored and sustained British rule but also altered its conditions of existence. The failure to explore this history runs the risk of portraying colonial India as a place scorched by the power/knowledge axis, leaving nothing of its past except the remains of what either was appropriated (consumed and normalized, made appropriate) or stood resistant to the incendiary combine of modern science and colonialism. To fall prey to this view is to suggest that the exercise of colonial power produced only mastery, that British India's history is nothing but a record of submission (or opposition) to trajectories charted by this mastery.

My interest is to explore the history lodged in the discordant life of dominance, to outline the interstitial zone of images and practices that took shape as an effect of the contradictory exercise of British power. While I focus in this chapter on museums and exhibitions in British India during the late nineteenth and early twentieth centuries, the general object of my inquiry is the staging of science as a sign of colonial power/knowledge. My aim is to trace the enactment of other performances in such dramaturgy and identify colonial power's dislocations at the point of its deployment. John Stuart Mill neatly captured the founding logic of these dislocations when he proposed that despotism was a legitimate means of achieving the "improvement" of "barbarians." A deep rift fractured the exercise of colonial power. On the one hand, the British desired to teach the "natives" that Western science was universal and instruct them to apply the new order of universal knowledge to their objects and practices. On the other hand, the British were compelled to represent the universality of science in the particularity of the imperial mirror: the "civilizing mission" was the means of instituting science as a general form of knowledge. Such was the split between the subject of representation (universal science) and the process (colonial and particular) by which it was signified. With the claim for science's universality underwritten by this particular history, scientific knowledge and institutions emerged pursued by the stigma of their colonial birth. Science's functioning as a technology of colonial governance and as an ideology of improvement overshadowed its representation as a body of universal laws of nature. There is a parallel here with Kipling's dilemma. Just as colonial conditions obliged Kipling to produce white identity and authority in Kim's "burned black" skin, so they compelled the British rulers to hatch science's universality from its particular, colonial double.

To dwell in doubleness was to dislocate the polarities—scientific/unscientific, universal/particular, European/non-European, and colonizer/colonized—through which colonialism functioned. My aim is not only to trace such dislocations but also to identify the new space of power that comes into existence from the undoing of polarities. How did the contradictory functioning of British rule produce a new arena of colonial dominance and indigenous agency? What took shape under the shadow of colonialism's double life?

THE DISCOURSE OF COLONIAL SCIENCE: CLASSIFICATION AND FUNCTION

To the British, India was an ideal locus for science: it provided a rich diversity that could be mined for knowledge and, as a colony, offered the possibility for an unhindered pursuit of science.[6] By the late nineteenth century, this sense of an unbounded opportunity was driving the establishment and expansion of museums and exhibitions in different regions of India.[7] Equally important in the rise of these institutions was the conviction that India needed a new form of knowledge. The matter was stated plainly in 1874:

> Local officers must be able to recognize with precision the various grains and other products of their districts, to enable them to deal with agricultural statistics in an intelligent manner. At present it is almost ludicrous to observe . . . how often the same things are called by different names, and different things by same names.[8]

To know was to name, identify, and compare—this was the frame in which the question of understanding India entered the discourse of colonial science. Museums were valuable because they provided an order of things by naming, classifying, and displaying Indian artifacts.[9] In this respect, museological practice differed from the cabinets of curiosities of the Renaissance: unlike these cabinets, museums organized objects to make them speak a language and reveal an order. From this point of view, the Oriental Museum of the Asiatic Society, founded in Calcutta in 1814, which was little more than a warehouse of rare objects, was no longer adequate by the 1850s.[10] Persuaded by the Society's argument that the existing separation of collections into detached parts robbed them of their scientific value insofar as it did not make visible "that series of links which actually exists in Nature," the government had the collections reorganized into colonial India's largest and most important museum, the Indian Museum, which opened in 1878 to the public in Calcutta.[11] The foundation of the Madras Central Museum has a similar history. Originating in a storehouse of curious objects, it was established as a museum in 1851 and began to function systematically after 1885, when Edgar Thurston was appointed as its first full-time superintendent. Thurston remained in charge until 1910 and expanded the museum greatly. He also became a major colonial ethnologist who pursued his special interest in anthropometry rather unusually: he kept his calipers and other measuring instruments handy, using them on native visitors to the museum—sometimes paying them, sometimes not.[12] A number of other significant museums were established during the second half of the nineteenth century, making them ubiquitous in urban India by the end of the century.[13]

As museums both spread and expanded their collections, the stress on natural history, on classifying, and re-presenting the order of nature, persisted;[14] geological and natural history collections were the predominant concerns of the older and larger museums from their inception. Important in this respect was the colonial conception that India was close to nature: its inhabitants lived close to the soil, it was home to numerous "tribes and races," and the state of its knowledge was chaotic—"same things are called by different names, and different things by same names"—and required persistent classification.

If colonialism amplified the importance of classification in the organization of museums, the imperial connection was visible also in the significant role given to order and naming in provincial and local exhibitions throughout India during the same period. The link between classification and colonialism had also marked the organization of objects at the Great Exhibition at the Crystal Palace in London in 1851.[15] Local exhibitions in India originated in the 1840s as part of the preparations for this event, but acquired a momentum of their own in subsequent decades. As instruments for promoting commerce and advancing a scientific knowledge of economic resources, they brought artifacts into the colonial discourse as classified objects. The emergence of these artifacts as objects of discourse, however, entailed the authorization of colonial officials as experts responsible for collecting information from native informants.

> A *general list* of Sections was made in advance, and in every district visited, at a meeting of cultivators, called whether by the District Officer or an important zamindar [landlord]; a *special list* was prepared in accordance with the general list of agricultural articles of special value for that district. In some districts, as in Burdwan, Bankura and Murshidabad, *Kabirajes* [indigenous herbalists and healers] were also consulted. The list so made out was made over to the District officer or to the zamindar concerned, and things were collected by actual cultivators and others, and sent to the Exhibition.[16]

If one aim of colonial pedagogy was to instruct peasants by exhibiting their own products and knowledge organized and authorized by the science of classification, its other aim was to render manifest the principle of function so that it could be applied to improve production. Indeed, the organizers of the Allahabad Exhibition of 1910–11 stated that the exhibition's purpose was to instruct viewers in different methods of production and in the functioning and benefits of machines.[17] For example, on entering the Court of Engineering, one found water-lifts and irrigation pumps of Indian and European manufacture at work. To demonstrate the working and power of water-lifts, a series of small, measured fields was laid out, demonstrating the actual area of land irrigated. Across from this Court was a working dairy, exhibiting everything from cows to butter, including modern dairy machinery, the best breeds of Indian milch cattle, a dairy farm for commercial use, a modern village dairy, and an Indian dairy using indigenous implements. To the north was the Agricultural Court,

Fig. 1. "Kim's Gun": Cannon (the Zam-Zammah) outside the Lahore Museum, c. 1920s. Phot. 66/8(96). Reproduced by permission of the British Library.

where agricultural machinery from all over the world was displayed, the number of exhibits limited so as to emphasize objects in actual use. With the aim to instruct and educate, an official was placed in the Court to answer questions and put agriculturists in touch with demonstration staff and experts. The object of these arrangements was to advance popular education and commerce by demonstrating the "science of the concrete," in practical and self-evident terms.

Exhibitions did not exclude classification—the division of the space into distinct Courts meant that there was a classificatory order also at work—but they emphasized the principle of function.[18] Function as a category of knowledge grew rapidly in importance after exhibitions made their appearance in the mid nineteenth century. Agricultural exhibitions, in particular, became a regular feature of the rural landscape.[19] In Madras province, for example, agricultural exhibitions were held in every district in 1855[20] and reappeared annually for several subsequent years. Some of the agricultural exhibitions were initiated locally and

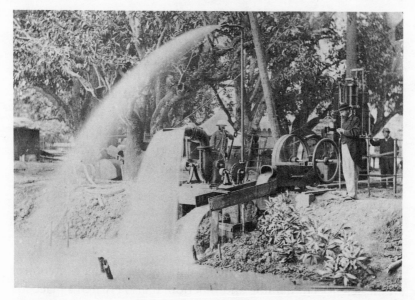

Fig. 2. "Exhibiting Science": Steam pump machinery in action at the Alipur Agricultural Exhibition, Calcutta, 1864. Phot. 1000 (4812). Reproduced by permission of the British Library.

grafted onto traditional fairs.[21] In addition to such local events, provincial and international spectacles were also staged, such as the Calcutta International Exhibition in 1883.[22] So important had these spectacles become by the end of the nineteenth century that even the Indian National Congress joined in, starting in 1901, by organizing an industrial exhibition to coincide with its annual meeting.

Organized with a great deal of pomp and show, exhibitions encapsulated the colonial staging of science as technology, as knowledge and techniques for improvement. Ordering and distributing objects to highlight function and use, they were successful in drawing a large number of visitors.[23] For example, the Nagpur Exhibition in 1865 reported 30,000 visitors over eight days; 50,000–60,000 visited the Fureedpur Exhibition in Bengal over eight days in 1873, and a million visitors went to see the 1883 Calcutta International Exhibition.[24] Museums, though sober and somber by comparison, were also successful in this respect. Between 1904 and 1914, the Indian Museum in Calcutta drew between 503,000 and 829,000 visitors annually.[25] The Madras Central Museum was equally successful, prompting Edgar Thurston to favorably compare the number of visitors to the Madras Museum to the number of visitors to the British Museum in London.[26] These numbers indicate the measure of success that colonial science had achieved in its pedagogical project. But what happened when Western science, embodied in native material, was staged before an overwhelmingly native audience?

THE LIMINAL MAN

As the colonial discourse assembled and staged India as an object of the sciences of naming and function, it also created a place for what it sought to appropriate; indigenous artifacts and "tribes and races" emerged in their native particularity as objects of scientific discourse. Forcing scientific knowledge to inhabit and emerge from the subordinated native objects, this was a process rife with ambivalence.

The liminality enacted in the performance of the colonial discourse can be seen in the "science of man" that occupied the attention of the Royal Asiatic Society of Bengal. In 1866, the Society informed its members that the curator of the Indian Museum had issued a circular soliciting the assistance of the colonial administration in the collection of human crania for the museum's ethnological section, and that his request had met with a favorable response. The Society had received some contributions from private donors, and several sources had promised further aid.[27] But the collection of skulls presented problems. One could buy skulls, as one ethnologist did when he persuaded an Andamanese widow to sell for one rupee her dead husband's skull that she had been wearing "as a sort of a locket"; but individuals could have a "not unnatural prejudice" against parting with their crania, and the "possessors of interesting skulls might not be willing to let us examine them, while still on their shoulders."[28] An alternative, superior on both practical and scientific grounds, was suggested by Dr. Frayer, professor of surgery at the Medical College, Calcutta. In a letter to the Asiatic Society, he argued that while the display of crania was valuable, it "fell short of the advantages to be derived by anthropological science from a study of races themselves in life."[29] Thus arose the idea of assembling for display "races" found in and around Bengal and other provinces at various local exhibitions, leading up to an ethnological congress of all the races of India.

Endorsing this proposal, George Campbell, ethnologist and later governor of Bengal (1871–74), recounted being "much struck by seeing men of most interesting and curious races carrying things down to the Punjab Exhibition two or three years ago; the men, who were *not* to be exhibited, seemed to me much more curious than the things they were taking to the exhibit."[30] Persuaded by Campbell, the Asiatic Society proposed to the government that an ethnological congress be held as a "fitting adjunct to the proposed General Industrial Exhibition of 1869–70."[31] Discussions at the Society's meetings now centered on practical aspects of the proposed exhibition. Campbell thought that an "exhibition of the Aborigines would be the easiest thing in the world," and that "as they are such excellent labourers, they might be utilised as Coolies to put in order the Exhibition grounds at certain times, while at others they take their seats for the instruction of the Public." Accordingly, he proposed that

an Ethnological branch should be added to the next Agricultural Exhibition, in which, without in any way degrading men and brethren to the position of animals, opportunity should be given for studying man at least to the same extent to which animals are studied; a study, which, in the case of humans, should extend to language and mental qualities, as well as to physical qualities. I would engage a suitable number of individuals of pronounced type, as Exhibitors on a suitable remuneration. I would erect a sufficient number of booths or stalls divided into compartments, like the boxes in a theatre or the shops in a bazar; I would arrange, that at certain hours, on certain days, the Exhibitors, classified according to races and tribes, should sit each in his own stall, should receive and converse with the Public, and submit to be photographed, printed, taken off in casts, and otherwise reasonably, dealt with, in the interests of science.[32]

Unlike exhibits in museums, living exhibits, suitably framed in classified stalls, could talk to visitors; they could be observed in motion, as functioning objects. Insofar as such an exhibit offered an understanding of life itself, a better breeding of "man" became realizable:

I hope, I need scarcely argue, that a movement of this kind is no mere *dilettantism*. Of all sciences, the neglected study of man is now recognised as the most important. The breeding of horses is a science; the breeding of cattle is a science; I believe that the breeding of short-horns is one of the most exciting of English occupations, but the breed of man has hitherto been allowed to multiply at hap-hazard.[33]

This haphazard multiplication was evident, according to Campbell, in miscegenation. "The world is becoming more and more one great country; race meets race, black with white, the Arian with Turanian and the Negro; and questions of miscegenation or separation are very pressing."[34] By providing the means for observing and understanding separate and mixed races, living exhibits held out the possibility of envisioning a more scientific breeding of man to replace and reorder the chaos of miscegenation—such was the heady lure offered by the science of life. Given such high stakes, nothing was too much to offer at the altar of science. When asked how much clothing was to cover these exhibited "wild creatures," Campbell replied:

With respect to clothing, I would only suggest that I think we should prefer to have them in their native and characteristic shape. . . . As cleanliness comes after godliness, so I think that decency must come after science; at any rate I would only satisfy the most inevitable demands of decency.[35]

The Exhibition Committee of the Central Provinces formulated a plan to seize a family of specimens rather than individual samples of "wild tribes," and to feed and photograph their "biped specimens." An official from the Andaman Islands, in preparation for the ethnological congress, sent two Andamanese boys with new names—Joe and Tom—to Calcutta, where they sang and danced at a meeting of the Asiatic Society.[36] A great deal of ethnological inquiry was carried out by district officers in different provinces, and a sizable number of reports on "races and tribes" accumulated. But by 1868, the plan for a grand exhibition of all the races had been scaled down, and in the end, due to lack of funds, such an exhibition was held in the Central Provinces only.[37]

Notwithstanding the whittling down of overly ambitious plans, the case of the ethnological congress of races shows that the science of man was inevitably contaminated by the objects in which it inhered and the mode of its staging. How could the science of man be separated from its representation in the "aborigines" placed in theater-like stalls? The ambivalence of the colonial science of man lay in the fact that it was produced on the borderlines of black and white, of Aryan, Turanian, and Negro—indeed, on the margins between man and short-horns! Could the category of man produced by fears of miscegenation be anything but disturbed and liminal? The traces of such a category are to be found in Campbell's plea that the human exhibits be "otherwise reasonably, dealt with, in the interests of science," and the embarrassment with which he concludes that "decency must come after science." Racism, to be sure, is overwhelming in this and other colonial texts; it empowered the colonialist to place the "native" in stalls, interrogate and photograph him, and refer to him as a biped specimen. But the predicament of the colonial science of race was that it could not escape the liminality produced in its own performance. As the colonizer staged the colonized as man, he disavowed the racist polarity—the European versus the "native"—that enabled his discourse. The subordinated "aborigine" emerged as the kindred of the dominant European, the biped specimen came to stand for man.

SPECTATORSHIP: SCIENCE TAKEN FOR WONDER

The question of viewership dramatized the ambivalence of the colonial staging of science. The problem for museums and exhibitions was how to make objects rise above their concreteness and their native particularity to reveal something more abstract and universal. How was a pure order of knowledge to emerge from objects of native provenance and strike the viewer as science? This problem could not be addressed at the level of the re-presentation of objects alone; it required the conception of a viewership that was capable of separating the pure science of classification from the impurity of "same things called by different names," one that was competent to isolate the science of man from the body of biped specimens. Thus the eye became responsible for obtaining the scientific knowledge lodged in objects of India's natural history, and the production and the authority of science became dependent on visual demonstration.

The eye as the privileged means of acquiring and demonstrating scientific knowledge was particularly important for museums in India because most Indians could not read. For illiterate visitors, captions on exhibits were of little use—least of all those written in English, as were customary in museums. Given these conditions, labeling was a neglected feature of museums; labels were poorly conceived, unimaginative, and often wrong, rendering the techniques of display all the more important.[38] The standards of display were superior by comparison, enhancing the importance of visuality in museums as an instrument of education. In the absence of a reading public, the museum could substitute for a book, and the observing eye could stand for the reading eye—so thought Dr. Bhau Daji, a Western-trained doctor and a Sanskrit scholar, who, addressing a public meeting of "Native and European inhabitants" held in 1858 to establish the Victoria Museum and Gardens, stated that

> to the unlearned especially—and in that class we must include a very great majority of our countrymen—a Museum is a book with broad pages and large print, which is *seen* at least; and by mere inspection *teaches* somewhat, even if it be not *read*.[39]

According to Dr. Daji, seeing was a poor surrogate for reading—it was not reading but inspection, capable only of "teach[ing] somewhat." But poor substitute though it may have been, the vast numbers of the "unlearned" left no alternative. Indeed, visuality became all the more critical:

> The Natives cannot understand a new thing unless it is held up before their eyes with something of a continuous perseverance. The first time they may wonder; the second time they may understand; the third time they may observe with a view to practice.[40]

The project of colonial pedagogy required the "unlearned" Indian whose education could be accomplished only by repeated visual confrontations with scientific knowledge embodied in objects. But addressing and reforming the eyes of such viewers demanded that science express itself as magic, that it dazzle superstition into understanding. Such a restaging defined the introduction of mesmerism as a science in British India during the 1840s. The chief proponent of mesmerism in India was a surgeon in the colonial medical service, Dr. James Esdaile. He was allowed to set up the Mesmeric Hospital in Calcutta as an experiment in 1846, subject to regular inspections by other medical officers to determine the scientific value of mesmerism. The inspecting medical officers concluded that Dr. Esdaile's claims on behalf of mesmeric science were untenable, but they noted that the hospital was popular with the "natives" of Bengal because of the existence of "superstition in its widest sense and in its most absurd forms." Those who had "the most implicit faith in witchcraft, magic, the power of spirits and demons, and the efficacy of charms and incantations" believed that Dr. Esdaile had supernatural powers, and the officers reported that "the common name under which the Mesmeric Hospital is known among the lower classes is that of *house of magic*, or *jadoo hospital*."[41] But how did Dr. Esdaile's hospital acquire its name as a house of magic? And why did the "natives" believe that mesmerism was magic? Is it possibly because Dr. Esdaile himself used the term *belatee Muntur*, "the European charm," to explain mesmerism to his Indian medical assistants?[42]

Magic also marked mesmerism's public staging, which was performed to establish its status as science. These public demonstrations were crucial, as Dr. Esdaile acknowledged, if mesmerism was to press its claim as a science before both Europeans and Indians.[43] At first he was skeptical of the utility of "public exhibitions for effecting a general conversion to the truth of Mesmerism" and believed that "performers in public are not unnaturally suspected to take insurances from Art, in the event of Nature failing them." In spite of his "natural distrust of public displays," however, he consented when senior officials pressured him to stage a demonstration. The performance, held before Europeans and Indians on 29 July 1845, was reported in the newspapers the next day: "The party was very numerous, two steamers having brought the curious from Barrackpore and Calcutta; and there was a large assemblage of the European and Native residents of Hoogly and Chinsurah."[44] Before the day ended, Esdaile had impressed the viewers with his many feats: Two women who were mesmerized separately in different rooms displayed identical symptoms of twinkling eyelids and swaying side to side while entranced. Mesmeric trance at long range was demonstrated on a man who, in his insensible state, evident in his cataleptic limbs, obeyed Esdaile's instructions, singing "Ye Mariners of England," "God Save the King," and "Hey Diddle Diddle." "Sleeping water" was administered—after clergymen and doctors had observed Esdaile "charming" the water—to men who turned cataleptic or became somnambulists after drinking it. Undoubtedly, the European account from which these examples are taken treated the whole spectacle as an amusing magic show, but it also

presented the show as a demonstration of the scientificity of mesmerism. Indeed it was in the public display of its magical effect
that mesmerism emerged as science, perched precariously between cold scientific inquiry and "superstition in its widest sense
and . . . most absurd forms."

If performance mixed science with magical spectacle, it also
enhanced the importance of visuality. Museums confronted observers with an orderly organization of fossils, rocks, minerals,
bones, vegetation, coins, sculptures, and manuscripts. Exhibitions, on the other hand, offered a feast to the Indian eye. De-
pending on the scale, no effort was spared to produce an attractive
spectacle: ceremonial arches, palatial structures, military bands,
lakes, fountains bathed in colored lights, food stalls, wrestling
competitions, pony races, and regional theater—all combined to
impress the public eye and draw it to agricultural products, manu-
factured goods, machines, scientific inventions, and new methods
of working and living. Dramatic display was so central to the success of exhibitions that when it fell short, public commentary was
sharp. This occurred when the Calcutta International Exhibition
of 1883 opened after an evening of pouring rain—a damp beginning compounded by the opening ceremony being plunged into
darkness when "owing to the wickedness of some wretch the electric wire was cut."[45] *The Englishman*, a newspaper always enthusiastic about colonial projects, could not refrain from commenting
that the scene was "very sad, the great ceremony was torn to rib-
bons, the superb ruby velvet canopy was dripping like a drill cloth
. . . Every Court leaked more or less—Victoria a good deal."[46] By
contrast, the opening of the Allahabad Exhibition of 1910–11
drew ecstatic public praise. *Saraswati*, a premier Hindi literary
journal, was moved to describe the layout and exhibits pic-
turesquely, declaring the event a spectacular success.[47] The *Pioneer*, an English daily, gushed that "sons and daughters of the
East and West" greeted the opening of the exhibition with cries
of "Kolossal!, Kya ajib [how amazing]! Bāpre bāp [oh my God]!
Wah [splendid], this beats Chicago! [referring to the Chicago
World's Fair of 1893]"[48]

33

What began as representations of science staged to conquer ignorance and superstition became enmeshed in the very effects that were targeted for elimination. We encounter this intermixture in the museum's evocation of awe in its visitors, in the exhibition's utilization of a sense of marvel, in mesmeric science's attempt to show magical efficacy, and in the miraculous powers evoked by public demonstrations of scientific instruments. In these stagings of science, the cold scrutiny of scientific knowledge confronted the magic of spectacles as part of its own process of signification, as difference within itself. Within this structure of difference, science aroused curiosity and wonder, not superstition: the "Wonder House" was not the museum's polar opposite but an interstitial space that accommodated a half-awake state of comprehension and incomprehension. In the cries of "Kya Ajib!" and "Wah!" we confront not blind faith but the wondrous curiosity of "this beats Chicago" that science's authorization in magic had brought about.

Second Sight

As colonial conditions turned the staging of science into a wondrous spectacle, a space opened for the subjectivity and agency of the Western-educated indigenous elite. Trained in Western schools and colleges, and employed in colonial bureaucracy and modern professions, this elite acquired a visible presence in principal Indian cities and towns by the late nineteenth century. In a sense, their emergence was attributable to the colonial project of re-forming Indian subjects. The exhibitionary institutions contributed to this process by acting as pedagogical instruments, by inviting Indians to identify and learn universal principles of classification and function in objects encased in colonial power and exhibited as spectacle. The elite emerged from their encounter with exhibits claiming that the experience had reoriented their vision, or endowed them with "second sight." It is significant that this second sight appeared on the cusp between the exhibition of

34

the imperial power to name and order artifacts and the representation of this display as the spectacle of science. Placed between the two, the power of understanding signified by second sight was rooted in curiosity and wonder. Signifying neither a superstitious eye nor a scientific gaze, it was a vision re-formed by its encounter with science's representation as wondrous and useful Western knowledge. Equipped with such a vision, Western-educated Indians surfaced as modern subjects who could claim to represent and act upon the subaltern masses from whom they distinguished themselves.

The emergence of the curious eye of second sight is observable in R. B. Sanyal's *Hours with Nature* (1896), which includes a chapter titled "Round the Indian Museum," a fictional account of a visit by schoolteachers to the Indian Museum.[49] Mr. W. (West?), inspector of schools in Bengal, instructs Pandit Vidyabhushan, a Sanskrit grammarian, in a dialogue that opens with the teachers expressing amazement at the sight of zoological specimens.

> 'What a variety of forms!'
> 'From all parts of the world!'
> 'The vastness of the collection is perfectly bewildering!'
> 'Not so much as those strange weed-like things,' said Vidyabhushan, pointing towards some really very plant-like objects kept in cases against the Western wall of the hall. . . . Mr. W. who was attentively listening to the conversation and had noticed Vidyabhushan's embarrassment, explained that though weed-like in appearance they were in reality *animals*.
>
> 'Truth *is*, as they say, stranger than fiction,' exclaimed Vidyabhushan.
>
> 'Let us hear something about these strange forms,' cried many almost in chorus.
>
> 'Well then,' resumed Mr. W. 'those weed-like objects are "Zoophytes or Plant-animals," so called owing to their superficial resemblance to plants.[50]

The text continues in this manner for several pages, bewilderment and amazement followed by explanation and understanding. The method of comparison and classification is demonstrated, leading to the following:

> 'I have been connected,' said Vidyabhushan, 'in one capacity or
> another with the education of children and young men for the last
> thirty years, and have read and taught a great many things about
> animals and their ways as related in story and reading books. I
> know, as every school-boy knows, that lions and tigers are formidable animals; that ostriches are very large birds that live in the
> deserts of Africa, and are remarkable for their speed; that elephants
> are very sensible and amusing to children, and have their uses. But
> then, this is learning things without method, and is, therefore, of
> no value. I am so glad that Mr. W. has hit upon this plan of teaching the teachers to value system. In fact, he has given us a *second
> sight* [emphasis mine]. When I first entered this great hall, I was
> perfectly bewildered at the vastness of the collection, and had not
> the least idea in what order and plan they were arranged. I have got
> at least some notion now of their arrangement, thanks to the interesting demonstrations of Mr. W.'[51]

After describing several other occasions of puzzlement followed by Mr. W.'s explanations, the text concludes with Mr. W. stating that understanding nature requires the simplicity and the purity of a child's heart, and "an ear of faith." This statement rejects colonial power's self-identification with universality and scales down its knowledge to a set of particularly Western values and attitudes. Vidyabhushan acknowledges the importance of these values but adds that "according to our old Hindu idea 'Reverence' is another essential quality for the training of the mind." With this invocation of a "Hindu idea," Vidyabhushan does not dilute difference but affirms it as the basis for negotiating a relationship with Mr. W.'s emphasis on "an ear of faith."

As the text sketches and negotiates the relationship of wonder with science and the relationship of childlike simplicity and the Hindu idea of reverence with a Western value system, it outlines a space for an educated elite, now possessed of second sight and able to absorb Western knowledge. Second sight emerges out of the bewilderment experienced when confronted with alien knowledge while encountering the objects in the museum. The emergence of this amazement and wonder is attributed to the performative process, not to prior scientific training—the museum-goers are "school-masters and Pandits," and the principal character, Vidyabhushan, is a scholar of grammar.[52] As a grammarian, he presumably brought logic and classification to his understanding of the museum, but this was not the same as the value system taught by the museum. Significantly, the Hindu idea of reverence invoked by the text, though part of Vidyabhushan's heritage, surfaces in the process of viewing objects in the museum. Outlined here is the notion of a Hindu conceptual system, or "Hindu science," that is not derived from or opposed to Western science. It arises as a different form of knowledge—divergent and autonomous from Western science, but not its polar opposite.

The text identifies the emergence of second sight in a museum, and historical records indeed suggest that museums took their educational function seriously. Almost all museums organized visits of groups of students and teachers to their galleries;[53] in addition many museums organized regular public lectures. In this regard, the Lahore Central Museum stands as a representative example.[54] Besides housing the Science Institute and allowing the Society for Promoting Scientific Knowledge to use its lecture hall, the museum also instituted a series of "Magic Lantern Lectures" in 1892–93 when John Lockwood Kipling, Rudyard's father, reported the purchase of a magic lantern and its apparently hugely successful use in a lecture. The topics of these lectures, delivered in both English and Urdu and by both Englishmen and Indians, varied, ranging from history to science. The best-attended lectures were apparently the "Zenana Lectures," reserved for purdah-clad women and delivered frequently in the 1910s and 1920s by Monorama Bose, a Bengali Christian woman who taught at the Victoria School, eventually becoming its headmistress.[55] She belonged to a family devoted to missionary work. Her father had converted to Christianity after graduating from the

Calcutta Medical College and joining the medical service in the
Punjab, where he met American missionaries in Ludhiana. Monorama, one of his four daughters, was sent to London in 1884 to
train as a teacher. While there she began to keep a diary in which
she recorded her visits to Kew Gardens, the Natural History Museum, the Crystal Palace, and to a demonstration of the magic
lantern.[56] On her return to India in 1886, she learned Urdu, Persian, and Bengali, joined the Victoria School as a teacher, and
lectured frequently in the series at the Lahore Museum. Her lectures were not on science but on such general topics as travel and
the education of women. The museum appears to have included
these subjects in order to enlarge the appeal of its series of
lectures.[57]

Finding and including activities with a wider appeal was a continuing feature of museums and exhibitions, and it provided the
means for marking and separating the elite from the subaltern.
We notice this process of marking emerging in Dr. Bhau Daji's
conception of the museum as a "book with broad pages and large
print" that taught through mere seeing the "very great majority
of our countrymen"—"the unlearned." We catch a glimpse of it
again in the response of Bhoobun Mohun Raha and Jadub Chandra Goswami, the two Joint-Secretaries of the Fureedpur Agricultural Exhibition, to criticisms of amusements in the exhibition: "If bands of music and other attraction are found necessary
in England, how much more so is something of this sort necessary in this country."[58] That this referred not to Indians as a
whole but specifically to the lower orders becomes clear when
Raha and Goswami state that the performances of *jatra* (Bengali
traditional theater) and nautches (dances) during the 1873 exhibition were organized "chiefly for the amusement of the lower
classes, who have still a great taste for these things." The lower
classes were not only marked by their taste for *jatras* and nautches
but were also defined by their poor understanding of scientific
agriculture. Thus these amusements were considered justified
for the sake of "the improvement of the agriculturists of this

Sub-division, who were so much in need of instructions and practical demonstration on scientific mode of cultivation and manuring."[59]

Awareness of the subaltern's need for scientific instruction runs through the writings of the educated elite. It appears, for example, in an article on the Alaska-Yukon-Pacific Exhibition of 1910, published in *Saraswati*. The author, impressed by the Agricultural Court and describing the demonstration of scientific methods of production, writes of his conversation with a friend:

> 'Doesn't the sight of these things teach a great deal?' Munshiram said in amazement.
>
> 'Undoubtedly, why not? This knowledge is relevant to farmers. They have gained much by coming into this building.'
>
> 'And then there is our country, where people are living in darkness. The same old ploughs and bullocks. These unfortunate souls believe that fate determines the poor productivity of their soil. They do not realize that their miserable condition is due to their own ignorance. The same land can grow a hundred times more if scientific methods were to be employed.'
>
> 'But who will teach them?'
>
> 'Our government should spend crores of rupees to teach peasants, just as governments here do.'
>
> I smiled. Munshiram understood the meaning of my smile. He took a deep breath and joined me as we came out of the building.[60]

The admiration for scientific agriculture, the bitter recognition of the Indian peasant's ignorance, and the smile and the deep breath—these were the gestures and expressions of the discourse in which the elite formed their identity, colonized like the subaltern but unlike them, enlightened. This identity can be seen coming to the fore even earlier, in reactions to the 1883 International Exhibition in Calcutta. The *Bengalee* welcomed the idea of an exhibition, acknowledging that it could be instructive, particularly when held on a small scale in districts, but observed that a grand one such as the Calcutta exhibition ignored the character of the people it was aimed at and the resources they possessed:

> If an Exhibition were held among the remote barbarians of the Sandwich Islands, the spectacle would create astonishment, the projector would probably be worshipped as a god—an honour that would perhaps be extended to some of his commodities—but nothing solid or substantial would follow. These barbarians have no capital, and even if their curiosity were deeply stirred, and their inclinations moved, there would be wanting the capital to manufacture.[61]

A similar problem existed in India. Here, too, "artisans and agriculturists will come from the moffasil to see the great Bazar," and though they would be moved by things they saw, nothing could come of it, as they were deeply in debt and had no capital. Once again, this commentary registers the educated elite's effort to distinguish itself from artisans and peasants, who were seen as similar to "the remote barbarians of the Sandwich Islands" and whose welfare and reform they claimed as their responsibility. Eighteen years after this commentary, in 1901, when the Indian National Congress began to hold industrial exhibitions to coincide with its annual meetings, this elite emerged, organized in a powerful institution, as a class apart from the subaltern masses and determined to change them.

SCIENCE AND THE SUBALTERN

If museums and exhibitions made a space for the emergence of the educated elite from which they could act and speak, what of the subalterns? They did not write books or letters to editors. They were spoken to and spoken for. We encounter them in the discourse of the colonizers and Indian elite as icons of the ignorance and darkness both wished to remove. But this was an impossible goal, for the colonial project hinged on the presumed and permanent existence of the superstitious as a subaltern object to be transformed by modern reason; the ignorant and irrational could never be fully understood or completely appropriated, for that would end the "civilizing mission." Thus, if the subaltern was silenced or made to speak only through superstition, the subaltern was also assured an intractable presence in the discourse of colonial science. At once completely known (stubbornly irrational) and entirely unknowable (who can understand the ways of unreason?), the figure of the subaltern occupies a disturbing presence in dominant discourses; it represents the limit of those discourses, a marginal position against which they defined themselves.

What did it mean to identify the self under the pressure of this unknowable, subaltern other? Let us turn to George Campbell's rueful acknowledgment of the subaltern as that ineluctable difference in which colonial knowledge sought its identification.

> I often stop and look at them ["tribes and races"], and I have tried to make something of them, but they don't understand me; I don't understand them; and they don't seem to realise the interest of ethnological inquiries, so I have not progressed much.[62]

As Campbell regretfully notes the unbridgeable gap between the colonizers and "tribes and races," he also makes clear that the progress of ethnological inquiries hinged on closing this gulf. This was an impossible project, not only because the discourse required the unassimilable subaltern, but also because the spectacle of science could not shake off its imperial connection. To subalterns, the staging of science appeared either as an expression of the government's intent, which was always suspect, or as Western novelty. Museums and exhibitions, therefore, were read as curious, miraculous shows and often generated rumors.

By perpetuating the destabilizing momentum of rumors, the intractable subaltern became a threat. The British were thrown into a panic when, wishing to dazzle peasants into improvement and progress with agricultural exhibitions, they were met with

41

rumors sweeping the countryside. In some Madras districts it was said that the British were plotting a new tax scheme: it was reported that while the landed gentry and traders cooperated in organizing exhibitions, others, due to their "unconquerable feelings," had "strange notions" that the government wanted to identify the best agricultural land and produce so that it could assess higher taxes.[63] Even more disturbing was the word going around the South Indian countryside during the 1850s that agricultural exhibitions were British plots to convert Hindus to Christianity:

> Superstition also lent its aid to fill the cup to the brim, and the most wild and laughably fanciful notions, were in some instances, I am inclined to think, designedly spread and seized by the people, one of which was so original that it deserves mention, *viz.*, that one of the great ends of the Exhibition was to convert the heathen to Christianity, that for this reason prizes were offered by the Government for the best paddy, that the *whole* in the District might be brought up and the natives compelled to eat boiled rice and become Christians, and that to celebrate the event, prizes were offered by Government for the best beef in the shape of cattle of all sorts, on which the Europeans were to regale at Christmas in token of thanks giving.[64]

We can read the strategy of normalization in references to superstition and "laughably fanciful notions." But this very strategy of showing the far-fetched nature of stories also opened a place for the subaltern's agency—rumors "designedly spread and seized." This contradictory process of both acknowledging and denying the subaltern a place in discourse can be observed in Edgar Thurston's description of his ethnological tours:

> The Paraiyan women of Wynaad, when I appeared in their midst, ran away, believing that I was going to have the finest specimens among them stuffed for the museum. Oh, that this were possible! The difficult problem of obtaining models from living subjects would be disposed of. The Muppas of Malabar mistook me for a

42

recruiting sergeant, bent on enlisting the strongest of them to fight against the Moplahs. An Irula of the Nilgiris, who was 'wanted' for some ancient offence relating to a forest elephant, refused to be measured on the plea that the height-measuring standard was the gallows. A mischievous rumour found credence among the Irulas that I had in my train a wizard Kurumba, who would bewitch their women and compel me to abduct them. The Malaialis of Shevaroys got it into their heads that I was about to annex their lands on behalf of the Crown, and transport them to the penal settlement in the Andaman islands.[65]

While the wry humor of "Oh, that this were possible" and the amused description in Thurston's prose present rumors as wild stories of wild people, his retelling of these stories—indeed, the general tendency of colonial officials to retail what they regarded as fanciful—is significant. The very strategy of defining and appropriating the other in rumors compelled the colonial officials to give life to rumors, to make a place for absurd tales. In accommodating them, the colonizers opened their discourse to the wild contagion of indeterminacy characteristic of rumors, to the menace of their shadowy origins, and to their reckless reverberations once they were set in motion. Registering the threat posed by such escalating indeterminacy, one official wrote that "the most absurd reports were in circulation, no one pretending to know or [sic] with whom [these rumors were] originating, still they were greedily credited, and the more grossly absurd the report, the more certain was it of belief."[66] The panic felt was real enough. The exhibition in Cuddapah opened with considerable apprehension because the British were unable to read people's intentions. On the one hand, they expected considerable apathy, prompting them to consider postponing the opening of the exhibition. On the other hand, since defiance was "also stated to be the intention of those inimical to the Exhibition, all thoughts therefore of postponement were abandoned." Thus, the authorities opened the exhibition on 26 May 1856. And in fact, in the event, it was noted, "nothing was forthcoming save a few cattle."[67]

Anticipating a similar outbreak of rumors due to the impending census operations, Abdul Luteef Khan, a Western-educated Bengali Muslim, recalled the atmosphere created by rumors at the time of the Alipore Agricultural Exhibition in 1864. Among many "absurd and ridiculous stories" was one that the real reason why cattle and horses were required by the exhibition was the outbreak of a war somewhere, for which the cattle and horses would be slaughtered for food or used to transport military stores. These rumors prompted Khan to launch a campaign of education. He issued a pamphlet in Urdu which, along with its Bengali translation, was widely distributed by the government. As a result, he wishfully concluded, the "bugbear called into existence by popular ignorance has vanished, and that which was once dreaded is now invited and welcomed."[68] It is true that later exhibitions did not record similar outbreaks of rumors, but the subaltern continued to occupy an unmanageable position in colonial and Indian elite conceptions. If the lower classes did not threaten the project of disseminating science by spreading rumors, they undermined its gravity by demanding frivolous amusements as the price of their participation.

The subaltern's "inappropriate" attitude also compromised the functioning of museums. Colonial officials feared that the popularity of museums with the lower classes had driven out the elite: "The Indian aristocracy look on a museum as something pleasing to the vulgar with which they are not concerned." Frequented by the lower classes the museum in India could not be "an institution of education and research," and the intended purpose of the museum seemed threatened. In Lahore, for example, a visit to the museum was a regular feature of lower-class wedding ceremonies.[69] In Madras, as in other places, days of the most important Hindu festivals drew the largest numbers of visitors. But, contrary to what we may suppose, these visitors did not go to museums to pay obeisance to the statues of deities housed there; at least no such mention is made in any document. Instead, Hindu festivals appear to have only provided an occasion for festive recreation, which might include a visit to the museum. Describing the day of the feast of Pongal, 15 January 1895, when 36,500 visitors flocked to the Madras Museum, Edgar Thurston wrote:

> The museum grounds presented the appearance of a fair, occupied as they were by a swarm of natives in gay holiday attire, vendors of sweetmeats, fruit, toys and ballads, jugglers, mendicants and others.[70]

Describing what visitors did inside the museum, Thurston does not mention any religious purpose:

> For the great mass of visitors to the museums in India, who come under the heading of sight-seers, and who regard museums as *tamāsha* [show] houses, it matters but little what exhibits are displayed, or how they are displayed, provided only that they are attractive. I am myself repeatedly amused by seeing visitors to the Madras museum pass hurriedly and silently through arranged galleries, and linger long and noisily over a heterogenous collection of native figures, toys, painted models of fruit, &c.[71]

Thurston adds that for these uneducated visitors, who called the museum a "stuffing college" and a *jadu ghar* (magic or wonder house), the main delight offered by the museum was "in the recognition of familiar objects, which they shriek out by name, *e.g.*, kākā (the crow), pachi pāmbu (the green tree-snake), āni (the elephant), periya min (big fish—the whale!), etc."[72] When Thurston pulled out his anthropometrical instruments every evening, a crowd would gather to watch him:

> Quite recently, when I was engaged in an enquiry into the Eurasian half-breed community, the booking for places was almost as keen as on the occasion of a first night at the Lyceum, and the sepoys of a native infantry regiment quartered in Madras, entered heartily into the spirit of what they called the 'Mujeum gymnashtik shparts' [Museum Gymnastics Sports] cheering the possessor of

the biggest hand-grip, and chaffing those who came to grief over the spirometer.[73]

THE SIGNIFICATION OF SCIENCE: AN ENIGMATIC ARTICULATION

The history of museums and exhibitions is inseparable from their functioning as signs of Western power. This holds true not only for the colonies, but also for the West. In the West too, these institutions named, classified, and displayed non-Western objects and peoples to showcase the power and knowledge of Western nations and to reform and discipline the working classes, who were often compared with the exhibited "savages" elsewhere.[74] But it was one thing to compare class and race, quite another to conflate them in placing "natives" for display in theater-like stalls. Colonies, after all, provided the infamous "elbow room" for experimentation unavailable in Europe. For this reason, museums and exhibitions in British India remained singularly concerned with science and natural history. This also meant, however, that it was precisely in the virgin, colonial space of India that museums and exhibitions as European institutions were forced to confront their intimacy with the "native." There, the colonial "supplement," to use Derrida's term,[75] enacted Europe's authority and identity, and emerged powerfully and disturbingly. As the British staged Western science in Indian material, as they signified universal knowledge with particular, colonial methods, the native supplement, hidden in Europe, made a forceful entry in colonial discourse.

It is tempting to see the "Mujeum gymnashtik shparts" as the price European science had to pay for its implantation in non-European soil. Indeed, this perspective frames Thurston's narrative, implying that European discourses, originary and normal in the metropolis, were perverted in the process of their tropicalization in the colonies.[76] Such a view overlooks the crucial fact that the representation of Europe's originality hinged on the "native" double. It also elides the scandalous history of the fashioning of Western knowledge's identity, initially in the foreign and exotic material accumulated in the cabinets of curiosities and later in the burgeoning colonial spoils displayed by metropolitan museums and exhibitions.[77] My point here is neither that there was no difference between Europe and India, nor that the two were locked in an implacable dialectic, now to be reversed in favor of the repressed other to explain Europe's originality. Instead, what I wish to highlight is the historical undoing of the self/other binarism, the unraveling of the narrative which posits that Western knowledge, fully formed in the center, was tropicalized as it was diffused in the periphery.[78] The paradox of the "civilizing mission" was that it was forced to undo the very opposition upon which it was founded. To achieve improvement through despotism, as John Stuart Mill proposed so baldly, was a Faustian bargain, the effects of which bedeviled colonialism; it dislodged the very civilized/savage opposition upon which colonial power depended. As the British used barbarism to deal with the "barbarians," as they also used science to mark the "burned black" Indian skin with white authority, they also undercut the very ideals of civilization and progress that legitimized their power. Such was the compulsion of empire: colonial dominance in British India had to operate through the undoing of its founding oppositions.

It was at the point of colonialism's unresolvable dilemma that an ambivalent zone of power and agency took shape. In this zone the universality of Western power and knowledge appeared in the mirror of magic and spectacle, and the sciences of classification and function instituted themselves in curiosity and wonder. From this arose the agency of the Western-educated elite, located in their "second sight" and expressed in their portrayal of science as a marvelous value system and useful technology that could be combined and enriched with indigenous traditions. Science's uncertain and other life can be also identified in the mixture of amusement and fear with which subaltern groups viewed the exhibition of artifacts, reading it as a collection of pleasing novelties and as a sign of malevolent designs upon their lives. If the British

47

regarded both elite and subaltern responses as less than appropriate, as proofs of the dictum that natives will always be natives, they could not ignore these altogether. Seeking from Indians the recognition of Western knowledge's authority but unwilling to acknowledge them as knowing subjects, the British had to regard Indians as always less than adequate, always lacking some key attribute. This justified colonial dominance, but it also conceded that the colonial project would never achieve complete success, that Indians would remain unconquerable in the last instance. It was precisely at the site of colonialism's necessary failure to resolve its paradoxes and prevent its knowledge from "going native" that the career of science charted another course in British India.

CHAPTER THREE

Translation and Power

*. . . all translation is only a somewhat provisional way of
coming to terms with the foreignness of languages.*
Walter Benjamin[1]

In 1896, a Calcutta journal published a poem entitled "The
Blessings of Science," registering science's cultural power in the
discourses of the Western-educated elite:

> Science! Thou mysterious Being! Through Thy aid we can know
> all:
> Man and Nature's mighty laws and what are hid in the Future's
> path.
> Through thy mighty aid we mortals filch the lightning from the
> clouds;
> Through thy aid immortalize our mortal voices low or loud,
> Through thy aid from hence I know what is made the lum'nous
> sun.
> By thy magic wand when 'tis touched light divides in seven hue:
> Red and violet, green and orange, yellow, indigo and blue.
> Through thy aid our fleeting shadows are imprisoned in the frame,
> Thus thou giv'st to "airy nothings" "habitation and a name."
> Through thy aid our optic powers are increased to such a height,
> Each of us, as it were, gifted with a second sight.[2]

Science's authority inhabits and animates the poem; its cultural
force emerges as it brings the hidden out in the open, as it re-
names "airy nothings," as it redirects "our optic powers" to act as
"second sight." Functioning as an aid for repositioning and re-
claiming an already-present indigenous rationality, science surfaces and is itself reconstituted in the realignments of objects it
achieves and authorizes. The dynamic at work in the poem invites
us to view the institution of science's authority as a process of

translation, not imposition. Translation meant a realignment of power, a renegotiation of the unequal relationship between Western and indigenous languages. To view the elite discourse in such terms is not to fixate on its content but to understand it as a syntactical rearrangement of power and culture, not fasten onto the mere presence of science in that discourse but to focus on the conditions under which it was authorized.

Significantly, Western-educated intellectuals themselves approached translation as an issue of renegotiating power. Consider, for example, the views of Rajendralal Mitra, the prominent nineteenth-century Bengali Orientalist and intellectual. Confronting the problem of rendering Western science into Indian languages, Mitra wrote in 1877 that it could not be resolved by a "system of servile verbatim translation, like a Chinese copy, with patch and all."[3] Nor could it be done by a wholesale importation of Western technical terms into Indian languages, because that would "create a new language foreign to people at large, and give an exclusiveness to the professors of science not much unlike that of Cabalists and Gnostics."[4] Neither a "Chinese copy" nor a massive importation, translation had to aim at more than the reproduction of words: it had to transfer the "secret power" of language, which was frequently undefinable and intransmissible, and whose evaporation it could not prevent entirely. The delineation of one language into another, then, worked as a process of dissemination, not dialectic, from which neither one nor the other could reappear with its original position and meaning intact.

Dissemination was generative; it produced an altered authority and identity. For this reason, it was vitally significant to determine the nature of power's dispersal and transformation, particularly since it involved languages with unequal status—English and Indian languages. At stake was the integrity of the Indian languages, which did not participate in the creation of modern scientific discourses but were obliged to incorporate them. What were they to borrow and assimilate successfully without losing their fundamental character? Mitra proposed that indigenous interests guide the Indian languages' unequal encounter with English.[5] Regretfully, he acknowledged, the importation of technical and foreign terms could not be avoided entirely, but their evil could be minimized by making them simple, logical, and easily intelligible. He also recommended the use of "well-understood, and easily accessible native terms, with such a judicious mixture of foreign elements as may be absolutely necessary, taking care that, in the first instance, it is so manipulated as to render it fit for the purpose for which it is to be employed."[6]

There is an intimation here of another history—a history that emerges from science's authorization in the language of the other and consists of a process of cultural appropriation that bears the mark of a contestatory negotiation between unequal languages and subjects. The contestation surfaces in Mitra's insistence that Indian interests must govern the translation of Western science, that the process of dissemination and hybridization must be subjected to the pressure and agency of subaltern languages.

Mitra's perspective urges another reading of the enunciation of the discourse of science by the middle-class elite; it asks us to view the elite discourse as what Walter Benjamin called an interlinear, or between-the-lines, translation.[7] Understood as translation, the enunciation of the discourse of science becomes a far more complicated matter than the colonizer's victory over the colonized. Translation involves the undoing of binaries and borders entailed in the authorization of the discourse, and it locates the formation of a modern Indian elite as a counter-hegemonic force in those productive in-between strategies and spaces that come into existence when "our optic powers" are relocated as "second sight." To think of science's authority in India and the modern Indian elite as products of a translation between the lines is to bring another history into view—a history of an irreducibly different Indian modernity forged in the interstitial spaces opened by the process of translation. Viewed as a product of translation, the elite does not appear as a copy of the original, but as a ghostly double that resists identification as a copy by asserting difference. This is a history that sits oddly beside both the heady celebration of modernity as progress and its stinging denunciation as the colonization of the mind, and reveals the emergence of the indigenous elite's counter-hegemonic aspirations in the translation of Western modernity.

THE DISTRIBUTION OF SCIENCE'S AUTHORITY

During the second half of the nineteenth century, the emergence and functioning of science as a form of cultural authority took a variety of forms in different parts of colonial India. New organizations were set up to foster a scientific culture, and existing public bodies included the promotion of science in their activities. Western-educated Indians published tracts on science with or without government patronage, and religious and social reform came to be seen through science's authoritative "second sight." From these organizations there emerged an elite, composed primarily of Western-educated upper-caste men of different regions, who represented themselves as an Indian "aristocracy of intelligence" engaged in the liberal project of cultivating and spreading new forms of thinking and living.

In this project, the establishment of the Asiatic Society of Bengal in 1784 marked an important watershed. Founded by British Orientalists and restricted to Europeans until 1829, it brought together the research of European Orientalists and the writings of British officials in a variety of different government bodies. It combined serious philological and textual scholarship with empirical reports on "tribes and races," folklore, and the flora and fauna of British India, prepared by the East India Company administrators and officers employed in such bodies as the trigonometrical and geological surveys, and medical and meteorological services. By the early nineteenth century, the Asiatic Society had established itself as the center of Western knowledge in India. It configured the new discipline of textual Hinduism and Hindu philosophy, influencing the emergence of the Bengali reformist intellectuals, and it set into place the investigation of India's natural history and the rediscovery of indigenous traditions in mathematics, medicine, and other sciences.[8] After it began admitting Indians in 1829, the Asiatic Society offered Western-educated Indians an opportunity to also pursue and publish academic studies. Among them, Rajendralal Mitra was the most prominent. He published a number of historical, archaeological, and linguistic treatises, and became the Asiatic Society's first Indian president.

The Asiatic Society, however, was an academic body; its activities offered little opportunity for Indians keen on propagating science as culture and as a sign of modernity. These goals were pursued instead by organizations established by Western-educated intellectuals to reform religion and society. The Brahmo Samaj, established in 1829 in the wake of the much celebrated Bengal renaissance, was the earliest and the most prominent of such organizations geared to reform Hinduism.[9] By the 1840s, the language of reform began increasingly to employ the belief in the universal laws of nature. As the most forceful and enthusiastic exponent of this view, Akshay Kumar Dutt, the editor of the premier Brahmo journal, *Tattvabodhini Patrika*, began a tireless campaign to demonstrate the fruits of science and technology. He taught natural sciences in the Brahmo Samaj school and translated text-books on physics and geography into Bengali.

The belief in the superiority of natural laws over "superstitions" also animated the famous reformer, Iswarchandra Vidyasagar. His organization, Tattvabodhini Sabha, and his campaigns for female education and widow remarriage in subsequent decades invoked rationalist arguments to justify their goals.[10] Such reformist activities of the upper-caste *bhadralok* (literally, "respectable folk," a term for the Bengali elite) men were directed at the growing middle class (*madhyabitta*), many of whom were located in district towns, where their income was drawn from government employment, new professions, and land tenures.[11] This middle-class constituted the social base of reform movements and participated energetically in the development of the new print culture. But the most prominent *bhadralok* intellectuals were centered in Calcutta where they attracted patronage and participation from some of the city's great nouveau riche upper-class Indian families.[12]

The Brahmo Samaj was only one, though the most celebrated, reform organization. By the mid-nineteenth century, the project to reorganize culture—not just religious beliefs and social customs as in the case of the Brahmo Samaj—witnessed the formation of one organization after another in Calcutta and in the district towns. These drew into their fold prominent *bhadralok* intellectuals, members of the grand families, "enlightened" landlords, and sympathetic British officials. The objectives of these organizations, some of which lasted no more than a few years, varied—the diffusion of new forms of knowledge, religious and social reform, female education, the promotion of vernacular literature, the improvement of agriculture. But all of them were formed by and functioned with a sense of the rediscovery of reason.[13] As science was part of this rediscovery, the popularization of its authority emerged as one of the key aims of such organizations.

The Society for the Acquisition of General Knowledge, for example, was one among many short-lived bodies gripped by an enthusiasm for science. Established in 1838 and lasting until 1843, it counted over one hundred and fifty members, including the famous and wealthy Tagores, Dutts, Mitras, and Mullicks of Calcutta, as well as some lesser known provincial gentry.[14] During the five years of its existence, it hosted lectures in English—the language of reform among the *bhadralok*—for its members. Bengali students of the Medical College delivered lectures with such titles as "On the Anatomy of the Eye," "On the Anatomy of the Ear," and "On the Physiology of Digestion," while others read papers entitled "A Short Topographical Account of Chota Nagpoor," "On the Present Condition, and Future Prospects of the Educated Natives," "On Matter," and "Answers to Agricultural Queries."[15]

The enthusiasm for science as a language of reform seized even such organizations as the Bethune Society. Known primarily for its advocacy of female education, the Society was established by the British and Bengalis jointly in 1851 to commemorate the memory of John Drinkwater Bethune, a senior colonial official who, like Iswarchandra Vidyasagar, was known for his advocacy of female education. The Bethune Society's Bengali membership, like that of the Society for the Acquisition of General Knowledge, consisted of the Calcutta elite.[16] Its regular meetings at the Medical College, where noted Europeans and Indians lectured on education, philosophy, arts and science, health and medicine, and sociology, attracted the educated Bengalis of Calcutta and visiting landed magnates from other parts of India.[17]

Intending to institute the bourgeois civil society, the Bengali elite, in addition to flocking to the meetings of the Bethune Society and the Society for the Acquisition of General Knowledge, formed organizations devoted to the public discussion of scientific knowledge. The earliest and most prominent of such bodies was the Burra Bazar Family Literary Club, formed in 1857.[18] Also notable was the Mahomedan Literary Society, established in 1863 by Abdul Luteef Khan. This body, like the Burra Bazar Family Literary Club, held addresses on science and demonstrations of scientific instruments and experiments, and organized regular "conversaziones" attended by Muslim "gentlemen" and the "*élite* of the European, Hindu, Parsee and Jewish communities."[19] The men who ran such bodies were not scientists themselves, but eminent Bengalis who regarded scientific knowledge and a scientific attitude as signs of enlightenment and education. Thus Khan, the most prominent Muslim in a Hindu-dominated Bengali elite, made lectures on science an integral part of the activities of the Mahomedan Literary Society, in order to develop well-rounded individuals who would not only grasp scientific concepts but also use them in their life and thought—like Khan himself.[20] A product of Western education and a government employee, he rose to become the Presidency Magistrate in 1877— no small achievement for an Indian under colonial rule at that time. His learning was broad and deep, and, like many of his contemporaries, his language of reform was profoundly influenced by science. Addressing the Bethune Society in 1865 on the impending census operations and explaining the basis for his claim that the knowledge of the density of population would enable better town planning and municipal services, he said:

> Who that has paid any the least attention to physical science does not know that carbonic acid, or the air we expel from the lungs during the process of respiration, is one of the most destructive agents in nature, and produces fatal results, when diffused through the atmosphere in the proportion of only ten per cent? Is not the physical debility of the native of Bengal, in some measure, to be ascribed to a direct violation of the laws of nature, the inevitable consequence of numbers crowding together within the scanty limits of a miserable hovel?[21]

The writings and speeches of men like Abdul Luteef Khan, as well as the glittering gatherings of Europeans and the *bhadralok*, were the most visible manifestations of the general distribution of the discourse of science. Less visible, though no less important, were obscure organizations and lesser-known intellectuals whose activities gave science its authority. Take, for example, the enthusiasm for phrenology—a science, then current, which analyzed mental faculties and character by studying the shape of the skull. To advance the science, the Calcutta Phrenological Society was formed in 1845 under the direction of Kali Kumar Das, a *bhadralok* intellectual who participated in the discussions of the prestigious Bethune Society but was not otherwise prominent.[22] His organization, run primarily with the help of his relatives, was distinct from a society formed twenty years earlier, in 1825, by British enthusiasts of phrenology in India. Das's principal purpose was to popularize, through practical demonstrations and the publication of a Bengali journal, the knowledge and the practice of phrenological science in order to regenerate India's society, religions, and educational system.[23] Although very little information on the subsequent activities of this organization survives, phrenology's continuing currency in the 1870s prompted Mahendra Lal Sircar, the best-known Bengali promoter of science and a graduate of Calcutta Medical College, to pen a tract offering a guarded endorsement of phrenology.[24] More important than the interest in phrenology, however, were the raging debates on the scientific claims of homeopathy that attracted many educated men, particularly after homeopathy was endorsed by Sircar.[25] Fed on these debates, minor Bengali intellectuals in Calcutta and elsewhere quietly promoted science as an instrument of social and cultural renewal. A good example can be found in the life of Pyare Charan Sircar. A descendant of a *banian* family employed by the famous booksellers, Thacker & Co., he was educated at the Hare School, where he wrote a prize-winning essay in 1844 on the effect of the steamship on India. He became a teacher in 1845 and was eventually appointed as a professor at the Presidency College. During his more than two decades of service in edcuation both in and outside Calcutta, he established an industrial school, instructed students on agriculture and botany, collaborated with district officials to give practical demonstrations on agricultural chemistry, planted a small botanical garden, practiced homeopathy, and subsidized the publication of Bengali tracts on this form of medicine.[26]

By the 1870s, so broad and deep was the distribution of science's prestige in the discourse of the *bhadralok* that it began to show up noticeably in the literary culture of Bengal. The conception of science as superior knowledge, for example, appears in the writings of the most canonical of all literary figures of nineteenth-century Bengal, Bankim Chandra Chattopadhyaya. Aside from contributing eleven widely read essays on popular science to the Bengali journal *Bangadarshan*, he wrote several novels, essays, and satires in which his belief in scientific reason in general and the influence of John Stuart Mill and Auguste Comte in particular are clearly expressed.[27] Although the appeal to scientific reason is present in virtually all his writings, a particularly pointed expression of science's authority occurs in his essay "Mill, Darwin and Hinduism" which, like many of his writings, was concerned with the subjection of Hindus and Bengalis to foreign rule, and provided an interpretation and defense of Hinduism through an appeal to science and rationality.[28] This essay, written to establish the scientific basis of the Hindu belief in a trinity (as the creator, the preserver, and the destroyer), begins with a reference to Mill's argument on God's existence, goes on to invoke Darwin's theory of natural selection to establish that functions of preservation and destruction are different from that of creation, and concludes that the Hindu belief in the trinity of Brahma, Vishnu, and Shiva is valid even if its existence cannot be proven.

> [I]t is true that there is no scientific proof of the existence of the Hindu trinity, but it must be acknowledged that this Hindu worship of the three gods is more natural and more in accord with science than the Christian religion supported by the scientific European people. Although the worship of the three gods may not be based on science, yet it is not contrary to science. But in the judgement of Mill . . . it is evident that belief in the omnipotent, omniscient and all-merciful Christian God is contrary to science. If, like the Hindus, one accepts the doctrine of *karma* or *māyā*, it would then be in accord with science.[29]

In his time, Bankim was the most famous Bengali man of letters to espouse the authority of science and express positivist beliefs. However, there were many other *bhadralok* men in Bengal, both celebrated and obscure, who were so attracted to Auguste Comte's ideas that they formed an organization in the 1870s to popularize positivism.[30] Positivist doctrines began to appear in Bengali journals and inspired the foundation of the Bengal Social Science Association in 1867, which over the next several years became a center for the research and exchange of ideas on sociology and science. The organization not only drew into its fold the elite of Calcutta and Bengali's district towns, but also recruited members among the Western-educated men from other provinces who were active in promoting modern education.[31]

Crucial to the influence enjoyed by positivism and other such theories licensed as science was the rise of a literati around the developing Bengali print culture. Beginning to develop in the eighteenth century, modern Bengali literature and a literary public had become forcefully present in the cultural life of the elite by the mid nineteenth century. This was reflected in the rapid growth in the number of published Bengali journals, literary magazines, and books. By the 1850s, the publications in Bengali included books by Akshay Kumar Dutt on Baconian natural philosophy; text-books on chemistry, medicine, anatomy and pharmacopeia; ancient Indian treatises on medicine and geography; and essays on agriculture and horticulture. During the next fifty years, the number of such publications grew substantially, and journals and tracts returned incessantly to reflect on science as a form of thought and on its relevance to religion and society.[32]

Building on the wide distribution of science's authority among the Bengali literati, the Indian Association for the Cultivation of Science (IACS) was founded in 1876 by Mahendra Lal Sircar. An important figure in the *bhadralok* milieu, he established the *Calcutta Journal of Medicine* in 1868 and worked along with Father Eugene Lafont, the Belgian missionary and professor of physics at the Calcutta St. Xavier's College, to popularize science. Often the featured speaker in the popular lecture-demonstrations on science that Lafont organized regularly, Sircar saw scientific training and research as crucial for national progress. Convinced that colleges, schools, and government bodies did not offer sufficient opportunity for nurturing and advancing scientific research and education,[33] he launched a campaign in 1869 to establish IACS as an institution that would both supplement existing institutions and function as an independent body devoted to promoting science for the national welfare. His efforts drew support from the same *bhadralok* intellectuals and wealthy families—along with a sprinkling of landed aristocracy—who supported nearly all elite projects of reform. Newspaper support poured in, and discussions were held at organizations to consider and further Sircar's scheme. With this backing, the IACS came into existence in 1876. Enlisting the support of the science faculty in Calcutta, the IACS organized a system of lectures for the students and teachers of science in the city. The IACS received the patronage of the government and the *bhadralok* consistently, becoming the most prominent organization of scientists and enthusiasts of science in Bengal.[34]

While Bengal was first to witness the distribution of science's authority in the elite discourse, this phenomenon was also observable in other provinces after the mid nineteenth century. As Western-educated Bengalis relocated to North India in pursuit of employment opportunities in education, administration, and the railways, they took the language of reform with them. There they found like-minded local inhabitants who were also educated in new schools and colleges, and employed in colonial government and new professions. In Banaras, Ramkali Chaudhuri, a junior official in the judiciary, along with other "native gentlemen" founded the Benaras Debating Club in 1861. Renamed the Benaras Institute in 1864, it at first consisted entirely of Indian teachers and students of English from the local colleges and schools.[35] So successful was this venture that the raja of Banaras expressed his desire to join, as did several other "native gentlemen," including Siva Prasad, a government servant of some repute as a promoter of vernacular education. In 1864, the club opened its doors to Europeans, including missionaries, who participated in its series of lectures on education, sociology, sanitation and medicine, philosophy and literature, and science and art.

In Bihar, where the spread of Western education and the emergence of the new elite was limited, science's position as the syntax of reform was nevertheless also evident. In 1868 a group of educated Biharis and Bengalis employed in colonial administration formed the British Indian Association, later renamed the Behar Scientific Society, in Muzaffarpur, a small district town in north Bihar.[36] The principal force behind this organization was Sayyid Imdad Ali, a minor official in the colonial government. A Muslim like Abdul Luteef Khan of Bengal, he, too, was moved by the language of reform and progress. His organization, which included both Hindus and Muslims, was founded at a meeting on

the advancement of education that was attended by Indian officials, landlords, merchants, and "men of independent fortunes."
By 1870 the Behar Scientific Society had four hundred members,
including some British officials, with branches in two districts.
With donations received from wealthy landlords, the Society
sponsored translations of textbooks on natural philosophy, physics, chemistry, mathematics, astronomy, and geology into Hindi
and Urdu.

The Behar Scientific Society was modeled on the Aligarh
Scientific Society, an organization established in 1864 by Sayyid
Ahmad Khan, the nineteenth-century Muslim reformer.[37] Khan
belonged to the genteel North Indian Muslim *sharīf* culture of
comfortable, large households served by a retinue of servants
with long-term ties to the family. The men of this culture studied
the recitation and memorization of the Qur'an, were educated in
traditional schools in Persian and Urdu, and amused themselves
with chess or parchesi, pigeon-raising, kite-flying, cockfights,
poetry, music, and dance and music performances by courtesans.
By the 1850s, however, the *sharīf* men were beginning to find a
new cohesion as a group through their increasing involvement in
the *kacaharī*, or courts, as minor officials, document writers, and
legal agents—*vakils* and pleaders. Involvement in the *kacaharī*
milieu brought about an appreciation for English education.
However, men like Sayyid Ahmad Khan did not see English only
as a key to employment; Khan championed English education
because he drew from the 1857 revolt the lesson that political
weakness could be removed only with the new knowledge imparted by Western education. The establishment of the Aligarh
Scientific Society, facilitated by the network of donors and pa-
trons available through the *kacaharī*, was an effort to remove this
perceived political weakness through English education.

The Aligarh Scientific Society's activities consisted primarily
of sponsoring Urdu translations of English textbooks on science.
Most of these were texts on mathematics translated by Zakaullah
of Delhi College, an intellectual associated with the reformist

ferment historians call the Delhi renaissance, of which Sayyid Ahmad Khan was an early representative and important figure.[38] This reformism, which preceded Western influence and is traceable to the eighteenth-century reformer, Shah Waliullah, responded positively to Western learning in the early nineteenth century and fostered an appreciation for science. One product of the Delhi renaissance was a simplified Urdu that the movement's intellectuals had developed as a vehicle for scientific thought to replace the courtly Persianized Urdu.[39] Zakaullah studied at Delhi College in the 1850s, where he came under the influence of Ramachandra, a Hindu convert to Christianity and a brilliant mathematician who wrote books and published journals in Urdu advocating the instruction of new sciences.[40] Although Zakaullah, unlike his teacher, did no original work in mathematics, he became a teacher of mathematics, joined the government's education service, translated mathematics textbooks into Urdu, and became an active promoter of scientific education in Indian languages.

By the late nineteenth century, the pervasive deployment of science's persuasive power in North India was no longer limited to the writings and activities of eminent individuals and exclusive bodies, but became discernable in the cultural milieu that was developing around Hindi language and literature, and Hindu revivalism. Originating in Banaras and Allahabad, the spread of this Hindi-centered intellectual culture through north Indian towns eclipsed the cultural influence and public leadership of the Bengalis in North India.[41] In the new environment, discussions and debates on Hindu religion and society acknowledged the authority of science as a privileged body of knowledge, and proceeded hand in hand with the vigorous growth of the Hindi language and literature.[42] Hindi journalism and literature proliferated all over urban North India, powered by the extraordinary literary productivity and creativity of men like Bharatendu Harishchandra. The Hindi literati mounted powerful campaigns advocating greater use of Hindi in education and administration, and also fostered the rapid growth of a print culture that engaged in spirited discussions of Hinduism and Hindi language and literature.[43] Such activities were aimed primarily at promoting Hindi as the language and literature of the learned. But, given that the knowledge of modern science was regarded as a sign of education and enlightenment, Hindi journals also published regular columns on the history and contemporary state of different sciences, written mostly, though not exclusively, by science teachers dispersed all over the region.[44] Explaining basic concepts of chemistry, natural philosophy, biology, physics, astronomy, and mathematics, these articles were popular expositions aimed at addressing and cultivating the scientific disposition that a Hindi-speaking literati was expected to possess.

This disposition could be cultivated and maintained only if Hindi became a language of science, equipped to convey and produce scientific knowledge. Therefore, the Nagari Pracharini Sabha of Banaras, an organization formed in 1893 to advance Hindi's claim as a self-sufficient modern language, sponsored translations of textbooks and the compilation of a scientific dictionary in Hindi.[45] Similar developments occurred in Allahabad, another emerging center of Hindi literature. Professors Ganganath Jha, Hamiduddin, Ramdas Gour, and Saligram Bhargava, who taught Sanskrit, Arabic, physics, and chemistry respectively at Muir Central College, formed an association, the Vigyan Parishad, in 1913 to further the dissemination of scientific knowledge in Hindi. The Vigyan Parishad drew support from the city's literary and social elite and from science teachers in schools and colleges to organize a popular lecture series, establish a Hindi journal, *Vigyan*, which is still in existence, and launch the publication of a series of introductory and specialized scientific tracts in Hindi.[46]

By the early twentieth century, then, the authority of science had become widely dispersed. Fields ranging from social and religious reform to literary writings, and urban spaces ranging from major colonial cities to small district towns witnessed the permeation of science as a grammar of transformation. This was manifested in the establishment of public bodies, the organization of popular lectures, and the publication of journals. These institutional forms drew vigor from and also shaped the network of Western-educated men brought together by opportunities opened by new professions, the colonial administration, and landownership. Though limited in size and differentiated by religion, region, rank, and language, the class formed by these men came to represent modernity and to achieve prominence in colonial India.

THE INSTITUTION AND ALIENATION OF SCIENCE'S AUTHORITY

There is no doubt that the modern West permeated the discourses of Western-educated intellectuals in India and empowered them to represent themselves as forces of reform and progress. If we are to read this as a sign of the "colonization of the mind," then we should also be prepared to recognize the alienation inherent in its enactment. To enunciate the power of modern science in British India was to ask that it express itself in the menace of difference, that it court subaltern knowledges and subjects as the stage for its performance of dominance. Science was asked to open itself to and also contain the pressures of indigenous cultures, to dwell in the religious dispositions and literary writings of the "natives." Only then could there be an indigenization of science's authority—the imperceptible exercise of colonial domination. If these complex strategies of hybridization and translation confirmed science's authority, they also required it to address indigenous knowledges and subjects, resulting in a paradoxical legitimation: the establishment of science's power in its estrangement.

An early example of this process can be observed in a Hindi pamphlet, *Bhugolsār* (1841).[47] The origin of this text lies in an "interesting experiment" conducted in 1839 by a colonial official, L. Wilkinson. He organized a school for Hindu and Muslim boys who were taught, among other subjects, mathematics and astron-

omy from the body of ancient Sanskrit texts devoted to these sub-
ects and known as *siddhants*. According to him, the latter were
"wholly free from the fables of the Poorans" (the Puranas, myths
and historical legends collected and compiled between 500 B.C.E.
and 500 C.E.), and thus brought the student "just to the point to
which the Science of Astronomy had been carried in Europe
when Copernicus, Newton, and Galileo, appeared to point out
and to establish that the sun and not the earth was the centre of
our system."[48] Wilkinson attempted to expose the "absurd ideas,
usually prevalent among the Hindoos from the authority of the
Poorans," the first effect of which was "to rouse a very keen and
general opposition among the Bramins in many parts of India,"
although opinion ranged from an outright and total defense of
the Puranas to acceptance of certain classical Sanskrit texts as
scientific.

Bhugolsār was written by Omkar Bhatt, himself a *jyotish* (astron-
omer), in response to this debate. Comparing Copernican astronomy with systems described in the Puranas and in *Siddhānta
Śiromaṇi*, a twelfth-century text written by the astronomer-math-
ematician, Bhaskaracharya, the text asserts the superiority of
Western knowledge through a dialogue between a guru and his
disciple:

Disciple: 'Revered guru, how is the earth defined?'
Guru: 'The earth is defined in many ways; the Jains call it an in-
finite unity; and revered Vyasa in his *Bhāgvat* [one of the Pu-
ranas] calls the earth an expanse of 500 million *yojanās* and like
a lotus leaf; and Bhaskaracharya calls the earth small and round
in his *Siddhānta Śiromaṇi*; the British also judge it to be round.'
Disciple: 'If the earth is one, then why are there so many opinions?'
Guru: 'There are many kinds of men, and everyone speaks as he
believes.'
Disciple: 'Which one is true?'
Guru: 'The truth is that the earth is round.'
Disciple: 'What method establishes the truth that the earth is
round?'

Guru: 'There are many ways, but the chapter on calculations of the sphere in *Siddhānta Śiromaṇi* establishes it in the following way. . . . If the earth was a mirror, and if the sun went around the earth, then we would have only days, no nights; the fact that this does not happen proves that the earth is round.'[49]

While presenting these different conceptions of the earth, the text declares its commitment to scientific understanding. It does not dismiss the sage Vyasa, but describes the Puranas, which he narrated, as great poetry and wonderful sketches of God's play, though not science. Bhaskaracharya's theory, on the other hand, is scientific not only because it converges with the British view but also because, as the text proceeds to claim, the origin of the *siddhants* goes back to Surya, the sun god, who narrated the *Sūrya Siddhānta* to Mayasur, a Puranic artisan-demon. Bhaskaracharya's *Siddhānta Śiromaṇi* improved on the earlier *siddhants*, correcting their imperfections just as the "Sahibs" further developed and perfected astronomy.[50]

Having identified astronomy as a science, distinct from the poetry of the Puranas, Bhatt proceeds to assert the superiority of Western astronomy by first anticipating a challenge: How could the Sahibs' knowledge be more accurate than the divinely revealed knowledge of *Sūrya Siddhānta*, even though it developed later than Hindu knowledge?

Disciple: 'While Hindu astronomy is ancient, the Sahibs' knowledge is more accurate, even though they acquired it recently and from several different countries; why is this so?'

Guru: 'Because the Sahibs, after observing the entire earth, traveling through and living in every country, have measured their latitude and longitude accurately. Because those who work hard are also right, their knowledge is more accurate. Cotton grows in India, the Sahibs take it across to their own country, weave it into cloth, then sell it in India, garnering everyone's appreciation; and selling more than indigenous cloth. In the same way, the Sahibs have taken knowledge from the Arabs, Greece, and India, and like cotton, they have woven the thread of knowledge gained from these very books into a better fabric of astronomy.'⁵¹

Colonial exploitation as the model for the progress of science, capitalist colonialism as the accumulation of knowledge—such was the re-presentation of history in discourse. The text identifies the work of empire as the desire for knowledge and improvement that animates the British importation of raw cotton for its textile industry. Staged here is the compulsion to represent the capitalist empire as an expression of the effort to weave "a better fabric of astronomy." To achieve this representation, the text opens colonialism's normalizing myth to questioning and contention. The text does not simply assert the authority of the Sahibs' science, but makes it emerge through the pupil's probing interrogation. How can the Sahibs' science be more accurate? How can it surpass Hindu knowledge? These questions allow the text to portray colonialism as a civilizing force, to depict the Sahibs' "traveling and living in every country" as the culminating stage in the onward progress of knowledge. It patches together a narrative of science's progress that assimilates the astronomy of Bhaskaracharya and the divine speech of Surya in the trajectory of the Sahibs' knowledge.

Assimilating the content of the subordinated's knowledge, however, does not erase the disturbing position given it in discourse; the subordinated, speaking sometimes through the divine speech of the gods and at other times in the archaic voices of ancestors and tradition, exercises a constant pressure on authoritative representations.

> *Disciple*: 'The disrespect of tradition is improper because everyone accepts its testimony, but you violate the brilliant and boundless *Bhāgvat* and some of the *siddhants* to establish new principles, explain why.'
>
> *Guru*: 'The error of the old and the truth of the new should be acknowledged when that is the case. Revered Bhaskaracharya followed this method too. . . . I have followed his direction, to the best of my understanding, in determining errors; besides,

because the Hindu Puranic treatises on geography do not deal with proofs and have been written by poets, we should overlook their descriptions and set our sights on demonstrable proofs alone as astronomy recognizes observable demonstration only. . . . [T]he geography of the *Bhāgvat* is mere description, and not all geographical knowledge has been produced by the Hindus. The *siddhants* do not even describe travels south of the equator. . . . The Westerners have seen the entire globe; in 1497, Vasco de Gama Sahib of Portugal discovered the route around the Cape of Good Hope for his journey to India and circled Africa.'[52]

Here, the narrative of progress goes awry. As the text uses the pupil's unrelenting questioning to demonstrate that Hindu traditions cannot equal Western astronomy, it must pose and answer a troubling question: What justifies the violation of "the brilliant and boundless *Bhāgvat*"? This is not asked inadvertently, for the text's clearly visible purpose is to stage a rigged confrontation between indigeneous traditions and Western knowledge. This question is a critical moment that forces the discourse to turn against its progressivist narrative of astronomy and identify knowledge with power. Set to establish Copernican astronomy as a body of science consistent with and surpassing Bhaskaracharya's methods, the discourse ends up representing the superiority of Western knowledge in acts of Western explorations and expansion. It offers the West's navigation of the world south of the equator, its explorations of the globe, Vasco da Gama and Captain Cook's travels, and the British explorations of Africa as signs of Western knowledge and as proof of its superiority over Puranic poetry and cosmologies.[53] In asking its readers to reject poetry for science and Vyasa for Copernicus because Western expansion had proven the accuracy of Copernican science, the text brings Western astronomy face to face with the colonial mode of its universalization. There is something charmingly naive about Bhatt's telling of the tale of Western expansion as the story of astronomy's progress. But the narrative loses its innocence when it opposes the poetry of the Puranas to the Sahibs' explorations and conquests. Staging the opposition between indigenous fables and alien science reflects the bitter reality that Western knowledge needed Western power to achieve mastery over indigenous traditions. Thus, to the pupil's persistent demand for the reason why Copernicus must supersede Vyasa, the teacher responds by pointing to the West as the victorious civilization, through the feats of its da Gamas and Captain Cooks.

Bhugolsār was not an isolated case. Insofar as the narrative of progress was compelled to identify knowledge and power in seeking to master the colonized, alienation was a general condition of its articulation. This was true even during the early decades of the nineteenth century, when intellectuals of the Bengal renaissance like Rammohun Roy sang the praises of British rule. Roy diagnosed the root of India's afflictions in its social and religious practices and, overlooking colonial oppression, portrayed the institution of British rule as the revival of the era of reason in India.[54] This was no different decades later when Mahendra Lal Sircar condemned the "despotism of traditional opinions"—that is, Hindu beliefs—and lauded British rule for having established liberty and free inquiry.[55] In much the same vein, Gosto Behary Mullick, the secretary of the Burra Bazar Literary Club in 1874, spoke of reviving

the days of Elphinstones and Malcolms, Thomasons and Metcalfs, of Joneses and Wilsons and Bethunes . . . who came to India not for its rice or cotton, indigo or jute, shell-lac or lac-dye, sugar or salt-petre, but to raise from the depths of ignorance and superstition—fruits of years of foreign [Muslim] domination—a race whose venerable relics of literature and science play fantastically like the dazzling coruscations of a polar winter athwart the mysterious gloom that shrouds the dark night of ages.[56]

Obviously, the small Bengali Muslim elite, gathered in the Mahomedan Literary Society could not share the belief that the "years of foreign domination" had produced "ignorance and superstition," but it, too, sang praises of British rule and claimed that the "new world of thought" had calmed the minds of the "ignorant and bigoted co-religionists."[57]

These celebrations of British rule were not blind to the colonial divide; but instead of succumbing to it, they restaged the British rule of India as an instrument of new knowledge. Crucial to this restaging was the idea that the truth of science did not depend on power. Father Lafont expressed this idea well in an address to the Burra Bazar Family Literary Club, in which he stated that he had chosen to speak on a scientific topic because "it was the safest topic to be discussed in meetings like this."[58] Science was "safe" because it was thought to be nature's self-evident truth, contained in its working, and, unlike faith, free from power.

Yet to claim, as Mullick did, that "Joneses and Wilsons and Bethunes" had been necessary to raise India from "the depths of ignorance and superstition" was to acknowledge power as the secret dynamic of the narrative of progress. There is something odd in his celebration of modern science as deliverance from despotism, as a sign of free inquiry, for he acknowledges at the same time that freedom resides in domination. This was no self-contradiction, but a deep division in the discourse produced by its functioning. The narrative of progress courted difference in order to demonstrate the necessity of implanting modern knowledge. Thus, Mullick spoke of the depths of ignorance and superstition in India so that he could portray the British Orientalists as savants motivated not by salt-petre but by scientific knowledge. Similarly, Sircar prefaced his plea for the establishment of the IACS by detailing the lapse of the Hindus into speculation and superstition. Science was expected to conquer their false beliefs and institute true knowledge of the laws of nature that would place devotion to the almighty on a new basis. But having normalized difference as superstition, the mocked traditions returned as a menace. Sircar claimed that the very success of science had bred lethargy and complacency, making people indifferent to the methods of science.[59] Condemned to achieve progress and recognition slowly, science faced the overwhelming power of complacency, superstition, and error. How could this error be controlled so that the authority of science could emerge? It is at this point that the discourse's attempt to contain and exclude the difference in which science was authorized ended up alienating the colonial ideal of science as free inquiry. Suddenly, British rule appeared necessary to establish free inquiry and to rescue the people from the depths of ignorance and superstition.

The narrative of progress, therefore, was not safe from the contagion of its colonial articulation. As the very enunciation of the narrative forced the idea of progress to speak in the languages of those sunk in the depths of ignorance and superstition, there emerged, along with the myths of Joneses and Wilsons, another story. Perched beside the heroic tales of Copernicus and the Sahibs' science, there appeared a troubled acknowledgment of the deep-seated incompatibility between modern science's image as free inquiry and its operation as an instrument of colonial domination.

Displacement and Renegotiation

Under colonial conditions, the ideal of science's freedom from power could not escape displacement. On the one hand, science was projected as a universal sign of modernity and progress, unaffected by its historical and cultural locations; on the other hand, science could establish its universality only in its particular history as imperial knowledge. Forced to speak in tongues, the colonial discourse was compelled to authorize the language of science in idioms of cultural and colonial difference. To recognize this division of science's position in the process of its institution is not to celebrate the boundless play of the signifier. Rather, the creation of difference or division, Homi Bhabha suggests, is "the sign of the productivity of colonial power, its shifting forces and fixities"; "the effect of colonial power is seen to be the *production* of hybridization rather than the noisy command of colonialist authority or the silent repression of native traditions."[60] From this point of view, the hybridization of science's identity in the divine speech of Surya does not stand as the truth that exposes the myth of science's autonomy and originality. Instead, difference and dissemination displace the position from which the authority of science's truth is asserted. The truths of Western astronomy are rendered dependent on and shown to reside in their transferability and transformability. The Sahibs' knowledge becomes one that is "acquired recently and from several countries" and developed from the "knowledge taken from the Arabs, Greece, and India." Western astronomy acquires the status of truth as it travels, changes its shape, loses its origin, and installs itself in its colonializing explorations and exploits.

The dissemination of the narrative of science, then, was a charged event. As it split open and lost its autonomy and originality in the indigenization of its authority, a space opened for the renegotiation of science's status as truth. Such a space emerges in *Bhugolsār*, where the strategy to situate Western astronomy in the context of indigenous traditions demands that the text justify its transgression of traditional authorities. In response, the text cites colonial explorations and conquests as the basis for the West's superior knowledge. This produces a breach in the narration of science as a free accumulation of knowledge, as a matter of the replacement of error with truth. If the truths of Western science were gained in the exercise of Western power, then why should Hindu traditions give way to Copernican astronomy? It is remarkable that the text gives voice to these demands, but this reflects its subtlety as a project of legitimation. Thus the pupil, acknowledging Western power but questioning its cultural claims, asks: "How can you consider Western treatises true and doubt our own?"[61] The text steps into the breach opened by its own question to offer another basis for the cultural preeminence of Western astronomy.

> *Disciple*: 'Revered Guru, explain what are the fruits of instruction in geography and astronomy?'

Guru: 'The knowledge of geography and astronomy offers many benefits in this world as also in the other world. First, let me tell you about its use in this world; it is certain that the Brahmins who study geography and astronomy will command greater respect than other astronomers. As people become aware that astronomy is the best of all knowledges, their doubts will disappear. Deeply held false beliefs—that there exists a country of one-legged people, and that Rahu [the Puranic name for one of the nine planetary deities] devours the moon at the time of the eclipse—will vanish. Now listen to how this knowledge makes God's greatness visible. The understanding of the movement of the sun and other planets, the difference between seasons, the marvellous movement of meteors will reveal God's greatness and help place our hearts at God's feet. This will free us from desire, anger, greed, and illusion, and make the heaven attainable.'[62]

The intrusion of theology into science, or vice versa, remarkable though it may appear today, was neither novel nor unique. Such interpenetrations can also be observed, for example, as early as the twelfth century in European naturalist texts.[63] Remarkable, however, was the mechanism of natural philosophy's expression in the colonial context. On the one hand, natural philosophy licensed *Bhugolsār* to mark the Hindus as people with "false beliefs," who were yet to realize the superiority of astronomy as a form of knowledge, unlike the Europeans who knew this already. On the other hand, the text inscribed the Hindus as people whose capacity to recognize that "astronomy is the best of all knowledges" rendered them fit to see God's greatness. Thus, natural philosophy appeared in discourse neither as a lingering survival of an old idea, nor as the adaptation of science to the cultural heritage of India. Its specific meaning was produced between the mark that stigmatized the Hindus as given to false beliefs and the re-mark that conferred on them the capacity to understand "the marvellous movement of meteors." The text renegotiated science's signification by relocating its cultural force as it spoke of science's "use in this world" and benefits "in the other world."[64]

The authorization of science in its functionality—its "use in this world"—was a manifestation and mechanism of its cultural relocation. This structure comes into view clearly in a lecture delivered to the Bethune Society in 1868 by Reverend K. M. Banerjea. Banerjea was one of the fire-brand followers of Henry Derozio's "Young Bengal" movement. A convert to Christianity, he was one of the most prominent *bhadralok* intellectuals, and wrote and delivered lectures frequently on a subject dear to Bengali intellectuals: the reform of culture. On this occasion, too, he spoke of reform. Inevitably, he turned to science, arguing that it must supplement the instruction in Oriental classics: "the one for introducing, the other for naturalizing the enlightenment of Europe in Asia."[65] Neither was complete in itself. The function of cultures in the discourse of reform emptied them of their purported wholeness and offered another basis for their reformed existence. Thus Occidental knowledge, dispersed as a supplement so that it could be naturalized in India, swiftly acquired the creative power to introduce enlightenment. Likewise, Oriental classics, rendered incomplete without the supplement, became, in a flash, the fecund ground of naturalization.

Such dispersals and reformulations of culture constituted the life of science as a grammar of reform in elite discourse. Thus, two years after Reverend Banerjea's address, the Bethune Society's deliberations at a meeting in 1870 witnessed the same process once again at work. Like many Society meetings, this one included a lecture-demonstration on a scientific subject—on this occasion on respiration. Following the lecture's conclusion, Kali Kumar Das, founder of the Calcutta Phrenological Society, rose to thank the speaker for having shown how the ignorance of common principles of ventilation were ignored in the construction of native houses. However, Das disagreed that respiration was an involuntary act. He cited the practice of yoga to argue that the ancient Hindu devotees of the practice had controlled respiration with their will, and went on to refer to an account published several years earlier of a *fakir* (religious mendicant) who had presented himself at the court of Maharaja Ranjit Singh of Punjab and had himself buried on one occasion for forty days, and on another for ten months, and was still alive when disinterred.[66]

A somewhat similar expression of science in translation and the transaction of cultures occurred at a meeting of the Burra Bazar Literary Club featuring a lecture-demonstration by Father Lafont on heat, electricity, and magnetism. Ashutosh Dhar, a lawyer, enthused by the lecture as a demonstration of the unity of forces, called for the removal of the distinction between the organic and the inorganic. Father Lafont angrily rejected Dhar's demand that the mind's functioning be attributed to the action of physical forces and chemical reactions: "No amount of phosphorous ever made or will make a single thought; let us be sincerely and frankly spiritualists and rest satisfied with the noble use of *mind* to study and scrutinise *matter*, without confusion of two widely different departments of science."[67]

The call went unheeded. In fact, the confusion of a variety of categories permeated the discourse of the predominantly Hindu elite as they commissioned the cultural force of science to revive Hinduism. In the last decade of the nineteenth century, all over India, there ensued reassessments of the Vedic texts, the Puranas, and various textual commentaries and religious sects, and as this Hindu revivalism gathered force, the crossing of boundaries became increasingly common. Texts like *Bhugolsār* and discussions like the Bethune Society's conversation on yoga and science proliferated. The close of the nineteenth and the beginning of the twentieth centuries witnessed a vast explosion of pamphleteering and organizational activity that assumed and deployed science's authority to achieve a syntactical rearrangement of religion.

TRANSLATION AND HINDU MODERNITY

The most striking element in these reshapings of Hinduism was the attempt to produce a rigorously monotheistic vision. This attempt was not new, of course. In the early nineteenth century, Rammohun Roy had declared that monism was the true teaching of Hinduism and its classical texts. Religious reform in later decades had also invoked the ancient texts to place popular Hindu practices under intense scrutiny. The belief in the worship of multiple deities, the practice of a variety of rituals, the caste system, the status of Puranic myths—all of these had come into question. What was new as the nineteenth century drew to a close, however, was the force of the language of science. Under its influence, earlier formulations of monotheistic Hinduism acquired a new dimension.

Hindu intellectuals across India advanced the idea of a monotheistic Hinduism by asserting a fundamental indivisibility of science and religion. The influence of positivism was palpable here, and positivist philosophers were often cited to legitimate "dispositions" that, according to Hindu intellectuals, Hinduism itself contained.[68] These dispositions were defined increasingly, with citations from Herbert Spencer and Thomas Henry Huxley, as the belief in the oneness of all phenomena and in the existence of one supreme power; just as science had one truth, so did the "essential religion"—but not superstition masquerading as religion.[69] Hinduism as this essential religion, it was argued, did not reside in its symbols and rituals but in its recognition of the laws of nature in which the almighty manifested itself.

The belief in the indivisibility of science and religion pervaded powerful movements of Hindu reform, of which the Arya Samaj was the best known in North India. Established in the 1870s by the charismatic preacher Swami Dayananda Sarasvati, it quickly won a large following among the educated elite in the Punjab for its vision of a pristine Vedic Hinduism, shorn of superstitions.[70] It was premised on the belief that the Vedas contained and were based on the laws of nature, and it summoned the authority of science in advancing its project of reforming Hinduism, eradicating it of superstitious ideas and practices. So widespread was the notion in the milieu of religious reform that Hinduism and science were inextricable that it showed up in the views of even as bitter an opponent of Swami Dayananda and the Arya Samaj as Pandit Shiv Narayan Agnihotri. Himself at first a Brahmo Samaj activist in the Punjab, Pandit Agnihotri clashed with Dayananda and the Arya Samaj, and eventually established his own organization, called the Dev Samaj, in 1887. The purpose of the Dev Samaj was to propagate a religion named Dev Dharma, defined as a doctrine "in Harmony with Facts and Laws of Nature and based on the Evolution or Dissolution of Man's Life-Power."[71] The Dev Samaj, like the Arya Samaj, advocated radical social reform, but developed a distinctive "science-grounded religion" that combined positivist ideas of the evolution of society and of stages of knowledge with a deep veneration and worship of Pandit Agnihotri.

No movement better illustrates the rediscovery of Hindu monism in the confusion of categories than the Theosophical movement. Theosophy, which became the most prominent vehicle for transmitting the belief in the indivisibility of science and Hinduism in South India, was different in tone and emphasis from the Hindu revivalism of the Arya Samaj. But it too assumed the authenticity of an archaic Hinduism authorized by science. Originating in the spiritualist movement in the United States, Theosophy was developed by Madame Helena Petrovna Blavatsky and Colonel Henry Olcott. It was formulated at the intersection of ancient religions and modern science, containing a heady mix of clairvoyance, mesmerism, and hypnotism. The Theosophists claimed that their doctrine surpassed the understanding offered by modern science and penetrated beyond the material realm to reveal underlying principles and consciousness.[72] Convinced that the origins of their occult science lay in Indian religions, particularly Buddhism and Vedic Hinduism, they brought Theosophy to India in 1878, traveling widely, delivering lectures, receiving great respect and response, and forming alliances with men like Swami Dayananda Sarasvati. In Dayananda's Arya Samaj the Theosophists saw a mission very similar to their own, namely, the reappropriation of ancient religions as a key to a rational and scientific understanding and restructuring of modern societies. However, their plan to incorporate the Arya Samaj into the Theosophical movement did not succeed because Dayananda resisted and denounced their pluralism. Nonetheless, Theosophy began to gather impressive support after 1882, when Madame Blavatsky and Colonel Olcott turned their Adyar estate in Madras into the headquarters of their movement.[73]

From the Adyar estate, Blavatsky edited the periodical *The Theosophist*, in which she presented the turn to the Vedas as the return of modern science to its ancient roots. Or, as she wrote in one article, whatever explanations and hypotheses scientists may offer, "modern phenomena are fast *cycling* back for their true explanation, to the archaic *Vedas*, and other 'Sacred Books of the East.'"[74] While Blavatsky concentrated on developing the philosophical doctrine, Olcott worked as a tireless organizer, promoter, and practitioner of occultism. Traveling extensively in India and Ceylon, Olcott campaigned relentlessly for the Theosophist combination of ancient wisdom and scientism, and practiced mesmerism to cure patients suffering from such ailments as facial paralysis, glaucoma, deafness, and hysteria.[75] Olcott's tour of South India in 1883 to establish branches of the Theosophical Society was successful beyond his expectations. He was received by huge crowds, carried in open palanquins in torch-lit processions led by temple elephants, bell-bearing camels, and bands of musicians, and he addressed packed audiences in town halls and temples.[76] "I knew perfectly well that not one man in perhaps a dozen there could understand English or really know anything more about me than the fact that I was a friend and defender of their religion, and had a way of curing the sick that people called miraculous."[77] Theosophy's defense of Hinduism against missionary attacks added force to and also drew strength from the movement for Hindu renewal championed by the educated elite. As the Theosophists promoted Vedic authority and Sanskritic knowledge, they both expressed and advanced the elite's move from religious skepticism and suspicion of inherited cultural practices to a critical revival of Hindu religion and culture.[78]

The Tamil Brahmin and high-caste non-Brahmin elites who found themselves caught between the languages of science, positivism, and Vedic philosophy were drawn to Theosophy. Appre-

ciative of Hinduism's Western champions, they flocked to meetings and discussions conducted by Olcott and, after 1892 by
Annie Besant. Thus began the enduring alliance between Theosophy and the "Mylapore elite" of Madras that proved to be of
crucial importance in the 1910s when Annie Besant turned the
regional branches of the Society into instruments of nationalist
mobilization.[79] These branches had been formed in the 1880s
and the 1890s when Olcott's tours sparked a great deal of interest
in Theosophy among the small-town elite intellectuals.

N. K. Ramaswami Aiya was one such Brahmin intellectual. His
autobiography offers a rich portrait of the discursive milieu in
which Theosophy was thrust and prospered.[80] Aiya came from a
deeply religious family; his grandfather was a *sannyasin*, a Hindu
ascetic, and his uncle was a follower of Vedanta the philosophy
based on the metaphysical portion at the end of the Vedas and
Yoga philosophy. Growing up in Tanjore where his father was a
deputy collector, Aiya was first attracted to Vedanta and the views
of the eighth-century Hindu philosopher, Shankara, and then to
Herbert Spencer, whose writings he read in college. In 1886, the
year of his graduation from college, he "gave up religion and accepted Herbert Spencer's monism."[81] Later, he read Charles
Bradlaugh and Annie Besant, and published his first philosophical work, *Multum in Parvo*,[82] in which he "attacked Religion and
advocated Monism." In 1896 he began publishing a journal, *The
Awakener of India*, to advocate Spencer's monism and refute Theosophy and Vedanta.[83] A chance meeting with Swami Vivekananda in 1897 convinced him that Vedanta and Theosophy accepted scientific monism, prompting him to reorient his journal.
He began to study Vedanta and Theosophy, but this did not deter
him from attacking Theosophy when he attended a discussion
chaired by Colonel Olcott in Chittoor in 1898.[84] In 1903, at last
thoroughly convinced that Vedanta and Theosophy were scientific, he joined the Theosophical Society. He continued to lecture
and write on science and religion,[85] and continued to have mystical experiences that had begun in his youth; only now not only
Shankara but also Masters M and K (the spiritual mahatmas who,

according to Theosophical legend, lived in Tibet) also appeared in his dreams.[86]

Aiya's frenetic movement between different bodies of thought and his mystical experiences make him a rather special case—indeed so special that the Theosophist leaders asked him to pen his experiences in an autobiography. But the volatility of his shifts and movements should not distract us from recognizing the combination of science and religion that characterized the Hindu revival extending from the Punjab to Madras. Powerful social movements and prominent reformists like the Arya Samaj Swami Dayananda as well as little-known intellectuals like Ramaswami Aiya blended positivism, classical Hindu texts, and modern science to authenticate a monotheistic Hinduism.

The significance of monism in the Hindu revival was that it permitted the discourse of reform to invade every area of thought and practice. The belief in the indivisibility of science and religion, formed in the confusion of knowledges and linking the condition of the human soul to the moral state of the social body, authorized an invasive program of reform. Swami Dayananda's program, for example, ranged from the elimination of idolatry to the eradication of the influence of astrology in the daily lives of the Hindus.[87] Pandit Guru Datta Vidyarthi, a leader of the militant wing of the Arya Samaj in the 1880s, prepared the philosophical ground for the program of total reform by offering a "scientific" explanation for a "central conscious being" called the *atman*, or the human spirit.[88] Such a scientific explanation then enabled him to offer "expanded intellect, and not prayer," as the cure for the afflictions in the "inner life."[89]

Arguments upholding natural laws and physiology as the basis for the understanding of mental phenomena and religious life had become quite common in the elite discourse.[90] In fact, even Mahendra Lal Sircar, no religious reformer himself, had argued in 1869, citing phrenological science, that physiology could place morality and religion on "stabler foundations."[91] About three decades later, the renowned physicist and hero of the Bengali *bhadralok*, J.C. Bose, addressing a literary conference, argued for the unity of knowledge. Stating that while the West was known to compartmentalize knowledge, the "Eastern aim has been the opposite, namely that in the multiplicity of phenomena, we never miss their underlying unity.[92]

The insistence on the unity of forces and the oneness of phenomena had a powerful effect when deployed in the realm of religion. And because this view enabled a critique of a variety of existing religious and social customs in the name of science, the orthodox reaction was also compelled to invoke science. Thus, U. P. Krishnamachari, who represented himself as a proponent of "Aryan orthodoxy" and published a fortnightly journal called *The Orthodox Dynamo*, delivered a series of fourteen lectures published as *The Tribunal of Science Over Reformation Vs. Orthodoxy*.[93] He reviewed the charges that orthodoxy created disunity through the caste system, produced moral decay by telling obscene Puranic stories, promoted physical and moral degeneration by enjoining early marriage, and was responsible for intellectual decline by breeding superstition and idolatry. He cited Darwin, Spencer, Malthus, Adam Smith, Max Müller, and Huxley, among others, as authorities whose opinions supported his refutation of the reformist charges.[94] His text ended with a "Judgement of the Tribunal of Science" that acquitted orthodoxy of all charges. Orthodox Hindu practices were adjudged beneficial, practical, and in conformity with scientific laws.[95]

It was in these confusions of categories that the elites conducted the debate over the reform of Hinduism. Their transgressions of cultural borderlines empowered them to forge an invasive discourse. Both reformers and the defenders of orthodoxy required Hinduism to accommodate the laws of nature, and both placed the Hindu soul and Hindu practices at the service of modern science. If this colonized the indigenous culture, then it must also be admitted that colonization required the renegotiation of knowledge and power. The authority of science as a sign of Western power was lost as it was compelled to explain the Hindu atman. The signification of science as a sign of modernity was renegotiated as it was articulated with the archaic, the other. Father Lafont recoiled in horror as he recognized the loss of science's Western provenance to the other—to the Muslim *fakir* and the Hindu yogi, to willed respiration and the unity of phosphorus and human thought. The science that resulted—indigenized, renegotiated, translated—appeared to Lafont as the production of an alien, grotesque difference. Confusion expressed and normalized the fear caused by the breach of cultural boundaries. Yet, it was precisely in such boundary-crossings that the discourse of science achieved its enduring insertion into the elite culture.

CULTURAL TRANSFORMATION ON THE BORDERS

Towards the end of the nineteenth century a debate broke out among the Western-educated elite over the adoption of European habits and ideas by Indian young men. Many felt that the educated youth were following European fashions blindly. They had taken to tea and coffee, for example, with a zest that disregarded the ill effects of these beverages in the hot Indian climate. The *Calcutta Monthly*, a journal of the Mohammedan Sporting Club, published an article in 1896 criticizing the imitation of European practices:

> Now a word or two about the hard and fast rules which our ancestors (I mean the hardy Arabs and the primitive Aryans) observed. . . . Plain living and high thinking was their motto. . . . Our ancestors discarded all luxury and artificiality. The great benefit they derived by never drinking anything but water and milk cannot be estimated by the unthinking and the sceptic. It is only when one takes into account the prostrating influence of the *sherbet* (which produces languor and lassitude), the unnatural stimulating effect of tea and coffee and the various diseases brought on by intoxicating liquids (especially in a hot country like India), that the great scientific value of never drinking anything but water and milk becomes obvious.

Again, take for example, the habit of our ancestors of wearing nothing but white apparel. . . . Of course, if you asked them why they did so, they would reply that because our ancestors did so, or because coloured clothes look childish. But look at the thing from a scientific point of view. White coloured substances reflect all radiant light and heat. Cotton is a bad conductor of heat. Such clothing is scientifically the best for both winter and summer.[96]

Evident here is a shift in perspective that discovers a modern scientific point of view secreted in the ancient faith of "hardy Arabs and the primitive Aryans." This shift away from traditional arguments to support cultural practices registers the extent of the distribution of science's authority: even the ancestral practice of drinking nothing but milk and water is now justified by its scientific value and the contemporary habit of consuming tea and coffee is criticized for its unnatural stimulating effect. But also registered is another subtle move: the legitimation of modern science in the startling language of ancestral reason and in discrete strategies to reform daily habits.

Encapsulated here is both the story of the powerful colonial transformation of the elite and an account of the elite's emergence as a force that called into question the terms of colonial dominance. It would be a mistake to characterize science's divided, hybrid authorization as a story of the cultural adaptation of Western knowledge to Indian conditions. "Adaptation" does not capture the contention and contingency of "translation"; it fails to recognize the renegotiation of knowledge and power forced upon Western science because its hegemony could not be established through imposition. To achieve hegemony, science was compelled to disavow dominance; it had to implode prior conceptions of Western and Indian identities and express itself in the media of the Hindu atman. What was remarkable in this process was not the strange content of the science of respiration that emanated from the breath of the buried *fakir*, but the estranged position from which the authority of modern knowledge was enunciated.

83

Hybridity refers to the implosion of identities, to the dispersal of their cultural wholeness into liminality and undecidability. Such a notion of a hybrid, non-originary mode of authority is profoundly agonistic and must be distinguished from the concept and celebration of hybridity as cultural syncretism, mixture, and pluralism. Hybridity, in the sense in which I have used it in this chapter, refers to the undoing of dominance that is entailed in dominance's very establishment. It highlights cracks and fissures as necessary features of the image of authority and identifies them as effects of the disturbance in the discourse that the "native" causes. Recall, for instance, Mahendra Lal Sircar's dispersal of Western science's identity as free inquiry when he defined colonial despotism as its enabling condition. Recollect also Father Lafont's recognition of the loss of science's safety to the contagion of confusion. Such dispersals and confusions formed the ground upon which the Western-educated elite wrenched free the science of Bhaskaracharya from the fable of the Puranas, spliced it with the Sahib's knowledge, and lauded its "use in this world" and benefits "in the other world." This was no free-floating hybridization, for what it renegotiated was power, what it advanced was the claim of the elite as a modern representative of indigenous traditions. Hybridization and translation addressed the relationship between languages and subjects positioned unequally.

To situate science in the language of the other was to hybridize its authority, to displace its functioning as a sign of colonial power. Hybridization, therefore, served as a counter-hegemonic ground upon which the elite pressed their entitlement to modernity even as they misrecognized their aspirations for power as imitation and loyalism. Late-nineteenth-century gatherings of Europeans and the *bhadralok* intellectuals in Calcutta may have been heavy with the air of gratitude and loyalty to British rule, but smoldering underneath it was the explosive cross-hatching of mind with matter, Vedanta with positivism. For, to locate the origin of reason centuries before the Enlightenment in Vedantic monism was to question Western claims. This was precisely what the elite did as they realigned contradictory representations to produce a grammar of reform that penetrated the depths of their culture. By the turn of this century, fields ranging from literature to religion were opened to science's functioning as a project for a syntactical rearrangement of culture. Shaped by these changes, the elite came to occupy the center stage of colonial India. Though limited in size and circumscribed by their use of exclusive linguistic mediums (including English) and by their reliance on the printed word, the elite stood as a counter-hegemonic force. Themselves a product of the translation that gave them agency and intelligibility as subjects, the elite gave ideological direction and force to the emergence of an Indian modernity, and defined it in a predominantly Hindu and Sanskritic idiom. It was thus that the elite staked their claim to represent subaltern forms of culture and staged themselves as a force that would guide India's march to modernity.

CHAPTER FOUR

The Image of the Archaic

Time past and time future
What might have been and what has been
Point to one end, which is always present.
T. S. Eliot[1]

To ADVANCE universal claims for a people stigmatized as metaphysical and out of touch with modernity was an act of enormous imagination and ambition. Precisely such a far-reaching project came into view in late-nineteenth-century British India as the Hindu intelligentsia began to identify a body of scientific knowledge in particular Indian texts and traditions. Denying that science was alien to India, they argued with remarkable ingenuity and deep cultural learning that the ancient Hindus had originated scientific knowledge, and that this justified the modern existence of Indians as a people.

This view won widespread support among the Western-educated elite and became a key nationalist belief, but not without sparking a lively and contentious ideological debate and struggle. Consider, for example, the bitter dispute that broke out in 1895 in the northern Indian town of Vazirabad between orthodox Hindu intellectuals and members of the Arya Samaj. The dispute centered around the rationality and legitimacy of *śrāddha*, the ritual of ancestor worship. The Arya Samaj denounced this and other associated rituals as manifestations of superstitious beliefs invented by priests and contrary to the scientific wisdom contained in the Vedas, the authentic source of Hinduism. The orthodox Hindu intellectuals of Vazirabad took exception to the Arya Samaj's relentless attack on *śrāddha* as unscientific and illegitimate, and agreed to a debate. The disputation was held in May 1895 over the question as to whether or not the ancestral ritual should propitiate only the dead or both the living and the dead.

86

Pandit Ganesh Datta Shastri, arguing the orthodox case, wrote an essay in Sanskrit defending the ritual. The Arya Samaj was represented by two scholars who jointly wrote an essay on the subject.[2] The two sides disagreed on the impartiality of the Indian Orientalist judges and forwarded the essays to Max Müller, the esteemed German Orientalist, at Oxford for arbitration.

Müller replied in September 1896, stating that ancestor worship, found among both Aryan and non-Aryan nations, arose "simply from a very natural human feeling to give up something that is dear to us, to those who were dear to us."[3] No one asked if the departed came back to eat the offerings made, and the ceremony was held when the members of the family gathered at a meal. As the living also partook of the meal offered, the *śrāddha* encompassed both the departed and the living. However, superstition had taken over and people had begun to believe that the departed returned in bodily shapes to partake of the offerings, and "then the scoffers began to say that the Shraddhas were absurd because the departed spirits were never seen to consume them or benefit from them." Müller then quoted from the Vedas to establish that the ceremony honored both the dead and the living.[4] Stung by Müller's verdict, the Arya Samajists hired drummers to pace up and down the town, drumming the charge that Müller's letter was forged.

Rationalist critiques of *śrāddha* were not alien to Indian textual traditions. Such criticisms, for example, defined the basic position of the Lokāyata school of philosophy, which is dated at least as far back as the fourth century B.C.E. Advocating a relentlessly materialist view of the world that insists on experimental verification of knowledge, the Lokāyata's powerful challenge to idealist philosophies throughout the history of the philosophical tradition in Sanskrit is reflected in the existence of extended refutations of its propositions penned by rival thinkers.[5] Stating that there was no other world but this one, the Lokāyata philosophers asserted that the body alone is real. They argued that there was no such thing as soul, or its transmigration to another world, thus refuting concepts that underpinned the *śrāddha* ritual.[6]

If the rationalist criticism of *śrāddha* enjoyed a long history, the late-nineteenth-century context of its articulation was new. As the solicitation of Max Müller's opinion demonstrates, it had now to contend with the influence Western Orientalism exercised over the discourse of Hinduism; the rationality and authenticity of traditions had to be proven under the shadow of Western power. It was this compulsion that also drove Hindu intellectuals to reinterpret the rationality of classical texts in light of modern science's authority, describing Hinduism as a body of scientific knowledge and practice, and as the defining heritage of all Indians. The present claims of Indians as a people rested, they argued, on their past as Hindus with scientific knowledge of their own. Religious reformers, litterateurs, philosophers, and practicing scientists alike spoke repeatedly and obsessively of a forgotten but true knowledge fashioned by the ancient Hindus. Seizing on Orientalist research showing that ancient Indian culture could rightfully boast of significant achievements in fields ranging from mathematics to medicine, they declared that their ancient texts embodied scientific truths, that science was Hindu. The "corruption" and "irrationality" of contemporary Hinduism, they argued, were due to the loss of the ancient Hindu science. The Hindu intellectuals pointed to the existence of the caste system, the deplorable condition of women, and the grip of the priesthood and rituals to demonstrate that irrationality and unreason had so overpowered the Hindus as to render them powerless before the West. The debate over *śrāddha* was part of this larger project to reconfigure the flawed body of contemporary Hinduism in the immaculate shape of ancient Hindu science.

What made this recovery extraordinarily important was that it sought to "restore" the Indian nation "lost" to myth and superstition in the image of Hindu science. This was of profound significance, for, as Benedict Anderson reminds us, to think the nation in the myth of origins is to forge a compelling sense of contemporary collective belonging that "loom[s] out of an immemorial past, and, still more important, glide[s] into a limitless future."[7] From this point of view, the significance of the artifice of an archaic Hindu science was that it composed an undivided origin for the contemporary nation, legitimizing it as the return of an original unity and purity. The definition of classical texts as scientific was crucial in this process because it permitted their representation as the embodiment of eternal and universal laws. Signified thus, Hindu texts could be projected as the basis for a unitary modern community of Indians, while the contemporary division of India into different religions, sects, and cults could be seen as corruptions introduced by the passage of time. The image of a universal and singular archaic Hinduism that was validated by science forged difference into unity, multiplicity into singularity. Thus, the idea of India as an expression of ancient Hindu science also ended up signifying the nation as homogenous, whole, and Hindu.

As important as it is to recognize the far-reaching implications of the idea of Hindu science, we should not read it too quickly as an expression of the organicity and atavism of nationalism. The enduringly powerful identification of Hindu traditions with India's cultural texture was rooted in the colonial predicament of Hindu intellectuals. While the West was enabled by its global expansion to assert the universality of its reason in spite of its particularity, the colonized were denied this privilege; their historical fate was to assert the autonomy and universality of their culture in the domain of the nation. Alien domination positioned the nation as the enabling basis for pressing the universal claims of the colonized's particular knowledge—the horizon within which the subordinated intellectuals could justify their entitlement to modernity. In the colonial context, the nation was an expansive and open-ended concept; it meant negotiation, not nativism. It was a space of translation, an arena where the colonized elite reinterpreted the Vedas and repositioned them in relation to modern science in order to establish Hindu culture as universal knowledge.

The obligation to translate casts another light on the projection of the Hindu past as the sign of India's holism and homogeneity. It urges us to rethink the idea that the notion of Hindu science could consolidate the vision of the modern nation without punctuating the latter's language of atavism and organicity. In this context, it is significant that nationalist intellectuals believed not only that ancient texts contained Hindu science but also that this science had been lost to unreason and superstition in the course of history. Their idea of the modern nation as the recovery of Hindu science could not but crack the image of cohesion and synchronicity, and hollow out the solidity of the Hindu past.[8] How could the modern nation emerge continuous with the past when it was evoked as a form of return, as a repetition of the past? What did it mean to maintain the notion of an organicist nation, developing harmoniously and continuously in accordance with its tradition, when the present appeared as a palimpsest of the past, when the modern nation was seen as a belated realization of the "before"? In such a representation, the past must appear as an anteriority, not as an origin. Unlike the organicist concept, which draws an unbroken line between the origin and the present, the idea of the modern nation as the return of the archaic introduces a sharp break between the past and the present: the past irrupts, it does not evolve, into the present. As the contemporary national self emerges in the differential sign of the return, as *its* time is expressed in the repetition of *another* time, an alienating otherness becomes the medium of expressing the fullness of the nation. In this sense, the idea of the modern nation as the return of the archaic disrupts the evolutionary language of origins and invokes the past as a strange "before" that is discontinuous with the present.[9]

This is not to restate the familiar refrain that origins are never undivided but always split, nor is it to conclude that the reality of heterogeneity explodes the myth of the homogeneous nation rooted in archaic Hinduism. Instead, it suggests that the focus on the disjunctive structure of the nationalist imagination illuminates how the belief in Hindu science as the universal heritage of all Indians could serve nationalism without turning it into nativism. To conceive the present as the repetition of the past, rather than as its growth and fulfillment, was to enable the discourse of

Hindu science to invade every contemporary context and every aspect of people's lives. The entire arena of contending cultural traditions and social forces became available for recovery in the image of the archaic. In this sense, the evocation of the past as an anteriority, not an origin, was a productive moment in the realization of the modern nation. By the same token the irruption, rather than progression, of ancient Hindu science into the present estranged the modern nation. The contemporary nation, reflected in the mirror of the archaic, could not but emerge disfigured and distorted. It was from this estrangement and distortion, from an experience of loss, that modern India had to be refigured as a form of translation.

The Search for Hindu Universality

The cultural representation of the modern nation in its past gathered powerful momentum during the second half of the nineteenth century and was expressed in the rise of Hindu revivalism. This revival, drawing to its fold the educated elite ranging from religious reformers to practicing scientists, entailed the valorization of certain ancient texts as Hindu and as the authentic and authoritative heritage of Indians. The intentions and arenas of activities of these intellectuals varied. Religious reformers focused on interpretations of canonical texts and the status of existing beliefs and practices, and they expounded their views through publications and religious discourses. Members of new professions, including scientists, on the other hand, rarely concerned themselves with theological questions; their principal interest in the past was to identify a body of ancient knowledge that conformed to modern scientific truths and methods. They published books and pamphlets, delivered public lectures, and formed modern associations in order to convince the emergent Western-educated elite that science was part of their heritage. But regardless of differences in motives and arenas of action, all of these intellectuals worked in the milieu of revival and reform. There

91

was general agreement that India's past was Hindu, and that Hinduism was more than just a religion. Its texts, when properly selected and interpreted, contained scientific knowledge and defined the cultural past of all Indians. This archaic Hinduism may have had a particular history, but as culture and knowledge it was universal, and defined and justified the modern existence of Indians as a people. Shaping and shaped by this Hindu revivalism, the expression of the modernity of the Indian nation in the science of the ancient Hindus became a pervasive and enduring feature of the nationalist imagination.

No leader exemplified Hindu revivalism better than Swami Dayananda Sarasvati, the charismatic and audacious preacher and reformer, whose program of reviving the Vedic Hinduism of the ancient Aryans spread across northern India during the late nineteenth century. Under his teachings and magnetic influence the Arya Samaj quickly made its mark among educated Hindus, particularly in the Punjab.[10] Asserting the superiority of Vedic Hinduism over all religions, the Arya Samaj's mission was to restore a pristine and classical Vedic religion cleansed of such "corrupt" accretions as priesthood, the caste system, idol worship, child marriage, and prohibitions on widow remarriage and female education. This vision of a pure, scientific Hinduism of the Vedas was based on the authority and originality that Dayananda claimed for Vedic texts. This was not new, for the assertion of the Vedas' absolute authority has a long history.[11] Neither was the claim new that, strictly speaking, the Vedas were not religious texts, but transcendent knowledge. Derived from the Sanskrit root *vid*, "to know," *Veda* means "true knowledge." Thus, the orthodox and pedagogical Brahminical tradition of Mimamsa philosophy argued that the Vedas contained timeless and absolute truths.[12] Dayananda, however, advanced these claims in a new context in which the Hindu intelligentsia was anxious to establish not only the Vedas as a canonical "scripture" on par with the Bible and Qur'an, but also superior to them as a body of knowledge, as science. The intelligentsia's predicament was that to accomplish this, a simple citation of Mimamsa philosophy on the

Vedas' transcendent truths, for instance, could not suffice, because traditional arguments operated in a different environment than the Western criticisms they had to confront. It was necessary, then, to invoke modern science to show that Vedic knowledge deserved the status of scientific truths.

Dayananda advanced his claims relentlessly in writings, speeches, sermons, and in several debates he staged with orthodox Hindu pundits, Christian missionaries, and Muslim theologians.[13] Brazenly charging his opponents with ignorance and superstition, he claimed that whereas modern science confirmed the Vedic understanding of the universe, other religions violated the elementary principles of reason. He thrived on creating controversy and provoking opposition, and his rhetorical strategy in the verbal combats he staged was to refute and ridicule his opponents with relentless appeals to reason and science. In one such verbal duel staged in 1877, the combatants included Dayananda, a Hindu representative, four missionaries, and two Muslim theologians. Its avowed purpose was to ascertain true religion by addressing several questions formulated by Dayananda.[14] One of these questions was: What did God make the world with, at what time, and for what purpose? One of the Christian representatives, Reverend Scott, replied that he found the question useless, but he went on to state his view: God created the world out of nothing because there was nothing but God in the beginning; He created the world by fiat, and though the time of creation is not known, creation has a beginning. Reverend Scott was followed by Mohammed Kasim, who declared that God created the world out of his own body. The question of when, he thought, was futile.[15] Then came Dayananda's turn. He is sharp and combative, and his appeal to the authority of science is revealing:

God has made the world out of Nature or atoms, which are thus the material cause of the universe. The Vedas and the profane sciences prove the matter or the aggregate of atoms to be the primary and eternal substance of the phenominal [sic] world. The Deity and nature are both unbeginning and endless. Not one atom of the underlying substance of visible things can be increased, decreased, or annihilated. . . . Now, what is the doctrine of the nihilists, who maintain that the world has come out into existence from nothing. They point out fiat or sound as the cause of the world. This theory, being opposed to science, is incorrect. . . . No science can prove that the effect follows from no cause. It violates the law of causation, the foundation of science, and subverts the law of association, the basis of reasoning.[16]

Dayananda was not wrong in attributing the concept of nature's eternity to the Vedas, but it is significant that he draws on the authority of "profane sciences" to establish the truth of Vedic knowledge. Here he departed sharply from a key proposition of the Sanskritic tradition that denied the epistemological value of human knowledge based on experience, experiment, invention, discovery, and innovation.[17] According to this tradition, theory was prior to practice, and the theory of the śāstras, especially the Vedas, was transcendent, needing no human confirmation. But Dayananda was constrained to confirm the Vedas' concepts with human knowledge, this being the price the non-Western tradition had to pay to authorize itself in a world dominated by the West.

Having claimed the superiority of the Vedas over other texts and traditions because they alone were consistent with science, Dayananda went on to assert their antiquity. Claiming that "formerly knowledge travelled from India to Egypt, thence to Greece, thence to Europe, and so forth," he declared that no other religion could possess "the genuine history of this country"; only the Aryans, the most ancient people of India and the possessors of "the most ancient records of knowledge," could answer questions about creation and offer their country's "genuine history."[18] Such a claim on behalf of the Vedas and for the Aryans' right to represent their nation's history could not be confined to philosophical matters but had to extend to the daily practice of Vedic religion if the modern Hindus were to be refashioned in the image of their scientific forebears. This meant that the Vedic rituals—of which the *homa*, or sacrificial fire, was the most important—had to be represented as scientific in inspiration and purpose. This was significant because Dayananda's reinterpretation of the Vedas was formed in opposition to popular Hindu rituals of worship and devotion. Anticipating that the Vedic sacrificial fire and the recitation of hymns might be subjected to the same critique that he had directed at popular Hinduism, Dayananda offered explanations that invoked the authority of science. In *Satyārth Prakāsh*, the canonical text of the Arya Samaj, Dayananda first recommends the *homa* and then poses questions that he answers:

> (*Question*) What is the use of *homa*?
>
> (*Answer*) Everyone knows that foul air and water breed disease, diseases cause unhappiness in human beings, whereas fragrant air and water promote health and the destruction of disease provides happiness.
>
> (*Question*) It is useful to apply sandalwood paste on someone's person and to offer clarified butter in a meal[?] The knowledgeable do not destroy and waste them in fire.
>
> (*Answer*) If you knew the laws of matter which state that a substance is indestructible, you would never say such a thing. Look, when *homa* is performed, men living in places far away from its site breathe the fragrant air just as surely as they take in foul air. This is because fire breaks matter into fine particles which mix with and are carried by the air to great distances, where they negate pollution.[19]

To suggest that the Vedic *homa* purified the atmosphere by fragmenting matter into fine, light particles was to throw science into the Vedic fire. Science emerged from this sacrificial fire with an ancient Hindu rationality, buttressing Dayananda's claim that only the Aryans possessed the most ancient records of knowledge. This also supported his assertion that they alone could write their country's genuine history. Such a staging of Vedic rituals as the performance of the modern nation underscored the nation's importance in the representation of traditions forced upon it by Western domination. In colonial India, to affirm that one's cultural tradition was universal was also to assert autonomy and entitlement to the modern nation. This appealed to educated Hindus, who in North India flocked in great numbers to the Arya Samaj. Their eager participation helped the Arya Samaj to run a successful program of education and social reform. Instruction in modern science was integrated into the Sanskritic education offered at the Dayananda Anglo-Vedic College, and research institutes were established that sent speakers on tours to deliver lectures on science and technology.[20]

This emphasis on science did not suffer when the organization split into moderate and militant factions in the 1890s. On the contrary, as the militant Gurukul wing stressed the Vedic rather than the Anglo part of education in nationalizing the curriculum,[21] the Vedas themselves were interpreted as science. The militant Arya Samajists emphasized Vedic education with the strident claim that the Vedas constituted the sole source of science. This was the guiding vision in the writings of Pandit Guru Datta Vidyarthi, a professor in the Lahore Government College who inspired the program of Vedic education imparted in the Gurukul school and led the militant faction until his death in 1890. Vidyarthi outlined his position in his collection of essays, *Wisdom of the Rishis*, by first refuting the argument that the Vedas were myths that embodied natural truths in an imaginative language.[22] Unlike myths, which are concrete, the Vedas, he argued, were abstract and philosophical; they gave birth to philosophy, and mythology evolved afterwards. Having thus established the Vedas as philosophy, he questioned the authority of the European Orientalists whose interpretation of the Vedic hymns as the mythology of a primitive people he dismissed as prejudiced and the product of mistranslations of Sanskrit.[23] The European Orientalists, Vidyarthi charged, did not understand the rules of Vedic Sanskrit grammar properly; they treated Vedic terms as nouns when they were actually *yaugika*, that is, terms that conveyed a derivative meaning consisting of a reference to a root together with modifications effected by the affixes. As an example of such a mistranslation, Vidyarthi cited lines translated by Max Müller:

> May Mitra, Varuna, Aryaman, Ayu, Indra, the Lord of Ribhus, and the Maruts not rebuke us, because we shall proclaim at the sacrifice the virtues of the swift horse sprung from god.[24]

Vidyarthi offered the following translation instead:

> We will describe the power-generating virtues of energetic horses endowed with brilliant properties, or the virtues of the vigorous force of heat which learned or scientific men can evoke to work for purposes of appliances (not sacrifices). Let not philanthropists, noble men, judges, learned men, rulers, wise men and practical mechanics ever disregard these properties.[25]

The purpose of the great difference of Vidyarthi's translation from Müller's was to demonstrate that Vedic religion did not enjoin the worship of deities. The Sanskrit term *devatā*, he argued, did not mean a deity but signified a process; Agni and Marut were not nouns but terms that referred to processes and properties. Through such subtle reinterpretation and relocation of terms, Vidyarthi realigned the relationship between the Vedas and science. He placed the philosophy of the Vedas in a scientific register. His essay on the Vedic term *vayu* is a treatise on atmosphere, on the "gaseous envelope" composed of molecules of air charged with energy. "Is not, then, a *light, mobile, tremor-communicating, effluvia-carrying medium* a better and a more exact appellation for this masterly creation of the Architect of Nature than the ugly, unmeaning, inexact and half-articulate word *air*[?]" he asked.[26]

As Vidyarthi housed the concepts of mobility and medium in the Vedic term *vayu*, he shifted both science and the Veda out of their respective domains. This changed their meanings. The Vedic *vayu*, when placed in relationship to changing temperatures and currents, revealed itself not in accordance with the opposition between science and religion but as a concept formed in their precipitous mix. It is thus that the Sanskrit word *ṛg* came to signify nature and its properties, and Vidyarthi construed the *Rg Veda* to mean the knowledge of the "physical, chemical and active properties of all *material* substances as well as the psychological properties of all *mental* substances."[27] Whether or not this is the real meaning of the Sanskrit term is irrelevant; what is pertinent is that the Vedas were infused with the authority of Western science, whose position, in turn, they invaded and dislocated. We can observe this double operation performed in Vidyarthi's assertion that "long before Cavendish performed his experiment on the composition of water . . . the true philosophy of the composition of water was recorded in the Vedas and perhaps understood by many philosophers of the east."[28]

The belief in the antiquity of Vedic knowledge was not new to the nineteenth century. Nor was Vidyarthi's following claim original: "The measure of Vedic truth is not its power to grow and spread, but its inherent power to remain the same ever to-day and to-morrow."[29] The Mimamsa philosophers explicitly denied the notion of progress and argued that knowledge could advance only by regressing to match the eternal and the original.[30] But it is telling that the claim for the timeless truths of the Vedas required Vidyarthi to cite Cavendish. He had to first acknowledge the authoritative status of Cavendish's experiment and then establish that the Vedic conception conformed to its results in order to assert that the philosophers of the east had always known how water was composed. Encapsulated here once again is the quandary that the authorization of indigenous traditions faced under colonialism: indigenous thought had to cohabit with Western knowledge in order to exceed it.

HINDU SCIENCE AND THE MODERN NATION

Inevitably, the modern nation impinged on the expression of Hindu universality. Because alien domination was structured as the rule of one nation over another, the colonized culture was obliged to express its autonomy and universality in the framework of the modern nation. To say that one's culture was rational and universal was to lay claim to nationness because it signified these cultural attributes. Recall Dayananda's statement that the Aryans' possession of the most ancient records of knowledge meant that they alone could represent their country's genuine history. The Hindu intelligentsia simply could not get around the looming presence of the nation. The revaluation of the past, therefore, led to the projection of Hindu science as India's national tradition.

The idea of Hindu science had originated in the Orientalist research of the late eighteenth century.[31] But a century later, the seeds sown by the Orientalists had come to bear different fruits. No longer did it satisfy only the hunger for the knowledge of the East: Hindu science now nourished the idea of a modern Indian nation. Helped by its status as the product of academic research, the notion of Hindu science won influence beyond the circle of religious reformers. References to Hindu medicine, mathematics, astronomy, and chemistry became ubiquituous in the elite culture. Journals and pamphlets returned to the past to search for the scientific contributions of the Hindus, identifying India with Hinduism and seeking Hinduism's transcendent value in its science. Kissory Chandra Mitra, a *bhadralok* intellectual, wrote that the Vedas demonstrate the great progress the Hindus had made in medicine, and "shew the high estimation in which the science and practice of medicine were held."[32] In a reversal of the colonial stereotype, he added: "It was in the East that medical philosophy was first cultivated; While it reposed in Asia on the solid foundations of induction and deduction, it rested in Europe on the baseless support of the supernatural, and was in fact obliterated in superstition."[33] He acknowledged that Hindu medicine, including *ayurveda*, originated in religion, was administered by priests, and did not come close to modern anatomical knowledge. But, he argued, it equaled ancient Greek medicine and "it was precisely what might be expected in a very early stage of a civilization."[34] "What might be expected" referred to the absence of modern science. Mitra maintained that it was anachronistic to compare contemporary Western medicine with the ancient *ayurveda*, although such a comparison was widespread and constituted the background for the criticisms that the practitioners of Western medicine directed at indigenous medicine and drugs.[35]

Ayurveda's vital presence as a therapeutic system enabled it to survive the weight of forces ranged against it, even attracting the government's patronage and regulation of its practice.[36] More importantly, it drew strength from its functioning as a sign of India's culture. The nationalist movement took up the issue of *ayurveda*, and *ayurvedic* practitioners advanced their craft as science.[37] They established popular journals in which they offered medical advice and disseminated *ayurvedic* knowledge, and wrote tracts defending the therapeutic system against the charge that it was unscientific.[38] These publications located the nation's genius in its scientific achievements and described India as the original home of science. For instance, the *Nagari Pracharini Patrika* published an article that drew on Orientalist research to argue that science originated in India. The Hindus, it claimed, had not only originated the sciences of medicine, chemistry, and grammar, but had provided the foundation of all sciences by inventing the decimal notation and introducing algebra.[39]

The notion of a Hindu science, widely circulated by middle-class journals and pamphlets, received authoritative interpretations in the writings of two individuals, Brajendranath Seal and Prafulla Chandra Ray. Born in 1864, Seal was a philosopher who, like many other Bengali intellectuals, was a member of the reformist Brahmo Samaj. But by the turn of the century, his interest in comparative religion and history had moved him increasingly to scientific positivism.[40] Influenced by Comte's ideas, he penned *The Positive Sciences of the Hindus* (1915), which actually began as part of Ray's project on the history of chemistry. Seal's aim was to establish that scientific concepts and methods underpinned Hindu speculative thought. With remarkable erudition and rigor, Seal identified a body of scientific knowledge and practices developed by the Hindus in the investigation of physical phenomena. Divided into seven chapters, his book offered a comparative assessment of Hindu mechanical, physical, and chemical theories, and Hindu ideas of mechanics, acoustics, plant and animal classification, and physiology. It located the formation of core scientific concepts and practices in the millennium from 500 B.C.E. to 500 C.E., and identified the existence of a precise Sanskrit philosophical and scientific terminology. The book concluded with an essay on the Hindu scientific method aimed to demonstrate that Hindu sciences were not random practices but formed a systematic body of knowledge that was governed by rigorous and explicit methods of observation, proof, and experimentation, and by theories of perception, inference, variation, and causation. This demonstrated, Seal argued, that the Hindus, no less than the Greeks, had contributed to the development of science and natural philosophy.[41] The reference to the Greeks was not incidental. So powerful and widespread was the nineteenth-century ideology that European culture and modern originated in classical Greece, that Indian intellectuals were compelled to formulate a classicism of their own. Orientalist research was reframed to position ancient India as classical India, and the culture of its early inhabitants as the heritage of modern Indians. This classicism spurred Seal's reconstruction of the ancient Hindu sciences, and sparked many other nationalist projects of "recovering" classical Hindu science.

Ray's work on the history of Hindu chemistry received greater notice than Seal's work, though it too was marked by a sober and academic classicism. His research on Hindu chemistry formed part of his activities as a nationalist scientist. His first nationalist act was submitting an essay entitled "India before and after the Mutiny" for an essay competition in 1885 in Edinburgh where he completed his doctoral work.[42] His essay did not win a prize, but this did not signal the end of either his nationalism or his scientific work. Upon his return to India, he became an influential teacher at Presidency College in Calcutta, where he taught chemistry from 1889 to 1916. He also established the Bengal Chemical and Pharmaceutical Works in 1893 as a commercial enterprise and as a research body to promote the indigenous production of pharmaceutical products.[43]

Ray's supreme achievement and fame as a nationalist scientist, however, rested on his two-volume *History of Hindu Chemistry* (1902–9), a meticulous, scholarly reconstruction of the history of the ancient chemical theories and practices, accomplished with a careful reading of Sanskrit texts.[44] Ray divided the development of Hindu alchemy into four periods: the Vedic and Ayurvedic age from 1500 B.C.E. to 800 C.E., the transitional period from 800 to 1100, the period of Tantric chemistry lasting from 1100 to 1300, and the iatro-chemical period from 1300 to 1550. Beginning with the knowledge of metallurgy evidenced on the pottery of the Indus Valley civilization, Ray set forth a history of chemistry in India—documenting alchemic notions developed around medicine in the Vedas and in *ayurveda*, tracing the transformation in Hindu medicine as it increasingly used metallic substances in the composition of drugs during the transitional period, depicting the evolution of Hindu alchemy along with the development of Tantric rituals, and describing the final stage of the growth of metallurgy before a decline set in towards the close of the sixteenth century.

This was not a work of nationalist cheerleading but a work of immense sophistication and erudition that assessed the achievements of Hindu alchemy from the point of view of modern experiments and observations. Ray never claimed that Hindu alchemy was an experimental science, but only that its development in India was owed to indigenous sources, not to Greek influence, as European Orientalists were wont to believe.[45] He patiently reconstructed the history of Hindu alchemy, including its knowledge of the science of mercury, through its different stages. India, more so than Europe, developed alchemy as a branch of medicine, which meant an inevitable connection of alchemy with faith in deities, because the full efficacy of drugs was believed to require the interposition of the gods. But the higher gods of the *Ṛgveda* were "almost always personifications of the elements and other natural phenomena, such as the fire and the wind, the sun and the dawn."[46] Herbs and plants were recognized for their active properties and were addressed as deities. Even the *Caraka-*

saṃhita, the foundational text of *ayurvedic* medicine, dated to the first century C.E., contained frequent references to Vedic gods. If this meant that Hindu medicine and chemistry were never able to completely shake themselves free from magic and alchemy, one could still identify, Ray argued, a scientific core in Hindu texts. *A History of Hindu Chemistry* was a scrupulously scholarly attempt to accomplish precisely this task.

Ray's labor of love attracted a favorable response from scientists and nonscientists alike. Lauded in the most prestigious scientific journal in India at the time,[47] his careful reconstruction of a Hindu scientific heritage was hailed as epoch-making and produced calls for pursuing modern science by resuscitating archaic knowledge: "Let us imitate the example of the ancient Hindus, let us follow the foot-steps of modern Hindus like Dr. Ray."[48] He became something of a cult figure and was invited frequently to deliver public lectures. These lectures drew on his *History of Hindu Chemistry* and concerned, not surprisingly, the theme of the Hindu scientific heritage. Thus, in a lecture delivered in 1918, Ray declared that the Hindus had developed their chemistry long before the Arabs or Europeans and that their achievements in chemistry formed a part of their general scientific accomplishments.[49] These accomplishments extended to several other sciences, proving that Hindu chemists, "far from being mythical, existed in real flesh and blood," although their attainments had remained unrecognized.[50] These forgotten Hindu chemists could be heard speaking again, demanding our attention, Ray announced to his audience in another lecture he delivered in Madras:

> Thus it is that even after a lapse of 7, 8, or 10 centuries, Govinda, Somadeva, Nāgārjuna, Rāmachandra, Svachchanda Bhairava and others appeal to modern India in eloquent terms from dust-laden shelves and worm-eaten tomes and manuscripts not to give up the pursuit of the Science they so dearly professed. As I find gathered round me the flower of youth in Madras, may I join in the appeal so eloquently given utterance to by the chemist Nāgārjuna some

1000 years ago: "For 12 years I have worshipped in thy temple, O Goddess; if I have been able to propitiate thee, vouchsafe to me, thy devotee, the rare knowledge of Chemistry."[51]

While Ray made an eloquent plea on behalf of Hindu chemistry, others rose to the defense of *ayurveda*, a system of medical ideas and practices first set out in the Vedas and elaborated subsequently in other treatises, most notably in the *Caraka-saṃhita* and the *Suśruta-saṃhita*. *Ayurveda* had come under increasing attack as quackery by the practitioners of Western medicine, and it was defended spiritedly as science not only by *ayurvedic* practitioners but also by those who regarded it as Hindu science.[52] One such able and influential defender was G. Srinivasa Murti, a Tamil Brahmin Sanskrit scholar and a doctor trained in Western medicine. Srinivasa Murti's combination of classical Sanskritic erudition and modern Western education drew him to Theosophy.[53] The Theosophical Society, after the establishment of its headquarters in Madras in 1882, was quick to win influence among the Tamil upper-caste elite, who read Theosophy's heady mixture of occultism, mesmerism, positivism, and Eastern philosophy as a strong defense of the ancient Brahminical order. Functioning in this milieu, Srinivasa Murti was well positioned to provide a scientific justification for *ayurveda* when he was appointed in 1921 by the Madras government as the secretary of a committee charged to study indigenous medicine. In the report he submitted in 1923, Srinivasa Murti defended *ayurveda* and the Hindu scientific method.[54] His purpose, however, was not to render *ayurveda* identical to Western science. He showed resemblance and convergence between the two but also asserted the irreducible difference of Hindu science. He did so not only by claiming that Hindu methods were superior to Western methods, but, more interestingly, by refuting the charge that *ayurveda*'s intimacy with religion and philosophy crippled its scientific status. He wrote:

To understand this position, we must first realize that, to a Hindu, "Philosophy" was not a matter of mere speculation or intellectual edification; from his standpoint, no subject of inquiry was worth the study, unless it helped the student to so regulate his life as to lead him to that state of perfection called Moksha. The modern Western conception of Philosophy as a pure speculative, theoretical study dissociated, as it were, from the actual problems of life had no place in his scheme of life; his justification of philosophy was not merely its excellence as a theory of speculation, but its intense practical value in regulating one's daily life; in other words, the great value to him of philosophy was that it served as the basis of certain ethical rules and physical practices, broadly included under the term "Religion," although modern Westerners would label some portions of it as "Ethics" and others as "Science."[55]

Although the Hindu scientific method resembled Western reasoning, its theories and concepts were different and could not be made to correspond to Western knowledge without violating their integrity: "We should not torture Ayurvedic texts to read into them Modern Allopathic teachings through forced comparisons and fanciful interpretations."[56] Based on its own principles and premises, Hindu science was ineluctably different.

Srinivasa Murti's claim for the ineluctable difference of Hindu science assumed the prior existence of a modern Indian nation, an assumption captured in his description of Ayurveda as an Indian system. At work here was the silent presence of the nation that empowered him to voice *ayurveda*'s irreducible difference and universality as a scientific system. And yet, it was Hindu science that produced and legitimated the national subject: modern India came into being as it listened, with Ray as the eloquent interlocutor, to the appeal of Govinda and Somadeva "after a lapse of 7, 8, or 10 centuries" and to the utterance of "the chemist Nāgārjuna some 1000 years ago." Thus, even as Dayananda, Seal, Ray, and Murti gave themselves the right to represent India, it was their pronouncements that retroactively validated this right. Through this "fabulous retroactivity," to use Jacques Derrida felicitous phrase,[57] the idea of Hindu science brought into being the nation for which it assumed a prior existence.

RECOVERING THE LOST NATION

In 1883, an article appeared in a Hindi journal published by the Rotilkhand Patriotic Association, extolling the technological accomplishments of the ancient Hindus:

> There are some admirers of contemporary life who doubt and ask what technologies flourished in ancient Aryavarta. Did it have steam engines? Did it have telegraph, photography, or heliograph? It would be appropriate for them to acknowledge the truth that the ancient Aryans knew the power of steam . . . and the Aryans and their descendants possessed telegraph instruments that did not require telegraph poles and wires. . . . The Aryans fought battles in air chariots.[58]

The invented memory of the Aryans' past scientific attainments caused deep anguish as the writer observed the present: the ancient sciences had disappeared; Brahmin supremacy, which had created oceans of knowledge in Asia, had vanished; the faculty to understand matter no longer survived; Indians had become ignorant and selfish; the population and, along with it, poverty had grown; and the whole country was divided and fractious. "In the gardens where the birds of different kinds once sang, now hoot the owls, and the gardener cries out in grief: here grew the plants, here bloomed the flowers."[59]

What are we to make of the unmistakable sense of ruin and desolation that the fabricated remembrance of the past produced? Could the Hindu past serve as the culture of the modern nation without producing a searing sense of loss? Bringing into existence retroactively what one assumed to be already present was a project fraught with tensions.[60] It introduced a trace of inadequacy in the national subject as its retroactive authorization deferred its a priori presence. We can observe the irruption of this sense of lack and defeat in the Indian intelligentsia's understanding of India's present. The image of the Hindu past not only evoked a compelling sense of India's homogeneity, solidity, and unity, but also produced a powerful experience of loss, degeneration, and difference. The glory of ancient Hinduism, far from projecting an origin that evolved harmoniously and seamlessly into the present, burst forcefully into the time of the modern nation and made the ignominy of India's contemporary subjection to British rule all too evident. The present appeared dark and adrift, and the nation's archaic knowledge survived as a dim presence, as a reminder of its loss to superstition, priestcraft, the dark middle ages, and Muslim invasions. The experience of loss became the fertile ground for the proliferation of strategies designed to regain the fullness of the ancient nation.

The loss of Hindu greatness formed a staple of the Orientalist diet, but its powerful function in the Hindu discourse was to bring the modern nation to life. Highlighting this function of the notion of loss, the Arya Samaj stated: "The main purpose of the Arya Samaj is to diffuse, to the best of its powers, those sublime truths which are contained in the *Vedas,* and thus *regenerate* [emphasis mine] the Hindu nation."[61] The idea of regeneration derived force from the belief that India was the cradle of civilization. All the sciences and arts and religions, Dayananda asserted, originated in Vedic India[62] But then came the Great War of the epic *Mahābhārata,* when learned men and philosophers were slain on the battlefield. Knowledge diminished; the religion of the Vedas disappeared or was perverted by the Brahmins, who had become ignorant; fraud, superstition, and irreligion flourished; and numerous religious sects were born. An Indian priesthood took root who convinced the Kshatriya warriors and kings that their word was the pronouncement of God himself, and they flourished in the lap of luxury. Idol worship, temples, and the idea of incarnations were invented to ensnare the masses and prevent them from accepting Jainism. Thus arose Puranic Hinduism, a system of false beliefs and idolatry.[63] How could such false beliefs overpower the true knowledge of the Vedas? According to Dayananda, Puranic Hinduism was victorious because people, "naturally prone to indulgences of imagination and ignorance," were unable to live the difficult life imposed by the science of the

Vedas. As people succumbed to the bewitching charms of poetry, "science gave way to the spell of mythology, which soon spread over the world with the speed of electricity."[64]

Pandit Guru Datta Vidyarthi continued Dayananda's attacks on the Puranas. He argued that because the fables told by the Puranas were more appealing to our "degenerate sense" than the dry, abstract truths of the Vedas, idolatry and the fanciful belief of reincarnation took hold. He wrote:

> The broad and universal distinction of all training into profes-
> sional and liberal has been altogether lost sight of in the Puranic
> mythology, and like everything else has been contracted into a
> narrow, superstitious sphere of shallow thought. The Vedas, in-
> stead of being regarded as universal text-books of liberal and pro-
> fessional sciences, are now regarded as simply codes of religious
> thought. Religion, instead of being grasped as the guiding princi-
> ple of all active propensities of human nature, is regarded as an
> equivalent of certain creeds and dogmas.[65]

In the cold light of the reason and science of the Vedas, the myths, legends, and deities of the Puranas that formed the stuff of popular beliefs and practices, appeared childish and deserving of ridicule. These fables had managed to even pervert the meaning of Vedic philosophy; "instead of being regarded as universal text-books" of science, the Vedas had become a body of "certain creeds and dogmas."

The Arya Samaj leaders pressed the claim that the Vedas were not religious texts but books of knowledge not to settle an incon-sequential and arcane theological debate but to establish the Vedas as the basis for India's entitlement to modern universality. This meant constituting Indians in the image of the ancient Ary-ans and attacking popular beliefs and practices. The personality and the daily life of Indians had to be refashioned if they were to be regenerated as true descendants of the ancient Aryans. This project drew inspiration from Dayananda's *Satyārth Prakāsh*, much of which was devoted to outlining rules of daily living. Da-yananda's bitter denunciation of astrology as superstition, for example, was animated by the concern to diminish the influence of the priesthood on the daily life of the Hindus. He argued that once people gained the true knowledge of the physical world contained in the Vedas, they would cease to depend on priests and astrologers who hoodwinked the ignorant by attributing diseases and misfortunes to planetary influences.[66] *Pānchāl Panditā*, the bilingual journal of the militant Arya Samajists devoted to women's issues hammered home the same message: astrology fed on ignorance and was contrary to the authentic texts of Hinduism.[67] The reform of daily life was also a principal concern in Guru Datta Vidyarthi's text, *Wisdom of the Rishis*, which devoted a chapter to the organization of the household and marriage, subtitled "A Scientific Exposition of Mantras Nos. 1, 2, and 3 of the 50th Sukta, of the first Mandal of the Rig Veda bearing on the subject of the household."[68]

The reform of daily life meant identifying and attacking rituals that the Arya Samaj read as the product of superstition and priestcraft. The favorite target was the ancestral ritual of *śrāddha*, against which it carried out a ferocious pamphlet war. To expose it as irrational, the Arya Samaj had to dislocate the ritual from its context and place it in a different register, where it could be judged according to standards of empirical proofs and scientific understanding. Take, for example, a Hindi pamphlet that the Arya Samaj published in 1893. Consisting of a fictional disputation between an Aryan and a Pauranik (a Puranic believer), the text rigs the discussion in favor of the Arya Samaj, demanding that the efficacy of the *śrāddha* ritual be proved and demonstrated with empirical evidence. The Aryan commands that the Pauranik explain how his ancestors return from the world of the dead to consume food offered in the ritual, and then goes on to dispute the explanation it manufactures.

Aryan: Okay, let us assume that they shed their gross bodies to reenter this world, as they did earlier to depart from it upon their death. I assume that just as we cremate a lifeless body, so do they in the world of the dead, or else the blood would cause the body to rot. If this is the case, then it seems you have committed a murder by performing a *śrāddha*, because now they are neither in the other world nor here. Where will they go now?

Pauranik: No, my view is that they live in subtle, spiritual bodies. They do not need gross bodies. Therefore, they can travel as they please.

Aryan: This is impossible because, if they did not leave this world of their own will, how can they now travel as they please? Besides, you believe in rebirth. If they left their bodies here, who would be reborn?[69]

Admitting his error, the Pauranik amends his argument, stating that ancestors do not reenter this world to accept the offerings made in the ritual; rather, the food offered to the Brahmin in the *śrāddha* ceremony is carried across to the ancestors. The Aryan then clinches the argument:

Aryan: This is very doubtful. If the fluid from the food consumed by the Brahmin is sent across, then it will not turn into blood, and the Brahmin will die. If it transforms into blood and reaches your ancestors, then they are guilty of drinking the blood of the Brahmins, committing their murder. Besides, the Brahmins should become weak from the lack of blood, but we observe instead that the Brahmins fed during the *śrāddha* become strong and healthy from the fifteen days of feasting. So, your argument does not make sense. Nor can you say that your ancestors consume the food offered them by inhaling the Brahmin's breath, because they could not possibly survive breathing the foul air, that is, "carbonic acid gas," that we exhale.[70]

The dialogue is set up to establish the writ of science and reason, but the Aryan's strident refutation of the Pauranik's beliefs is attained through distortions. Having placed *śrāddha* in the incongruous arena of empirical proofs in order to demonstrate its falsity, the text is committed to ask questions one does not ask of rituals. The Aryan must ask: How do the ancestors travel? Do they shed their gross bodies? How can they be reborn? Does food turn into blood before its consumption by the ancestors? Such questions are rigged with the intent to establish the vision of an authentic and scientific Vedic Hinduism, but to fulfill this intent the Aryan must first allow the Pauranik to cut into the discourse, permitting his ancestors to gnaw at its authoritative core. Only then, after the Aryan has explored and exhausted every one of the Pauranik's explanations, contorting his discourse to follow the mythic meandering of the bloodthirsty and Brahmin-murdering ancestors, can the Aryan display the sign of his authority. The recovery of the identity of the Hindu nation lost in difference necessitates distortion and vulgarization of the ritual's context and meaning—"it seems you have committed a murder by performing a *śrāddha*."

Stereotypes were modes of the existence of the Hindu nation; they were the distorted forms of its own self produced by the project to constitute Indians with the culture of the lost Hindu past. To recover Vedic knowledge as the science of the nation was to revive something that had never existed. Invented in the present but dressed in the garb of the past, the representation of the Vedas as the cultural text of the Indian nation instituted itself through misrecognitions and mischaracterizations. Its distorted life can be identified in a Hindi pamphlet from 1895. An allegory that accuses the Puranas of fanciful imagination, this text describes the deliberations of a fictional special committee (a "subject committee") instituted in heaven to register complaints and investigate charges against the Puranas.[71] A correspondent describes the preparations for the meeting: Upon receiving notice of the meeting, the deities came from all over—from Calcutta and London, and from Bhopal and Nainital, crossing rivers ranging from the Ganges to the Thames and mountains from Meru to the Himalayas. Riding on swans, bulls, buffaloes, and railroads, the deities of everything, including tables and chairs, and numbering nine hundred million ("the population of the deities had increased greatly in the most recent census"), arrived at the meeting to air their complaints.[72]

Every deity lodged a complaint that the Puranas' fanciful tales had done them untold harm. Lord Brahma proposed that Vyasa, the sage who is said to have composed the Puranas, should be expelled for writing defamatory accounts of the gods. Lord Krishna joined in, stating that he had been greatly embarrassed by the Puranas; he had never stolen butter or carried on amorous relationships with milkmaids. Lord Vishnu endorsed the proposal for Vyasa's expulsion, charging that he had been smeared by Vyasa's accusation that he had left his consort to make love to a demon's wife. Lord Shiva complained that Puranic stories had turned his lock of hair into a water spout; people expected to see the Ganges flow out of his hair. After all had aired their grievances and asked unanimously for Vyasa's expulsion, the president of the committee agreed that the Puranic myths had made a mockery of the deities and reduced them to curiosities displayed in a museum. Vyasa, he agreed, must explain his conduct. But Vyasa pleaded innocence. "I never composed even a single Purana. If I had, why would I have given a slanderous account of my own birth?" Then, engaging in a grotesque distortion of the history of Sanskrit philosophy, the text has Vyasa charge that the atheists (the Charvaka philosophers of the Lokāyata school) were responsible for composing the Puranas. "I trained my disciples only in the Vedas and composed the Vedantic texts to determine truths, in addition to writing a short historical account of the Mahabharata consisting of 24 thousand verses."[73]

Every deity and each story tells the tale of the loss of Vedic reason to fanciful myths in order that the authentic religion of the ancient Aryans may be recovered. But as each deity lodges complaints against the Puranas and acquiesces to the authority of the Vedas, the language of satire, distortion, and ridicule becomes the medium of the ancient religion's reappearance. So, as Vyasa declares his allegiance to the Vedas, his speech mimics the language and tone that the text mocks. The text stereotypes the Puranas and distorts the Lokāyata philosophy in order to establish the authenticity of the Vedas. But the bewitching spell of the Puranas exerts a constant pressure, which the text attempts to contain through distortions and stereotyping. It is in such a warped fashion that the the text authorizes the Vedas as the constitutive text of Indians.

Such contortions speak eloquently of the discourse's ambition. They point to its attempt to assimilate difference and constitute it as an identity. The recovery of an invented past produced distortions and deformations because modernity and tradition were compelled to masquerade as each other. But this testifies to the discourse's far-reaching aspiration to represent in the image of Hindu science everything that lay outside it. This was as true for the Arya Samaj's project as it was for P. C. Ray's scholarly reconstruction of Hindu science as India's national heritage. Ray, too, spoke of the loss of Hindu science. He believed that the ancient sciences of the Hindus had declined as the *Manusmṛti* or laws of Manu, and the later Puranas drifted in the direction of glorifying the priestly class. As the caste system became rigid and as Brahmins began to view as contaminating any physical contact with a corpse, the scientific procedures of observation and experimentation suffered. The intellectual classes withdrew from active participation in science, the spirit of inquiry died among "a nation, naturally prone to speculation and metaphysical subtleties, and India bade adieu to experimental and inductive sciences."[74]

The reference to "a nation, naturally prone to speculation" points to the uncertain emergence and functioning of the concept of rupture in Ray's thought. On the one hand, his conviction regarding the antiquity of Hindu science was evident in his scholarly *History of Hindu Chemistry*, and in his other writings and lectures. In a lecture delivered in 1918 he spoke movingly about the pride and satisfaction he felt when "old, worm-eaten Chemical Manuscripts" began to "pour in from every quarter of India" during the twelve years of his research in the history of Hindu chemistry.[75] These showed, he suggested, not only that the ancient Hindu theories and practices of chemistry and medicine were guided strictly by observation and experimentation, but also that the communication of the original insights of Hindu science sparked the development of the Arab and European knowledge of physical sciences. By contrast, in a lecture two years earlier at Calcutta University, Ray had asserted just the opposite: "India has been a *tabula rasa* so far as the cultivation of physical sciences is concerned for the last 1000 years or perhaps more."[76] The Hindu traditions, content for so long with metaphysical speculations, could offer little inspiration for the development of the physical sciences. Ray reminded his audience that James Mill, and even Rammohun Roy had warned that Sanskritic training bred ecstatic meditation, not science.[77] Calling Bengal "the land *par excellence* of scholasticism and logic-chopping," Ray declared that physical science was an "exotic plant" in that province."[78]

Having proclaimed that the Hindu heritage was metaphysical and inimical to scientific inquiry, Ray changed gears abruptly, closing his lecture by denying that science was alien to Indian soil.

> I spoke of Physical Science as an exotic plant in India. Perhaps, I should modify or qualify that expression. Ancient India was the cradle of mathematical and chemical Sciences. . . . Remember, it is to India that the place of honour has been assigned by the illustrious French chemist, Jean Baptiste Dumas. I hope it will be hers once more to hold aloft the torch of Science and assert her true place in the comity of nations.[79]

Ray elaborated on this amendment two years later in another lecture:

> It is generally taken for granted that the Hindus were a dreamy, mystical people given to metaphysical speculation and spiritual contemplation. . . . But the fact that the Hindus had a very large hand in the cultivation of the experimental sciences is hardly known in these days.[80]

The awkwardness of this discourse, as it oscillated abruptly between the acknowledgment and the denial of the effect of Hindu metaphysics, points to the ambivalence of producing modern

India as the reemergence of ancient Hindu science. The structure of emergence as re-emergence required that the great Hindu past decay and degenerate, not evolve and progress, in the tragic unfolding of history so that it could be regenerated. To accomplish this narrative requirement, Ray, like other nationalists, painted a picture of the decline of Hindu science brought about by the Puranas. But Ray went further. He incorporated in his recounting of the story of the nation the formulaic statement that "Hindus were a dreamy, mystical people given to metaphysical speculation and spiritual contemplation." This was a bold attempt to inhabit the stereotyped other within the nationalist discourse, to make a place for and rescue the Hindus, who were "naturally prone to speculation." Recuperation working through repetition—this is a profoundly unstable structure that requires that the truth of a general statement emerge in its repetition in specific acts and contexts that, in turn, can rearrange the general proposition. Thus, the general trope that the Hindus were given to scholasticism and logic-chopping was repeated in Ray's nationalist text. Repetition, however, opened this general statement to the influence of its specific context. Thus the Hindu mind became "equally propitious for the cultivation of Physical Science," as the India that was the "cradle of the mathematical and chemical Sciences" crossed and re-marked the stereotype of the India where physical science was an exotic plant.

It is in these movements and shifting relations of statements, not in their specific content, that Ray's text acted as the work of the nationalist imagination. The content of one statement did not negate the other; the propensity for physical science did not deny the metaphysical predisposition of the Hindus. Ray juxtaposed and interpolated these contrary evaluations of India to reach far into the Hindu mind "naturally prone to speculation" and extract a mind capable of scientific inquiry:

If I could for a moment command the organ voice of Milton I would exclaim that we are a Nation not slow and dull, but of a quick, ingenious and piercing spirit, acute to invent, subtle and sinewy to discourse, not beneath the reach of any point the highest human capacity can soar to.[81]

Ray's text was inconsistent and moved awkwardly between contrary positions because its nationalist project sought to recuperate Indians from the Vedantic predilection for logic-chopping. Not content with recovering the archaic kernel of the modern nation lost to Manu and the Puranas, Ray's text stretched across, recovered, and transformed every sign of India's nationness, including the Hindus' spiritual disposition. Such an enactment of the nation was undoubtedly uncertain, but so was the whole project to produce the modern nation in the remembrance and recovery of a past that could only appear as lost and forgotten. This uncertainty, however, was the site and the source of the strength of the nationalist imagination. Ray himself exemplified the productivity of such an ambivalent restaging of the nation. His writings established the rise and decline of the archaic Hindu science as the enabling plot for the nation's coming into being. His Bengal Chemical and Pharmaceutical Works, established to manufacture indigenous drugs with modern scientific precision, was a concrete effect of the effort to restage the nation as a form of recovery.

The liberal vision of self-help and the complex program of cultural recuperation and renegotiation of the Hindu nation can also be witnessed in Srinivasa Murti's 1923 memorandum to the Madras government on *ayurveda*. His memorandum, while outlining a program of health education, proposed a scheme for the revival of *ayurveda*. The idea of revival was based on the recognition that the "palmy and progressive days of *ayurveda*" were followed by "dark and decadent days for Indian Medicine as for many other branches of the learning and wisdom of India."[82] The loss of state recognition and the government's patronage of Western medicine in recent times, he argued, had worsened the state of *ayurveda*. However, it constituted the cultural heritage of India and was a science that still benefited the poor, and therefore deserved to be revived.

Ayurveda's revival could not avoid negotiation with Western science, but this did not mean the dissolution of its identity and authority. Murti advanced this argument by first acknowledging that *ayurveda* needed the language of modern instrumentation. The Hindu method, which was based on the perfection of the senses of observation to a degree that only a few could achieve, could benefit greatly from the external aids to observation developed by Western science. This scheme constituted, in his view, the statement of ancient wisdom in the language of modern science. He illustrated his view with the example of J. C. Bose, the Bengali scientist whose research in plant physiology had won much acclaim.

> With the aid of his marvelous instruments of great delicacy and precision he demonstrated to an astonished world that the response to stimuli of both the so-called living (*e.g.* animals) and the so-called non-living (*e.g.* plants) were so strikingly similar as to suggest One common Life animating both Kingdoms of Nature; but, he was never tired of proclaiming from the house-tops that what he demonstrated was nothing new but was only a part of that ancient wisdom which our great forefathers taught many millennia ago on the banks of the Ganga. This is certainly true.[83]

Murti then described the ancient Hindu theories that converged with Bose's demonstration, concluding that Bose's instruments functioned as a language appropriate for our time. Poetry, which had once expressed *ayurveda* so effectively, was no longer appropriate; now Hindu medicine required the rhetoric of modern instruments to communicate its science to the modern world.

If *ayurveda* could now be expressed effectively only in translation, in the language of modern Western instruments, then what remained of its functioning as the sign of the Indian nation? Murti faced this question squarely, arguing that *ayurveda* was ultimately untranslatable. He pointed out that "while we may attempt some sort of equating at the level of physical matter known both to *ayurveda* and Allopathy, there is as yet nothing in the latter in terms of which things at the levels of vitality and psychic

117

principles could be explained."[84] Translation ("some sort of equating") meant not dissolution but demonstration of irreducible difference, the expression of Hindu science's untranslatability. Ideas of loss and decay produced uncertainty, distortion, and translation that empowered the ambitious imagination and assertion of India's identity.

NATION AND NEGOTIATION

Hegel could confidently present the history of the modern West as universal history, placing scant value on the claims of other cultures and histories. Cultures under Western domination did not enjoy this option. In fact, they had to come to terms with precisely this universalization of the West as History if they were to express the universality of their cultures. It was this historical compulsion that drove the Hindu intelligentsia of British India to negotiate the relationship of classical knowledge with Western science and to represent their traditions as scientific. If the modern nation emerged as a frame for this negotiation, this is not surprising. Alien rule had thrust upon India the framework of the nation as the enabling condition for formulating and advancing the tradition's entitlement to modern authority and universality. This does not mean that the idea of Hindu science was reducible to nationalism. Although the concept of an ancient Hindu science could not do without nationalism, it derived its motivating force from the desire to fashion its cultural resources into a living tradition. Thus, as Hindu intellectuals with different backgrounds and agendas reevaluated and advanced the claims of traditional knowledge, they also ended up projecting Hindu science as the past of the Indian nation.

The nationalist imagination drew its compelling ideological force from negotiation, not nativism. When Dayananda or P. C. Ray described India as the original home of science, this was not a nativist boast but an attempt to resignify traditions to position them as knowledge relevant to their contemporary world. This was an act of enormous significance and enduring implications, for it involved identifying certain traditions as authentically Hindu and as the culture of all Indians. Its scripting of India in Hindu texts proved so compelling that even secular nationalists such as Jawaharlal Nehru could not entirely escape. His *Discovery of India* (1946), the canonical text of modern Indian nationalism, is a case in point. Written as a quest for India in history, Nehru identifies the emergence of the nation in the ancient culture and polity, in archaic sciences and philosophies. He denies the equation of Indian culture with Hindu culture, but his search for the culture and knowledge that define India as a nation leads him to describe ancient sciences as its vital force. Thus, while describing the end of the first millennium of the common era as a period of the loss of the scientific spirit to formalism and sterile logic, he writes: "as the millennium approached its end, all this appears to be the afternoon of the civilization; the glow of the morning had long faded away, high noon was past."[85]

The image of ancient Hindu science provided a certain depth and texture to the cultural representation of the nation, yet it also introduced a sense of uncertainty and lack. Thus Nehru wrote that the nation's heart seemed to "petrify, its beats are slower." This was an enduring trope whose origins went back to Orientalism. In the discourse of nineteenth-century Hindu intellectuals, however, it had acquired another meaning. For men like Swami Dayananda and P. C. Ray, the decline of the scientific spirit signified not only Hinduism's failure but also that of the nation. Such an irruption of the archaic into the present speaks eloquently of the uncertain construction of India as a modern, rational form of cultural and political affiliation. With its "homogenous, empty time" interrupted by another temporality, India does not evolve effortlessly out of the Hindu past but emerges with its wholeness unsettled, its seamlessness frayed. The persistent pressure on the discourse exerted by the spell of Puranic myth and poetry and by the image of the dark ages suggests that locating Hindu science as the culture of the nation was not an easy task, but was a difficult and contentious struggle to establish identity in difference. The Hindu intelligentsia waged this struggle by distorting and stereotyping otherness, by using the fabricated memory of loss to myth and superstition to stage the recovery of Hindu science. If distortions, inventions, loss and recovery bear testimony to the tortured language the discourse had to adopt in negotiating the relationship of indigenous knowledge with Western science, they also bring to light the far-reaching ambition of signifying India in Hindu science. What Hindu intellectuals claimed was nothing less than the right of Indians to the autonomy, authority, and universality of their national culture.

PART TWO

SCIENCE, GOVERNMENTALITY,

AND THE STATE

Body and Governmentality

> In contrast to sovereignty, government has as its purpose
> not the act of government itself, but the welfare of the
> population, the improvement of its condition, the increase
> of its wealth, longevity, health, etc.
> *Michel Foucault*[1]

JANUARY 10, 1836, was a special day in Calcutta. As Madhusudan Gupta, a student at the newly-established Medical College, plunged his knife into a human body, a taboo was broken. Indians, it was said, had finally risen "superior to the prejudices of their earlier education and thus boldly flung open the gates of modern medical science to their countrymen."[2] Fort William celebrated modern medicine's assault on the body and its onward march by firing a gun salute.

A century later, in 1936, Mahatma Gandhi referred to another kind of assault on the body by writing frankly about his unsuccessful efforts to conquer desire. Describing his condition in Bombay where he was convalescing, he wrote that whereas all "my discharges so far had occurred in dreams . . . the experience in Bombay occurred while I was fully awake and had a sudden desire for intercourse."[3] For Gandhi, the conquest of sexual desire was an important part of his philosophy of self-control. He believed that *brahmacharya*, or the practice of celibacy, was crucial not only for the maintenance of healthy bodies but also for achieving union with God.[4] *Brahmacharya*, he insisted, liberated one to pursue selfless action, free from desire and motivated entirely by the urge to pursue truth.

There is much that unites and separates Fort William's gun salute and Gandhi's failure-ridden effort to control the body through the suppression of desire. Both share a concern with the disciplines of the body. If the combination of the knife, the

123

dissected human body, the broken taboo, and the gun salute brings to mind Foucault's analysis of modern disciplines of the body as a form of war, so does Gandhi's struggle; his too was a war—against desire—a battle to establish *brahmacharya*'s command as the national discipline of Indian subjects. But there was also a stark difference. While one celebrated modern medicine, the other considered it evil. "Hospitals are institutions for propagating sin," Gandhi wrote.[5] In place of Western medicine, which he regarded as an instrument of India's enslavement, Gandhi advocated the discipline of *brahmacharya* as the true and universal means of achieving liberation.

What are we to make of the body's embattled history as it emerges between the war to regulate the life processes of the aggregate population through modern medicine and the battle to discipline the sexual life of the Indian self through rules of continence? Foucault's concept of governmentality illuminates the processes at work in the formulation of disciplines directed at preserving life and governing bodily conduct. He distinguishes governmentality from sovereignty, which is concerned with territory, legitimacy, and obedience to law, and from disciplines, which are elaborated in such institutions as prisons, schools, armies, manufactories, and hospitals. Locating modern power in a sovereignty-discipline-government triangle, he defines governmentality as a mode of pastoral power aimed at the welfare of each and all that functions by setting up "economy at the level of the entire state, which means exercising towards its inhabitants and their wealth and behaviour a form of surveillance and control as attentive as that of a head of a family over his household and his goods."[6] The application of economy at the level of the state was rendered possible by the appearance of population as a category. Population, with "its own regularities, its own rates of deaths and diseases, its cycles of scarcity, etc.,"[7] was irreducible to family, and became the object of schemes to promote its health and wealth. There emerged "a sort of complex composed of men and things . . . men in their relations, their links, their imbrication with those other things which are wealth, resources, means of subsistence,

the territory with its specific qualities, climate, irrigation, fertility
. . . in their relation to that other kind of things, customs, habits,
ways of acting and thinking, . . . in their relation to that other
kind of things, accidents and misfortunes such as famine, epidemics, death, etc."[8]

Governmentality in British India, like governmentality in Europe, also developed in response to the outbreak of epidemics,
death, and famines, and was directed to act on the population,
nurture its health, and cultivate its resources. But colonial
governmentality had to be radically discontinuous with the Western norm. Foucault pays little attention to colonialism in outlining governmentality. In fact, as Ann Laura Stoler points out, his
concept of biopower as a set of practices and institutions acting
upon the body remains resolutely blind to its imperial frame.[9] His
historical account also acquires an unmistakable Whiggish drift
as he defines modern biopower as the resolution of the centuries-
old confrontation between biology and history. According to
him, the French Revolution marked the beginning of the end of
thousands of years of the pressure exerted by the biological on the
historical: "Western man was gradually learning what it meant to
be a living species in a living world, to have a body, conditions of
existence, probabilities of life, an individual and collective welfare, forces that could be modified, and a space in which they
could be distributed in an optimal manner."[10] Signifying society's
threshold of modernity, biopower established its full presence in
the West, while the non-Western world remained vulnerable to
famine and biological risks to the species. Given Foucault's Eurocentric view that biopower was constituted fully within the borders of the modern West, its career in the colonies, marked by
their failure to achieve the "threshold of modernity," can only be
seen as a dim reflection of its metropolitan original.

Colonial governmentality, however, could not be the tropicalization of its Western form, but rather was its fundamental dislocation. Utilitarian theorists from Jeremy Bentham to Fitzjames
Stephen, including James and John Stuart Mill, had maintained
that British rule in India must necessarily violate the metropoli-

tan norm: only despotic rule could institute good government in India, only a Leviathan unhindered by a Demos could introduce and sustain the rule of law in the colony. Produced at the point of such estrangement of Western rule in despotism, British India was marked by the absence of the elegant sovereignty-discipline-government triangle that Foucault identifies in Europe. Fundamentally irreconcilable with the development of a civil society, the colonial state was structurally denied the opportunity to mobilize the capillary forms of power. Colonial governmentality was obliged to develop in violation of the liberal conception that the government was part of a complex domain of dense, opaque, and autonomous interests that it only harmonized and secured with law and liberty.[11] It had to function also as an aspect of coercion, that is, instituting the sovereignty of alien rulers.

The violation of the metropolitan norm was a productive breach, not a restrictive liability; it initiated a generative dislocation, not a paralyzing limitation. For what it set into motion was a powerful process of bureaucratic expansion and rationalization under which the population's economic, demographic, and epidemiological properties were surveyed, enumerated, measured, and reconstituted so as to bring into existence a *colonial* "complex of men and things"—that is, a population constituted as subordinated subjects, whose health, resources, productivity, and regularities were the objects of governance. Characterizing this process as the colonization of the body, David Arnold writes that British India demonstrates, "in a manner unparalleled in Western societies, the exceptional importance of medicine in the cultural and political constitution of its subjects."[12] With an extraordinary involvement of state medicine, the body was colonized, inserted in a new field of tactics and institutions aimed at achieving mastery over life.

Arnold is right to stress the extraordinary importance of state medicine in British India in the production and subordination of subjects, but the colonization of the body requires another specification if we are to understand the nature and the field of knowledges and practices opened up by Western therapeutics.

We must ask: What was colonial about the colonization of the body? How was the materialization of the body in institutions, knowledges, and tactics affected by conditions of alien rule? To govern Indians as modern subjects required colonial knowledge and colonial regulation to function as self-knowledge and self-regulation, but this was impossible under colonialism. The British were obliged to practice governmentality as an aspect of imperial domination. They introduced sanitary regulations, established Western medical therapeutics and institutions, and campaigned against epidemics, but such practices of governance had to operate as acts of colonial rule. The pressure to enact coercive rule as the welfare of the population forced colonial governmentality to occupy two positions at once—Western and Indian. The body rendered knowable by physiology, pathology, and surgery, and visible in diseases, epidemics, and deaths, was required to also materialize itself as the body located in the knowledge of Indian conditions and dispositions. The colonization of the body had to operate as the care of the native body.

It was at the site of this predicament that British India witnessed other contending strategies. Gandhi's advocacy of *brahmacharya* was an example of this, and it formed part of the nationalist effort to seize upon and resignify the body as it had been materialized by the plunge of Madhusudan Gupta's knife. Arising squarely within the historical arena of colonial power relations, the nationalist insistence on Indian therapeutics and indigenous cultural norms was not a defensive reaction to governance but a powerful attempt to change its terms. This is how Hindu culture and the masculinist ascetic ideal of *brahmacharya* appeared as cultural forms with hegemonic claims on the Indian body politic.

COLONIAL INSTITUTIONS AND THE EMERGENCE OF THE BODY

While medicine and colonial power were linked together soon after the establishment of British rule, it was not until the late nineteenth century that this relationship produced the native body as an object and effect of medical attention.[13] It was then that the effort to control and contain the alien environment of India, to regulate and reform the "tropics," where the unhealthy climate combined with the fevered irrationality of the people to unleash virulent outbreaks of sickness and death, gave rise to a new network of knowledge and tactics. This emergent regime of knowledge conjured up the image of a spectral body composed of unhygienic habits and superstitious beliefs upon which modern knowledge and tactics were to be applied in order to reform it and restore its health and well-being. Similarly, indigenous medicine and materia medica, previously incorporated as inferior but useful supplements to Western therapeutics,[14] appeared as a collection of unscientific and inaccurate beliefs under whose misrepresentations there lurked a real body. The reading of indigenous therapeutics as mistaken and imprecise signs of the existence of the body as a real object justified the application of strategies that materialized the body in a different set of institutions and effects; it posited the body as an a priori object, as an entity whose existence preceded the discourse within which it appeared as a matter of medical scrutiny and regulation.

Predictably, it was anxiety about the security of the empire that aroused interest in the health of the population. Initially, this interest focused on the army, whose indispensability for the maintenance of the colonial order had been driven home by the 1857 Revolt described by the British as the Mutiny. Shaken to its foundation by the upheavals of that year, the British government became concerned about the well-being of its army. The British troops in India had experienced a death rate of 69 per 1,000 (three times the rate in Britain), and epidemics had severely affected the conduct of military operations during the Mutiny.[15] With sanitation and hygiene in the military placed under the spotlight by the Crimean War, the bleak record of sickness and death in the British army in India caused alarm. Under the pressure of Florence Nightingale's resolute campaign, the British Parliament appointed a royal commission in 1859 to inquire into the sanitary

state of the British army in India.[16] The commission issued its
report in 1863, stating that fevers, dysenteries, diseases of the
liver, and epidemic cholera were the most injurious diseases in
India for British soldiers and that science could offer no relief
because it had been unable to determine their causes. But, the
commission declared, a "rational mode of inquiry" had discovered that improved drainage and sanitary conditions could counteract the intensity of the transmission of diseases. A meticulous
attention to hygiene, habitation, and habits could protect Europeans from the risk of epidemics in a place like India, where the
unhealthy effects of heat and moisture had to be assumed and
where malaria was an ever-present danger.[17]

The magnified attention to sanitation represented a shift in the
colonial medical discourse that occurred as part of the victory of
the Anglicists over the Orientalists in the 1830s. Out of this victory came the triumph of the liberal imperialist vision, which
opened the floodgates of contempt for Indian beliefs and knowledges, and led to the replacement of the Native Medical Institution with the Calcutta Medical College in 1835. The emergent
discourse broke with the Anglo-Indian medical tradition of the
late eighteenth and early nineteenth centuries, which had shared
much with the humoral pathology of *ayurvedic* and *yunani* medical systems and had found them useful, if not altogether correct.
By the mid nineteenth century, while the belief in India as a distinctly disease environment was not abandoned, the possibility of
incorporating indigenous practices into Western therapeutics
and acclimatizing European constitutions to Indian medico-topographical conditions was ruled out.[18] Both the Indian environment and Indian knowledges appeared so utterly alien and un-
remittingly perilous to health that only their containment and
suppression could preserve the well-being of the colonial order.
The discourse of sanitation both contributed to and reflected this
change insofar as, unlike climatological determinism, it brought
into existence objects over which control could be exercised.

Sanitation represented a new order of knowledge and power.
Florence Nightingale articulated its specificity when she enthusi-

astically described the sanitary inspectors' reports as "bringing to light what is the real social state of the mass of Indian peoples." These reports had removed "the veil of romance woven by poets over Hindostan," she added, and revealed "peoples to be numbered by tens of millions living under social and domestic conditions quite other than paradisiacal." They lived "amidst their own filth, infecting the air with it, poisoning the ground with it, and polluting the water they drink with it," and "some even think it a holy thing to drink filth."[19] This description was consistent with the prevalent theory of climatological determinism, according to which soil and air produced miasmas that caused and communicated diseases, but it also marked a departure insofar as it rendered human habits and habitation into objects of medical attention and regulation. Filthy cities, open drains, decomposing animal carcasses, rotting vegetable matter, irrational beliefs, and unscientific therapeutics appeared as errors that signified the truth of the Indian body. The "real social state of the mass of Indian peoples," after all, was revealed by the disclosure that Indians, "numbered by tens of millions," lived amidst their own filth, trapped by their unhygienic habits and beliefs. Muck and misunderstanding were read as signs that pointed to the existence of the body as an object prior to the dirt, disease, and dogma in which it was buried, and independent of the discourse that brought it into view. Such a positioning of the truth of the Indian body, as a specter of filth and error, set the stage for the sanitary policing and regulation of the population. The British appointed sanitary commissioners in Bengal, Bombay, and Madras Presidencies, and in the provinces of the Punjab, Burma, United Provinces, and Central Provinces, and charged them with the responsibility of preparing monthly and annual returns on diseases and drawing up plans for the sanitary regulation of the population.[20] The establishment and expansion of municipalities followed, the state apparatus grew, and the sanitary policing of the population became regularized.

Sanitary policing in India followed a design different from the metropolitan pattern. Considering the model of the English municipal institution "unsuitable and inefficient" for India, the British stressed centralized control rather than local self-government. Inspector-generals were to preside over local sanitary inspections which, unlike those in Britain, were to be carried out by low-level "lay" inspectors, not by well-paid medical officers of health, and they were "to see to the abatement of nuisances and to the bringing of cases of nuisance before the magistrates."[21] Administering a system designed and controlled by the center, local sanitary officers in India, again unlike their counterparts in Britain, did not work in just an advisory capacity; instead, they operated as executive officers with vast powers and responsibilities. They supervised the conservancy work, controlled a large subordinate staff and laborers, administered the registration of births and deaths, investigated the causes of deaths and epidemics, addressed public complaints, and advised on sanitary requirements of buildings.[22] A bureaucratic machine was found necessary for sanitary work because the state considered the colonized to be incapable of self-governance. As Nightingale put it, the state in India had to accomplish single-handedly what was achieved in Britain in conjunction with the "habits of self-government."[23]

When Lord Ripon, the Viceroy of India, did introduce local self-government in 1882, his Gladstonian liberalism made sure that it was extended only to Europeans and a small group of wealthy Indians. The size of the municipal electorate was tiny; in most provinces it was less than two percent of the population.[24] Additionally, local self-government was seriously undercut by the fact that provincial governments and district officers were committed to implementing policies determined by the central administration. Based, as municipalities and district boards were, on alien institutions of government rather than indigenous traditions, they existed as apparatuses of the colonial state, having very little to do with the surrounding Indian population. As one observer has commented, local government in India was "as incongruous as the bizarre Victorian Gothic Town Halls which adorn so many of the larger Indian cities."[25] The limits of local self-government meant not only an enlarged role but also an

131

altogether different positioning of the state as it sought to make up for the effacement of the colonized. In this regard, Nightingale's bold declaration that "Government is everything in India" neatly captured the ineluctably colonial nature of the governmentalization of the state in India.[26]

Sanitation in colonial India functioned as the knowledge and regulation of the other; it was deployed as a Western discipline for the governance of indigenous habits and habitation. In the first instance, this produced a discriminatory sanitary order which constituted Indians and the Indian environment as sources of diseases from which Europeans had to be protected. Descriptions of filth figured prominently in colonial investigations of "fevers" in Indian cities.[27] The focus on unsanitary conditions itself was understandable in view of Sir Edwin Chadwick's *Report on the Sanitary Condition of the Labouring Population of Great Britain* (1842), which had placed cities under the spotlight as centers of squalor and disease in Britain.[28] But the report's focus on filth and putrefaction has a telling origin. It reflects the thought of a group of Benthamite social reformers that included Chadwick and whose views on public health were articulated most effectively by Southward Smith. Margaret Pelling points out that Smith's view that dirt, filth, and the putrefaction of animal and vegetable substances caused fevers was widely shared by these reformers and was based largely on reports from India and Egypt.[29] In highlighting the unsanitary conditions prevalent in industrial cities and areas inhabited by the working class as the cause of fevers, Chadwick was drawing a comparison between putrefaction in the colonies, and dirt and squalor in working-class quarters in Britain. Indirectly, this confirmed India's representation as a cesspool of diseases.

Colonial reports projected dirt and disease as signs of India's otherness. Thus, when the sanitary commissioner described Calcutta in 1864 as a "scandal and disgrace" to "civilized Government," he blamed the native population as a whole, not just the poorer classes.[30] Colonial officials returned repeatedly to remark on the open and clogged drains, on the stench and the ugly sight of night soil that greeted the unfortunate visitor to the "black towns," on the gut-churning piles of garbage heaped in bazaars, on the crowded, ill-ventilated, haphazardly designed native houses. Not just colonial prejudice was at work in these denunciations, but a language of governance, a knowledge and discipline of the other. These representations justified the creation of hygienic European havens located in military cantonments, civil lines, and hill stations, that were separated from swampy, malarial grounds and the native population, and governed by sanitary standards prevalent in Britain.[31] Such hygienic enclaves were expected to reduce the threat to European health posed by Indians, but the British also recognized that their sanitary protection could not be fully secure unless Indian habitations were also regulated.[32] So, as municipal authorities favored the civil lines and cantonments inhabited by Europeans, they also realized the necessity of extending sanitary regulations to "black towns," which had acquired a menacing meaning since the Mutiny.[33]

As colonial officials set out to control the recurrent outbreak of epidemics during the second half of the nineteenth century, statistics came to occupy a prominent position in the developing medical profile of the indigenous population. The use of statistics was not peculiar to India. By the mid nineteenth century, as Ian Hacking has shown in his *Taming of Chance*, Europe had already witnessed statistics acquiring an important role in making the world apprehendable.[34] Statistical data and laws rendered chance less capricious; they discerned order and regularities in such indeterminate events as epidemics, thereby offering a mode of understanding and controlling natural and social processes. Such a conception of statistics achieved widespread influence in Britain after the 1830s, largely under the energetic leadership of William Farr. During his employment in the General Register Office between 1839 and 1880, Farr used his official position to relentlessly and successfully advocate statistics as a precise instrument of medical knowledge and public health reform. Sharing the belief of other influential public figures, such as Chadwick, that diseases originated in the environment, he forged an alliance with Florence

Nightingale, and served as a member of the royal commission appointed in 1859 under her influence to inquire into the health of the British army in India. His work for the commission as a member and as a paid consultant—he promised Nightingale "a New year's gift of tables"— lent the prestige of statistics to the campaign for sanitation.[35]

Undoubtedly, Farr's association with the commission and with Nightingale helped to spread the influence of statistics in the consideration of public health in India. Consider, for example, *A Manual of Practical Hygiene* (1864), the standard medical text for British officials in India. Its author, Edmund Parkes, had served as assistant surgeon in the British army in India from 1842 to 1845, investigating cholera and dysentery. Writing of the government's duty to maintain "watchful care over the health of the people, and a due regulation of matters which concern their health," he had recommended the use of "figures which admit no denial."[36] However, the use of statistics had begun even before Parkes' call for it. Joseph Ewart had already published a statistical study in 1859, providing figures on mortality among European and native troops. Ewart had intended to publish a short paper for publication in a scientific journal, but as "his researches advanced to maturity, the great importance of the facts elicited, the wide range of their application to different classes of our own, and to a large section of Asiatic race" convinced him to publish his findings as a book of raw facts.[37]

In British India, colonialism shaped statistics because they were produced in the exercise of alien power. Not surprisingly, the government's "watchful care" in India produced a colonial knowledge of the population. The data on the outbreak of epidemics was organized to show their differential effects on Europeans and Indians. Ewart's study, for example, contained vital statistics on sickness among European and native troops, which was analyzed in relation to the average rates of sickness and mortality in each Presidency.[38] These revealed a disturbingly high rate of mortality among European soldiers in India compared to Indian sepoys, leading to Nightingale's successful campaign for the appointment of a royal commission. The commission never visited India but pored over the substantial statistical data accumulated by Farr to understand the condition of army sanitation and to make its recommendations. The reliance on statistics grew and became more complex and sophisticated in the late nineteenth century as the British were called upon to cope with the ravages of cholera, smallpox, plague, and enteric fevers vastly aggravated by urban crowding, rapid and increased communication facilitated by railroads, and the malarial environment bred by irrigation works.[39] Colonial officials collected detailed numerical information on sickness and fatalities. They investigated the relationship of the outbreak of cholera and plague to race, region, climate, and habitation; measured the success of vaccination versus inoculation in resisting smallpox; and assessed the rate of mortality of Europeans and Indians in hospitals and clinics. Through all this, they hungered for more accurate data in order to enhance the "taming of chance" in the alien and hostile environment of India.[40]

The desire to bring diseases and deaths under the statistical gaze represented an effort to relocate the indigenous population, to bring it under the colonial "complex of men and things," where its regularities in relation to climate, topography, habits, and habitation could be observed and acted upon. Government officials searched for agencies that reached down to the village in order to collect vital information on births and deaths, and complained that inaccurate diagnoses and medical treatments provided by indigenous practitioners enabled sickness and mortality to escape the net of statistics.[41] The volume and complexity of statistical information grew with the regularization of the collection of mortality figures of the civil population and the institutionalization of the decennial census in the 1870s. These, together with systematic meteorological records kept by the government, extended the reach of the colonial establishment and enabled the formulation of a discursive formation that represented the body in different combinations and correlations of diverse statistical series.

The body was thus firmly located in India, and yet it was scientifically observable only through the knowledges and practices of colonial medicine which developed different and conflicting ideas about diseases and their treatment. As cholera raged, so did debates between the proponents of climatological determinism and the contagion theory. The theory that miasmas caused and communicated cholera received powerful support from J. M. Cunningham, the sanitary commissioner of India from 1868 to 1884, and was elaborated in a number of monographs that used and generated data that situated bodies and diseases in relation to climate and topography.[42] The opposing contagion theory, expressed originally in John Snow's *On Continuous Molecular Changes, More Particularly in their Relation to Epidemic Disease* (1853), found less support in India, but it was also elaborated with the help of statistical data.[43] Disagreeing over the understanding of the etiology of cholera and methods of its prevention, both theories used statistics to dislodge the body from indigenous beliefs and practices and materialize it in a new set of knowledges and tactics.

Statistics constituted an element of the wider discourse concerned with the medical specification of India's difference. This concern generated debates and theories, but the state's "watchful care" remained focused on formulating knowledges and identifying objects of governance. Thus, when the colonial government finally accepted the contagion theory in the mid 1890s—a decade after Robert Koch, the German bacteriologist, had discovered the cholera bacillus in a Calcutta tank in 1884—the Indian environment as a factor in disease did not drop out of focus. In fact, as Harish Naraindas's sharp analysis demonstrates, the British medical establishment reworked the function of climate in establishing the peculiarly colonial discipline of tropical medicine.[44] This discipline faced obsolescence even at the moment of its birth in 1898. For the contagion theory was already established in Europe, and germs, helminths, and parasites had been discovered as etiologic agents of disease, and were known to transcend climatic boundaries. Appearing in a context in which the contagion theory had already undermined the importance attributed to climate in the understanding of diseases, tropical medicine did not simply repeat an old and outdated dogma. Rather, it reworked the function ascribed to climate, creating the category of "tropical diseases" that was unavailable in the earlier obsession with climate as the original cause. The new discipline privileged etiology over pathology, which permitted it to analyze disease as the product of a microbe's combination with the tropics. In this way, social customs and environmental conditions of the "native" coupled with microbes to produce the discipline of tropical medicine, which could justify on "scientific" terms the representation of the tropics as a fertile soil for disease.

So entrenched was the belief that India was the breeding ground of diseases that the anti-contagionists were willing to entertain a compromise with the contagion theory even before it was firmly established. "In their insistence upon the physical or climatic idiosyncrasies of India," Arnold remarks, "the environmentalist school was in curious accord with its contagionist opponents with their eyes firmly fixed not on the heavens or the soil, but on pilgrim hordes."[45] The International Sanitary Conference at Constantinople in 1866 had placed its sharp attention on Hindu pilgrims as sources of cholera epidemics, causing great embarrassment to the British. At the same time, the government itself feared the large gatherings of Indians at religious fairs and pilgrim sites. An official report traced the cholera epidemic in northern India in 1867 to the Kumbh fair in Hardwar, attended by three million people—a number swelled by the recent introduction of the railways. The administration had made sanitary arrangements, including the disastrous one to bury the night soil from the latrines in the banks of the Ganges River. As pilgrims bathed in the river, they were exposed to the cholera bacillus. They in turn transmitted cholera to others, and as a result more than a hundred thousand died.[46] To combat the epidemic, the government prohibited fairs, established and policed sanitary cordons, and set up cholera hospitals and camps. Dead bodies were cremated or buried as soon as possible, and the clothing of victims was destroyed. The returning pilgrims were diverted from large towns and detained in quarantine camps for as long as five days, and they were obliged to wash and have their clothes fumigated before being allowed to reenter their villages and towns.[47] Cholera broke out again during the fair in 1892, in spite of elaborate sanitary arrangements made by the administration, leading the government to disperse the pilgrims, empty the lodging houses, and prevent dips in the holy waters of the Ganges. These measures helped prevent the spread of the disease, and positioned the colonial state as a form of pastoral power under whose watchful care indigenous religious observances were regulated in secular, medical terms.[48]

Even more so than cholera, the outbreak of smallpox and plague epidemics sparked the development of knowledges and practices to seize the body from its indigenous cultural location. Unlike cholera, smallpox brought the British face to face with a traditional method of treatment, that is, variolation, which entailed inoculation with live smallpox matter in order to induce a more manageable presence of the disease in the body.[49] Reports demonstrated to the government that, while areas "notorious for their crowded, filthy, ill-ventilated and ill-condition were the chief receptacles and hotbeds of this contagion and disease," variolation was as destructive and prolific as the natural occurrence of smallpox.[50] The government's investigation disclosed that the Hindus practiced variolation as a religious duty, prompting the circulation of questionnaires to Hindu pandits to determine its textual status. The replies by pandits were equivocal, suggesting that law books did not enjoin variolation specifically, but included it as part of religious ceremonies recommended for those struck by smallpox.[51] In British eyes, however, variolation was not a harmless religious ceremony but a "murderous trade"; it was not prescribed by "Hindoo Law and Theology" but was perpetrated because there was no shortage of "bigots to mislead the ignorant Hindoos, and to prejudice their credulous and simple minds, against whatever may be falsely represented to them as an innovation, or an interference with their religious privileges.[52]

As Arnold shows, a battle ensued to suppress variolation and replace it with vaccination. Coopting the inoculators (*tikadars*) as vaccinators, the government steadily increased the number of annual vaccinations in British India from 350,000 in 1850 to 8 million by the end of the century.[53] This did not happen without resistance. The opposition was provoked by the arm-to-arm method that remained the predominant form of vaccination in British India until World War I, when it was replaced by the cowpox vaccine. Unlike inoculation, this method involved the transferral of body fluids from one individual to another, causing higher castes to fear that they would be ritually polluted by the bodily matter of lower castes. Undeterred by this resistance, and following the recommendation of the smallpox commission, the British outlawed variolation and enacted laws for compulsory vaccination.

The process of removing the body from areas "notorious for their filthy, ill-ventilated and ill-condition," and freeing it from "credulous and simple minds" achieved an exceptional dimension during the bubonic plague epidemics of the late nineteenth century. As Arnold points out, plague brought to the fore an unparalleled state intervention because the disease "was specifically identified with the human body and thus occasioned an unprecedented assault upon the body of the colonized."[54] The list of instructions that Waldemar Haffkine, the Russian bacteriologist, prepared for the use of municipal authorities to identify the disease required examination of the body for fever, trembling limbs, pain and swelling of the glands, delirium, constipation, and diarrhea. To diagnose whether or not these were plague symptoms, the skin over a gland was to be washed with carbolic lotion and pricked with a needle to reach the gland. The gland was then to be pressed to squeeze out a whitish substance, which was then to be placed under the microscope.[55]

Because only physical examination of the body could identify the presence of plague, the interdiction of the body became necessary for understanding and controlling the disease. Thus, the outbreak of the 1896–97 epidemic in Bombay prompted the municipal commissioner to issue a notification claiming the right to enter any building to disinfect it and remove any item, to remove

139

Fig. 3. "Teaching the Body": Hospital morgue, Calcutta, c. 1900. Phot. 311/2(12). Reproduced by permission of the British Library.

any person suffering from the disease to a hospital, and to isolate any house in which the disease existed.[56] The British authorities examined passengers at railway stations to detect if fleeing residents of the plague-stricken areas were carrying the disease, segregated and hospitalized plague victims, and carried out extensive cleaning and disinfection of drains. Such interventions sparked widespread opposition, particularly in Pune, where the military carried out much of the house-to-house inspection to detect if plague victims had been shielded from hospitalization.[57] B. G. Tilak, the Maratha nationalist leader, portrayed the plague operations as an unacceptable interference in Indian life, and the fervent hostility to the government's policies led to the assassination of W. C. Rand, the chairman of the plague committee, in 1897. Elsewhere, the government's "assault on the body," as Arnold puts it, did not provoke assassinations, but the practice of seizing plague victims from their relatives and hospitalizing them met with violent opposition.[58] Faced with sustained opposition, the

Fig. 4. "Welfare of the Population": A plague inspection party led by a justice of peace, Bombay, 1896–97. Phot. 311/1(110). Reproduced by permission of the British Library.

British had to moderate their draconian policies, and eventually they were able to win at least the support of educated Indians.

Inspection, segregation, vaccination, and hospitalization dramatized both the general process of the elaboration of the state's concern with the governance of Indians and its colonial nature. On the one hand, the urgent need to combat epidemics mobilized and brought into play a range of knowledges and techniques—sanitary laws and tactics, studies of diseases and strategies of control based on statistics, vaccination, quarantine, hospitalization, municipal government—that had been develop-

Fig 5. "Identifying Diseased Bodies": Inspection of railway passengers for plague symptoms, Bombay, 1896–97. Phot. 311/1(125). Reproduced by permission of the British Library.

ing in a variety of locations over several decades. The epidemic victims in hospitals and clinics furnished details on the pathology and treatment of diseases, and these were combined with sanitary laws and statistical facts to render the body as an organism, as a constellation of functions, designations, symptoms, ailments, immunities, vulnerabilities, and therapies. On the other hand, epidemics were a flashpoint for the confrontation entailed in tearing colonized bodies away from native habits and habitation, and materializing them in disciplines and technologies of colonial governance. The development of governmentality as the knowledge of the other could not but position the application of disciplines as a battle. P. C. H. Snow, the municipal commissioner of Bombay wrote: "The people would not believe that the hopeless condition of their own dark, damp, filthy, overcrowded houses was their real danger, they raved about the sewers and became phrenzied if a scavenger was remiss . . . [E]very form of obstruction was resorted to when the Municipality attempted to deal with their dwellings." The municipal employees had to carry out their work "in the face of hostile, and sometimes violent crowds, and almost invariably in the teeth of sullen, if passive opposition."[59] Colonial officials attributed such hostility and indifference to ignorance, misinformation, and the hopeless inability of Indians to appreciate the value of sanitation and scientific therapeutics. The British officials told each other that Indians were driven to opposition by the rumor that hospitals killed the patients, took out their hearts, and sent them to Queen Victoria to appease the wrath aroused by the disfigurement of her statue in Bombay; that they distrusted hospitals because a large number of patients, having been brought to hospitals in a moribund condition, died soon after being admitted; that they misconstrued the subcutaneous injection used to resuscitate patients as an attempt to kill them to prevent the spread of the disease.[60] If such retellings of rumors underscored the unavailability of capillary forms of power to the colonial state, they also reinforced the British resolve to continue with the impossible task of re-forming Indians as self-governing subjects in spite of their will. The irreducible difference of Indians both limited and empowered the development of colonial governmentality; if rumors and misconceptions bedeviled the application of disciplines, they also justified the effort to place Indian bodies in the colonial grid of knowledges and practices.

BODY AND THERAPEUTICS

The British were fully aware that they ruled as an alien power and that their therapeutics functioned as an alien discipline. But they also exercised power and applied disciplines as if these could bridge the unbridgeable gap between the colonizer and the colonized, as if the absolute otherness of Indians was also knowable. This effort to achieve what was structurally impossible produced an embattled zone of governance, a space of practices created but not contained by the state. This sphere of governance was a peculiarly colonial space of political practice created by sanitary regulations, measures to control epidemics, the statistical representation and organization of the population, and medical knowledge and tactics. Here, it is pertinent to refer to Partha Chatterjee's concept of the political society, which he defines as a mediating space between the people and the state. This mediating space is created by governmentality and is founded on the idea of population, which is an empirical and descriptive category, rather than a normative category like civil society. In British India, the concept of population permitted the application of modern technologies on inhabitants who were otherwise seen as unfit for and incapable of reason and progress, thereby creating a space for practices connecting the state and the people.[61]

The Western-educated Indian elite were quick to recognize this new space of mediation, and sought to intervene by placing themselves as agents of modern transformation. This was true even of those who largely concurred with the colonial representations of Indians, such as Dr. S. G. Chuckerbutty (Chakrabarty), a professor at the Calcutta Medical College and a respected figure in the *bhadralok* milieu. Speaking at the Bethune Society in 1852 on the issue of sanitation in Calcutta, he placed the entire mode of Indian living under scrutiny. Food, drink, cooking, clothing, housing, drainage, sports, leisure activities, and intellectual pursuits—all were examined from a sanitary point of view. From this examination he concluded that, unlike Europeans, "East Indians" were living examples of "the passive exercise of bodily and mental powers." He illustrated these "passive" East Indians and their "diseased habits" with pictures of the idle, fat zemindar, the philosopher so given to mental culture that he neglected even the most elementary bodily exercise, the half-clad Brahmin without gloves or stockings, the dirty and damp dwellings, and the open gutters and sewers.[62] Such representations were directed at pointing out the need for more reliable and authentic information to facilitate the state's planning and implementation of sanitary policing of the population. They did not differ in content from colonial disciplines, but, insofar as they were descriptions of "our countrymen" by Indians, they posited that the Western-educated elite would act as a mediating force between the state and the people, diffusing knowledges and practices with which Indians would constitute themselves as modern subjects. Distancing themselves from the fat zemindar and the ill-clad Brahmin, the elite represented themselves as agents of modern transformation, as a force that would assist the state and educate the people in the regulation and improvement of the health of the population. When smallpox, cholera, and plague epidemics raged between the 1870s and the 1890s in the United Provinces and in the Bombay and Madras Presidencies, the elite swung into action to offer advice and relief.[63] The focus of their effort centered on the body brought to light by colonial knowledge, that is, a body manifested in filth, statistics, unhygienic habits, and superstitious beliefs.[64] The elite incessantly highlighted and criticized the Indians' allegedly characteristic neglect of their bodies and their supposed fatalism in order to diffuse a knowledge of the laws of health without which municipal laws and sanitary reforms could not combat epidemics.[65]

The attempt to educate the public in health and hygiene, and to disseminate colonial disciplines as self-disciplines, however, could not avoid the question of difference. Indeed, colonial governmentality was founded on the notion that the body in India was a peculiarly complex effect of environment, habits, beliefs, and knowledges. British medicine in India, David Arnold points out, was not simply the practice of Western therapeutics in a non-Western location but a peculiarly colonial discursive formation.[66]

The attempt to address Indian difference opened Western medicine to revision and reformulation, and precipitated a debate on the status of Western medicine in India. Dr. U. N. Mukerji, a

145

Bengali doctor, published a pamphlet in 1907, calling for the establishment of a system of national medicine. Offering a trenchant critique of the practice of medicine in Bengal, Dr. Mukerji stated that he was tempted to put an advertisement in the daily papers stating: "Wanted urgently a treatise on medicine, for treatment of Indians, written by an Indian." Why was an Indian treatise needed? He acknowledged that the "question may be asked if it is really necessary to have medical books written by Indian doctors, seeing specially . . . that a disease is a disease all over the world and a remedy is a remedy everywhere, just as a man is physically at least a man wherever he is found." Declaring that "the truth lies exactly the other way," Dr. Mukerji went on to outline a number of differences between an Englishman and a Bengali. Whereas the average pulse rate of an English adult is seventy-two beats per minute, it is eighty for a Bengali; whereas the liver of an Englishman commences two inches below the right nipple, the Bengali's liver lies three and a half inches below. If a Bengali were to be examined in Britain, the diagnosis would be that he was suffering from contraction of the organ.[67] Diseases differed, as did the functions of the organs in India. But colonial medicine, according to Dr. Mukerji, failed to take this difference into account. Medical colleges and English books in India produced an "endless regurgitation about eastern apathy, dirty habits, and oriental custom and oriental prejudice."[68] These did not teach Indians medicine but trained them to function as a class of medical subordinates to the British.

Expressing similar sentiments, Jadu Nath Ganguli's *A National System of Medicine in India* (1911) described the Indian practitioner of Western medicine as a foreigner in his own land. He was aware of the limitations of Western medicine, but he had no knowledge of either the medicinal properties of plants in India or of *ayurveda*, which for centuries had cured millions.[69] This is why India needed its own medical system, which, unlike colonial therapeutics, could take into account the particular conditions and resources of the country. The concept of a national medicine, however, emerged under the shadow of colonial medicine's authority, and it sought to act upon a body brought to surface by the knowledges and practices of colonial governmentality. For these reasons, it operated as a strategy of reinscription, not rejection, of colonial therapeutics. Thus, Ganguli, in specifying a "system of medicine on national lines," did not rule out allopathy but proposed its combination with homeopathy, *ayurveda*, and *yunani*.

While the call to include *ayurveda* and *yunani* was an attempt to invoke Indian cultural resources, the enthusiasm for homeopathy was a challenge to the supremacy of colonial medicine. Both Western-trained doctors and non-medical practitioners in cities took to homeopathy, and pitted it against allopathic medicine. Its initial stronghold was in Calcutta, where its endorsement by Mahendra Lal Sircar in the 1860s engulfed medical practitioners in a bruising debate. The controversy was all the more fierce because Sircar had been trained in Western medicine and was a well-known doctor and public figure in Calcutta. Sircar did not reject Western medicine but held that because the body was subject to various laws and conditions, the modes of treatment must also be multiple.[70] But this did not satisfy his critics in the colonial medical establishment, who saw his defense of homeopathy as a betrayal and bitterly attacked him and his new cause. Homeopathy nevertheless struck roots among the educated elite, profiting from the fact that its practice did not require institutional apprenticeship and certification. Thus, members of the educated middle class, with varying degrees of training and expertise, took up the practice of homeopathy either as a full-time practice or as part-time charitable work. When epidemics broke out, they combined homeopathy with *ayurveda* and Western medicine to formulate a system that reinscribed colonial therapeutics.[71] Journals and newspapers published health columns, invoking multiple therapeutic sytems and offering advice on topics ranging from epidemics to pregnancy and childcare.

The reform of households, particularly through the agency of women, received a prominent place in the reinscription of colonial governmentality. In this arena, the Arya Samaj was the most conspicuous in North India. From its very inception, this religious and social reform movement had focused on women, setting them up as symbols of Vedic virtues and the Hindu nation, and establishing a regulatory ideal of conduct for them. In addition to promoting female education, the Arya Samaj published journals addressed to women and directed at applying medicalized disciplines. One such important journal was *Pānchāl Panditā*, which started in 1897 as a bilingual English and Hindi periodical but became an exclusively Hindi publication in 1901. It focused on diffusing modern knowledge authorized by the invocation of the Vedas, and published articles regularly on healthy diets, cleanliness and hygiene, the care of children, the follies of astrology, and other such topics.[72]

The project to assemble a code of action for women extended beyond the Arya Samaj. Middle-class women themselves participated actively in this project. An example was Yashoda Devi of Allahabad, who ran an *ayurvedic* clinic along with her husband. She was also a prolific writer and publisher. She started a journal for women in 1908, followed it up with two more in 1910, and started yet another in 1930.[73] She published a book in 1924 that gives ample sense of the nature of governance aimed at women.[74] It concerned food and offered directions on cooking based on rules of health and hygiene, not taste. Yashoda Devi established the justification for the rules of health and hygiene by narrating a fictional tale of a man who comes very close to death because of eating his food at an improper time. The man's near death provides the basis for a dialogue between two women who, drawing lessons from this incident, discuss the nutritional qualities of different kinds of food and the rules to follow in cooking and managing the household.

This dialogue on ill-health caused by ignorance becomes the grounds for Yashoda Devi to outline what constitutes proper Indian womanhood. The boundaries between health, hygiene, morals, and social institutions blur as instructions on preparing healthy food lead to the injunction that women must take full responsibility for maintaining the health of the household. A responsible Indian woman, the text suggests, rises early, takes charge of the household, and prepares food according to the laws of nature and the season. She must not depend on the servant, who has no knowledge of the rules to be followed. In fact, the servant's services should be dispensed with because these encourage indolence and detract women from their responsibility. Disciplined living requires the total devotion of women to their responsibilities. No sleeping late, no lazing about, no gossiping with neighbors after the husband leaves for work and the children have gone to school; make the beds, bathe, cook food appropriate for the season, look over the household accounts, and perform other household chores. The evening routine is more of the same—cook, manage, and facilitate the running of the household.[75]

Yashoda Devi produced this extraordinary prescription for women by seizing on the fictional near death of a Hindu male caused by the neglect of the rules of nutrition by his wife. Curing the body, however, served as the ruse for the formulation of rules and routines calculated to render the body useful, healthy and productive. It was in this network of rules and tactics directed at the body that a project emerged to reform the Hindu wife, to reproduce the gender hierarchy. As the scrutiny and subjection of the body redeployed and renewed the family, the medical gaze became inseparable from that of gender. The boundaries between the two were crossed, and transgression became the site for transforming both body and gender relations. A blueprint for a modern middle-class Hindu family appeared imprinted on a body anchored in gender hierarchy and disciplined by an economy authorized by science.

What shaped the language and provided an arena for the reconstitution of gender relations was the attention to governance, the concern with the health of the population that developed during the second half of the nineteenth century. The middle class debated the status and relevance of Western medicine, homeopathy, *ayurveda*, and *yunani* in its search to define what was appropriate for India. In this search, a range of therapeutics—some new, some old, and some of different provenance—found eager enthusiasts concerned to produce disciplined bodies. These included chromopathy (a system of therapeutics based on colors), mesmerism, hypnotism, and mechano-therapy, and were circulated widely among the middle class through the nineteenth-century print culture.[76] Books, pamphlets, and newspapers frequently advertised and discussed these systems, and the efficacy of different patent medicines were items of urban middle-class conversations. Such discussions were not always systematic and learned, and they did not seriously threaten the dominance of Western medicine. But they were important for an elite obsessed with defining an appropriate therapeutics for India. For at issue in this definition was the body materialized by state institutions. Insofar as the body was produced as an effect of knowledges and tactics, attempts to reinscribe colonial therapeutics were efforts to intervene in the relationship between the state and the population. Believing that nothing succeeds like excess, the elite produced a surfeit of therapies that exceeded and estranged colonial science in delineating their own intervention on the body. These excesses and transgressions did not negate colonial domination but sought to renegotiate its terms in order to administer a nationalist remedy.

SEXUALITY AND ASCESIS

The strategy of recoding colonial therapeutics could not stop at the level of national medicine. To the extent that therapeutics formed part of a set of practices concerned with specifying and regulating India, the strategy of reinscription had to bring under its purview the entire process of subject formation. This meant not only interventions in the field of medicine to outline medical knowledge and hygiene along national lines, but also the assimilation of indigenous forms of self-subjection into the field of governmentality. It was an ambitious project whose object was to produce a national subject that was different at once from both the "superstitious" and "ignorant" masses and the "foreigner in his own land." The elite sought nothing less than pressing claims for an Indian rationality of governance. It was in this context that elite nationalism produced what Milind Wakankar calls a Hindu nationalist ascetics. At the center of the effort to outline an Indian modality of governmentality was the claim that one possessed a self lodged in a body that must be refigured to serve the nation.[77] The possibility for this strategic combination of body-as-self and nation-as-ascesis was opened by colonial governmentality, but what elite nationalism attempted to identify was a national mode of the governmental relationship between the biological body and the body social. In this process, there emerged the idea of the Hindu origin of the nation, expressed by men ranging from prominent nationalist writers like Bankim Chandra Chatto-padhyaya in Bengal to powerful religious reformers like Swami Dayananda in North India. These men identified a Hindu past of the nation and found in it cultural resources for self-knowledge and self-constitution that both incorporated and exceeded the disciplines of Western medicine and colonial public health regulations.

The conception of the Hindu origin as a forgotten "before" of the nation's present permitted the logic of modern governmen-tality to appear as archaic Hindu disciplines of self-subjection. The notion of an origin, however, produced a sense of lack in the nation's present, as I have argued earlier.[78] As nationalist intellec-tuals cast their eyes on India's present, they saw a deep chasm in the nation's plenitude, the past lost and the disciplines of national self-subjection forgotten. The language of Hindu ascesis always functioned under the pressure from corruption and error, always embattled and struggling to restore the body to its original Hindu-national condition. It was through such a pulsating de-ployment of Hindu signs that elite nationalism acted on the medicalized, corrupt, and enfeebled body to render it healthy and Hindu-national.

The Western-educated elite had internalized the colonial rep-resentation of Indians as effete weaklings. It was to transform this weak, disease-prone body that Gandhi had secretly experimented with eating meat during his youth.[79] A body culture developed that was aimed at sculpting strong, vigorous physiques, and brought within its ambit traditional arenas of wrestling, gymnastics, and other sports.[80] Attention also turned to sexuality as several Indian intellectuals argued that India had fallen to foreign rulers because Indians had been rendered weak and passive by self-indulgence and vulnerability to the seductions of sensual and materialist enjoyment. Sharing these views, prominent late-nineteenth-century religious reformers like Swami Vivekananda and Swami Dayananda advocated the practice of sexual discipline as a means of national regeneration.[81] Such attempts to sculpt Indians into a muscular nation produced prescriptions for self-disciplines that were authorized by the invocation of traditions and were widely circulated in the middle-class culture.

Consider, for example, the Hindi pamphlet, *Ārogya Vidhān: Vidyārthi Jīvan* (1929), a book of advice focusing on sexual discipline authored by Yashoda Devi. Her *ayurvedic* practice, which included a small hospital in Allahabad and clinics in Banaras, Patna, Muzaffarpur, and Gaya, specialized in the treatment of infertility. The focus of her publications was more general, dealing with bodies gone awry because of the neglect and loss of principles which she presented as scientific and Hindu. The purpose of these texts was to promote a nationalist discipline of the body in order to restore its health. Like her middle-class contemporaries, she was also troubled by the physical weakness of Indians, and by their self-indulgence and vulnerability to the seductions of modern life. The text on sexual discipline was addressed to students and offered advice on how to maintain healthy bodies and dispositions. It began with a depiction of the physical weakness and sexual diseases that she encountered commonly in her patients. Her female patients complained of their husbands' weakness, of their lack of sexual desire and prowess.[82] The cause was masturbation, a practice the men had picked up as students when they read "dirty literature" and fell into bad company. Such men not only produced weak offspring but also infected their wives with venereal diseases.

Yashoda Devi also encountered the debilitating effects of this habit among young men. A twenty-year-old son of a wealthy man wrote her that he had become forgetful, suffered from dizziness, body ache, backache, and constipation. When she began treating him, she learned that he had been masturbating since the age of ten, not missing a single day. In addition, he often had wet dreams, rendering him so weak that he dared not go near a woman. This was a widespread condition among the youth, she argued. Many young men had become so diseased by the habit that they no longer had the capacity to approach a woman, let alone have intercourse with her. She combined the denunciation of masturbation with a blistering condemnation of homosexuality, noting with regret that even women had become victims to the habits of masturbation and homosexuality.[83] Lost in sexual pleasure, Indians had destroyed themselves.

Yashoda Devi's tirade shares only a passing resemblance with the "masturbatory hypothesis" that surfaced as a moral issue in eighteenth-century Europe and quickly became associated with mental disorders.[84] Moral outrage characterizes her strident critique as it did the European critiques; however, she did not see masturbation as a sin in the Christian sense, but rather as a blot on the culture and health of the nation. The medical language of her critique was also different insofar as, unlike European doctors, she did not associate masturbation with insanity. Because she viewed masturbation as a sign of the nation's weakness, her prescription for its cure was a cultural self-discipline. Thus, the denunciation of masturbation, homosexuality, and sensuality was followed by the recommendation that young men follow *brahmacharya*. By *brahmacharya* she did not mean prohibition of sexual intercourse but the preservation of sperm. Men could have intercourse for procreation, but they should not destroy their strength in masturbation. Her text proposed a set of rules to guide young men: Do not think of women; do not listen to accounts of their beauty; do not try to meet women, certainly not alone; do not read books that describe women or recount love stories; do not consume garlic, onions, and spices excessively; do not smoke cigarettes because they contaminate the sperm. The function of these rules of sociability and dietetics was to teach young men to conserve their semen, to develop a celibate disposition.[85] The production of such a disposition was not just a matter of the corporeal; it involved thoughts, reading, speech, and social relationships as well. Only when the relationship between men and women was governed by *brahmacharya*, only when the strength of the corporeal body was controlled and redeployed by the will of the spirit, could the nation cease to destroy itself.

It is tempting to read the recommendation of *brahmacharya* as the resurgence of tradition, and indeed Yashoda Devi extols it as a practice authorized by traditions. Unlike classical texts, however, the regimen of *brahmacharya* she proposed did not concern the religious status or the celibate student's lifestyle or relations with the ritual world of the community; rather, she dislocated *brahmacharya* from its classical context and situated it in the present to make it speak the language of health, treating the body as a constellation of not just ritual and religious signs but also of medical facts.[86]

Also posing *brahmacharya* in terms of health, Gandhi wrote: "Many are the keys to health, and they are all quite essential; but one thing needful, above all others, is *Brahmacharya*."[87] This is not to say that Gandhi was unaware of the religious significance of *brahmacharya*. On the contrary, he considered it a practice necessary for spiritual self-control and self-realization that restored human beings to their God-given natural state. But he also regarded sexual intercourse that did not have procreation as its aim as deeply injurious to health. Sexual pleasure in itself was evil. The difference of opinion among doctors over whether or not "young men and women need ever let their vital fluid escape," according to him, could not be used to justify sensual enjoyment. "I can affirm, without the slightest hesitation, from my own experience as well as that of others, that sexual enjoyment is not only not necessary for the preservation of health, but is positively detrimental to it."[88] *Brahmacharya* signified purity of thought—a spiritual cleanliness that was just as essential for the maintenance of health as clean air and water.

Gandhi viewed the practice of celibacy as more than a set of rules for maintenance of the body in a narrow sense. While he was willing to advance it on popular or current terms of health, for him the concept's wider significance lay in its meaning as the control over all senses in the search for Brahma (God).[89] This conception of health did not endorse modern Western medicine; Gandhi was a well-known and outspoken opponent of modern Western therapeutics, including vaccination and inoculation, and he advocated "natural" forms of treatment. But the regimen of sexual and dietary behavior he proposed assumed the existence of the body as a site of medical facts and tactics. Whether he accepted Western medicine or not, he had to come to terms with its authority in understanding the body—thus his willingness to speak of *brahmacharya*'s popular or current meaning though he believed that it had a wider significance. So, even as he conceived of celibacy as part of a larger discipline of self-control, he came to accept sexuality as an instinct, as an expression of the body's "animal passion." Bhikhu Parekh notes perceptively that Gandhi viewed sexuality as an impulse, not as a relationship, and had no conception of love that included passion and sensuality.[90] Desire appeared as a physical instinct, and *brahmacharya* represented the triumph of spiritual discipline, of soul over animal passion.

The suppression of sexual desire as a strategy for the recuperation of enfeebled bodies applied to both men and women, but it was profoundly masculinist. While women were also asked to restrain their sexuality, the ideology of *brahmacharya* identified energy and strength in the semen alone, and its discipline of restraint was designed to conserve the vitality that the male body contained. Men were to husband their semen with rigid self-discipline and transmute it into energy and power.[91] Such a perspective had no conception of sexual desire, let alone of women's sexuality. Despite Gandhi's wish to overcome the male/female distinction and his description of himself as "half a woman," he could not recognize female sexuality. He represented women in the desexualized images of mothers, sisters, and wives whose pure conduct was to serve as a model for men, who possessed the "animal passion" for sex.[92] The feminine virtues of chastity and purity were to be used in controlling virile male bodies, in conserving semen and transforming it into a source of power and energy, and in achieving the self-control that Gandhi associated with freedom. This set up a normative and regulatory bodily discipline that excluded all but procreative sex as the ideal.

This discourse represented the body in a "traditional" frame of cultural intelligibility. Its attribution of power to semen and the recommendation of sexual restraint as a means of spiritual control and energy reiterated ideas and norms contained in such ancient and authoritative sources as the laws of Manu. These ideas were formulated originally in a Brahminical context and referred specifically to the lifestyle of Brahmin students. The modern discourse of *brahmacharya* departed from this specific concern with Brahmin students and generalized the practice of chastity as a strategy for all Indians. Projecting Brahminical ideals as normative principles for all Indians, it implied a deeply hierarchical vision of sexuality, society, and religion. Importantly, this projection operated as a strategy of recoding the body and reconfiguring governmentality along national lines. Accepting the positioning of the body as an object of medical attention, the nationalist discourse sought to bring it under a different cultural regime of conduct, one that would be more authentic to India's Brahminical heritage. It operated in the same field as sanitation, hygiene, statistics, and therapeutics because, like them, it functioned as a tactic for forcing together the body-as-self and the body social. Like them also, nationalist discourse focused on the body as the locus of the Indian self, but found that its weak, vulnerable, oversexed, and decaying state was the basis for prescribing the conservation of semen as the strategic national goal.

BODY AND COLONIAL/NATIONAL GOVERNMENTALITY

To identify a certain intimacy between the plunge of Madhusudan Gupta's knife and Gandhi's confessions of the flesh is to push

Foucault's concept of biopower beyond its Eurocentric frame and to recognize that the formation of modern subjects in the colonies was necessarily embattled. Reinscription was central to the political technology of the body because it was obliged to operate in and rearticulate the colonial divide.

Thus, the operation of biopower in British India from the very beginning was based on a strong sense of Indian difference and on a deep awareness of the unbridgeable gap between the state and the people. It was to bridge this unbridgeable gulf, to appropriate the otherness of Indians, that the British were driven to erect an elaborate grid of knowledges and practices that sought to produce a colonial complex of "men and things." Through sanitary regulations, statistical enumeration and representation, measures to control epidemics, and colonial therapeutics, the state opened a vast new field of practices connecting it to the population. This field treated the body as a complex configuration of the effects of habits, habitation, race, climate, topography, religious beliefs, and cultural dispositions. Western medicine, established in British India through such a combination of knowledges and practices, achieved power and exercised influence on the lives of the people, but there remained always an uncloseable gap between state medicine and the colonized population.

The necessary failure of the British to achieve the object of producing self-subjecting individuals created opportunities for Indian elites to intervene in this field. Mediating between the people and the state, they sought to develop an Indian modality of governance. This was never a matter of simple negation of colonial governmentality, but always meant its reinscription. Through subtle practices of transgression and repetition, nationalism subverted colonial governmentality and pursued its own program of the welfare of the population. Acting squarely within historical power relations in the field of colonial modernity, the nationalist discourse intervened to deflect governmentality along different lines. The measure and significance of this deflection can be gauged from how utterly different the project to institute

157

brahmacharya seems from Western medicine's concern to determine the etiology and pathology of disease in India.

This great distance between the two registers nationalism's success in delineating an alternative set of disciplines for Indians without altogether rejecting Western modernity. This urges us to rethink Partha Chatterjee's influential formulation that anticolonial nationalism constructed an image of the nation's "inner" sphere of spirituality and culture that rejected the "outer" sphere of modern science, technology, and materialism associated with the West.[93] As the colonial career of *brahmacharya* shows, nationalism constituted the inner sphere of family, women, tradition, and spirituality under the shadow of the outer domain of modern governmentality. In fact, it was precisely because the inner and uncolonized tradition arose in the outer arena of public health and medical science that its emergence was so subversive. Nationalist resistance thrived on transgression and translation, not insularity and confinement. To speak in the language of modern governance was to make hegemonic and universalist claims on behalf of the colonized culture.

Reinscription as the condition of resistance, however, also meant that the category "India" could never enjoy certainty and stability. To render the inner sphere of the nation in terms of the outer, to advocate *ayurveda*, *yunani*, and *brahmacharya* as "Indian" disciplines, was to acknowledge that something was lacking in the nation's present. The nationalists, like the colonialists, were confronted with objects that always threatened to slip out of control, forever vulnerable to filth, dirty literature, lust, and ignorance. Its disciplines of self-subjectification, therefore, were always deeply hierarchical; they were poised constantly to identify and eliminate the enemies of the nation. Formed on the borderlines of such political, social, and cultural differences, "India" emerged embattled. But it was precisely in conquering sexual desire and battling degenerating modern influences that what began with the Fort William gun salute in 1835 became an expansive and hegemonic project to seize the governance of Indians from alien hands.

CHAPTER SIX

Technologies of Government

The more we thought about this planning business, the
vaster it grew in its sweep and range till it seemed to embrace
almost every activity.
Jawaharlal Nehru[1]

THE ESSENCE of modern technology, Martin Heidegger wrote,
is not technology itself, but a form of revealing, an "uncon-
cealment" that occurs as technology "sets upon" and challenges
nature to yield energy, to be available as a "standing-reserve."
"The earth now reveals itself as a mining district, the soil as a
mineral deposit. . . . Everywhere everything is ordered to stand
by, to be immediately on hand, indeed to stand there just so that
it may be on call for a further ordering."[2] The truth of modern
technology, according to Heidegger, resides in an "enframing"
(*Ge-Stell*) that not only encloses nature but also gathers human beings in the ordering and challenging of all beings as resources. "If man is challenged, ordered, to do this, then does not
man himself belong ever more originally than nature within the
standing-reserve?"[3] Human beings form part of the enframing
and are worked into the system of revealing and challenging that
renders all natural, human, and technical forces into resources,
always available and completely manipulable. To think of technology in this fashion, as an enframing that acts upon and orga-
nizes the world so as to make it available as a resource, is to situate
power in the "setting upon," and challenging of all beings. This
is not technological determinism; it is not a claim that power and
social hierarchies are reducible to the autonomous logic of technology, but rather that the rendering of the human and natural
world as resources contains political imperatives.[4]

In British India, the political imperative unleashed by this "setting upon" nature and the gathering together of human beings

159

can be identified at the level of the state, which, after the mid nineteenth century, acted as the primary instrument of India's technological reorganization. Forging India into a productive, interlocking network of irrigation works, railways, telegraphs, mines, and manufacturing, the colonial state introduced and oversaw the establishment of modern technics. In an important sense, however, technology was not only the instrument but also the substance of state power. For, as the state's shape and functions came to rest in constituting India as a productive colony—that is, as technologies of the state came to reside in the technological organization of the territory and its people—the rationality of governance acquired another definition. Increasingly, state power meant the growing technological configuration of the territory; it became inseparable from the modern India it engineered into existence.

Technology forged a link between space and state, making the newly configured India part and parcel of the institution of its technological configuration. This was of profound consequence because it meant that to press one's claim on the one was also to demand a stake in the other. Thus, as Indian nationalism asserted its authority over the engineered space of colonial India as the territory of the nation, it also staked its claim to state power. Beginning with demands for a greater representation in colonial administration, nationalist politicians mounted a relentless criticism of the administration's economic and industrial policies, and eventually demanded state power itself. This steady escalation of political demands, which equated the capture of state power with the achievement of nationhood, appears natural in the wake of the nationalist triumph and the influence of its historiography. But this was not a simple matter, for it entailed restaging the political means of alien rule—the modern state—as the expression of the nation; it meant rescripting the rationality of colonial governance as the logic of the nation. Above all, it obliged the nationalists to visualize that the order of rational artifice fulfilled the coming into existence of a people. The nationalist campaign for state power to exert control over the space constituted by technics, therefore, involved a profound ideological struggle to negotiate the breach between the cultural imagination of the nation as an archaic community and its existence as a space of modernity. Such was the process unleashed by the reconfiguration of India by technology.

SINEWS OF POWER

It was Lord Dalhousie's ambitious public works program that produced the momentum for what can be called, following Michel Foucault, the governmentalization of the state. Dalhousie assumed control as the Governor-General of the East India Company in 1848, and immediately set about extending and re-constituting British rule. Over the next eight years he deposed indigenous rulers and annexed their dominions under one excuse or another, and oversaw the construction of a grid of public works to forge the conquered territory into a unified, secure, and productive colony. As he departed from India in 1856, he boasted that he had harnessed India to the "great engines of social improvement, which the sagacity and science of recent times had previously given to Western nations—I mean Railways, uniform Postage, and the Electric Telegraph."[5] A year after his departure from India in 1856, North India exploded in the 1857 rebellion, which had been sparked by his annexations. The rebellion suspended the construction of public works, but it also demonstrated the military value of telegraphs and railroads. After the suppression of the revolt, the British took up the construction of public works with renewed vigor. Over the next several decades, as the British planned and put into place one project after another to shore up the foundations of their rule, the operation of the colonial state became deeply enmeshed in a network of technological apparatuses, institutions, and practices. Thus, when the colonial government declared in 1915 that it must develop India into a "manufacturing nation" and appointed a commission of inquiry to study and make recommendations for this purpose, this was not only because the outbreak of the First World War had demonstrated the importance of industries: it was also a recognition of the density that the technological organization of power had come to acquire in British India.

The construction of public works, which began in the 1840s, marked an important step in situating the exercise of colonial power in the exploitation of the territory and the people as resources. The Company, realizing that its political health required secure fiscal resources, assumed the responsibility of repairing and maintaining old irrigation works. Maintenance and repair soon escalated into the erection of modern, large-scale projects, such as Major Arthur T. Cotton's reconstruction of the Grand Anicut on the Kaveri delta in South India, which, when completed in 1846, increased the irrigated area from 270,000 to 410,000 hectares.[6] Even more gigantic in scale was the Upper Ganges Canal, built to stem the tide of declining revenues caused by recurring famines in North India. Although Captain Proby T. Cautley submitted a design for the canal as early as 1840, it received active official support only with the arrival of Dalhousie. At a capital outlay of £2.15 million financed by loans raised in London, and consisting of a main canal of 568 miles length and 3,293 miles of distributory channels, the Upper Ganges Canal opened in 1854 as the largest canal in the world. The canal suffered from a serious design flaw—its slope was excessive—provoking a bruising debate between Cautley and Cotton.[7] The entire public works establishment became engulfed in the scalding controversy as the two legendary builders, each with loyal followings among the engineers, locked horns. But more was involved than the reputations of the two engineers, for the integrity of the canal had to be secured. So, treading gingerly, the colonial government instituted a careful examination of the design and functioning of the canal and carried out the necessary repair work. This closed the chapter on the debate over the Ganges canal but brought to surface the government's growing stakes in the application of technics.

Commensurate with the growing stakes, the responsibility for irrigation passed out of the control of the Military Board in the 1850s and came to rest with the newly established Public Works Department, though the army continued to be the primary supplier of irrigation engineers through the end of the nineteenth century. Illustrative of the deep intertwining of politics and economics were canal projects in the Indus basin in the Punjab and in Sind that sought to engineer a stable, prosperous, and loyal political and social order through technical means.[8] Of these, the most ambitious was the massive Lower Chenab Canal project in the northern Punjab in the 1890s. Comparable in scale to the Ganges canal, it reclaimed large arid tracts to agriculture. New "canal colonies" arose on these lands, settled by carefully screened peasant communities from the densely populated parts of the Punjab. While these canal colonies represented an effort to raise productivity and foster a wealthy and loyal peasant community, other canal projects were undertaken to prevent the distressingly frequent occurrence of famines. Following these different though complementary state goals, by 1903, 18,588,000 acres, or 42 percent of all irrigated lands were under canal irrigation.[9] This in turn entailed mapping and classification of the territory of India according to soil, topography, rainfall averages, natural facilities for irrigation, and population density.

Overseeing the incorporation of the differentiated regions into a network of water-delivery systems were professional engineers, who pushed for ever larger projects and stressed efficiency and engineering control and solutions. As David Gilmartin shows, this brought them into conflict with the nexus of local social hierarchies and practices, including notions of custom and privilege, that the British land settlements had installed in order to institute the colonial administrative and political order.[10] This was evident, for example, in the engineering solution they devised for the problem of the annual silting of waterways. Annual silt clearances, which were carried out by unpaid labor mobilized by elites, were viewed as unnecessary and as evidence of defects in the design of canals. Instead of focusing on the removal of silt, engineers mathematically defined irrigation channels as a balance between scouring and silting, based on a formula for slope and water velocity. This solution excluded the local society from the administration of canals and devised a system of engineering adaptation, remodeling, and management to maintain a scientifically defined balance between silting and scouring in the waterways. The emphasis on efficiency in water distribution also ran up against structures of social privilege and hierarchy because it relied upon the spatial distribution of outlets, timing, and quantity, instead of local structures of power, in regulating access to irrigation. Such a technological reconfiguration of the countryside not only reshaped the local social relations but also recast state power. Not only did professional engineers increasingly staff irrigation departments, irrigation itself was seen by the British as a system in itself, extending from canal works and water distribution to revenue management.[11]

The most important project in the technological reconstitution of India and the colonial state was the railways, which attracted approximately £150 million of British capital during the nineteenth century, making it the single largest sphere of investment within the British Empire.[12] Though the capital was British, Indian taxpayers bore the risk of investment because the East India Company guaranteed a five percent rate of return to investors. Under this guarantee system, the work began in 1849 with approval for construction of two experimental lines. The first, the Great Indian Peninsular Railway (GIPR), officially opened in 1853 and ran thirty-five miles from Bombay to the Western Ghats. The next year, near Calcutta, a thousand miles to the east, the East India Railway (EIR) began operations on its thirty-seven miles of track. By the end of the decade, the GIPR had built 297 miles of track and was proceeding with the construction of another 787 miles up the difficult terrain of the Western Ghats and beyond, the EIR had 368 miles open and another 761 approved, and railway construction had started in other parts of the subcontinent.

This was achieved at great expense. The guarantee system did not encourage cost control, and, at an average cost of £18,000 per mile, the Indian railways were some of the costliest in the world. Rising concerns about the costs of construction impelled the government to assume responsibility for construction in 1869. Managed by civil engineers of the Public Works Department, railway construction proceeded with speed. By 1910, the subcontinent had 30,627 miles of track in operation, making it the fourth largest railway system in the world.[13] More importantly, railroad density in India, though lower than in the United States and Europe, was higher than in South America, Africa, the rest of Asia, Australia, Canada, and the USSR, indicating a relatively high penetration and integration of the territory by railways.[14] Criss-crossing the subcontinent, running through tunnels cut into rocky plateaus at great expense and huge labor outlays, steaming over rivers on bridges built with remarkable ingenuity and engineering, the railroads carried rapidly growing amounts of freight and numbers of passengers.[15]

A contemporary British observer remarked that the state in India was fortunate because it was free to devise the railway system without "frivolous oppositions" and the interference of parliamentary committees encountered in Britain.[16] Free to operate without interference, the state directed and supervised all aspects of railways in India. This was true even before it brought railway construction directly under its control. Thus, during the 1850s and the 1860s, when private companies built and operated railways under the guarantee system, government engineers supervised and guided all aspects of the operation. After 1869, when the state entered directly into the construction and management of railways under the departmental system, a complex mix of railway ownership and management developed; there were railway lines constructed and worked on by the Government of India, provincial governments, district authorities, railway companies under contracts, and princely states. In spite of the complexity of construction, ownership, and management, state direction remained a constant with regard to sketching the routes, determining the size of tracks, and controlling the opening of rail lines to traffic. The state built lines to defend strategic points on the frontier, constructed otherwise unprofitable tracks to connect certain parts of the colony, opened the so-called "famine lines" to transport grain to poor regions, and connected cotton-growing regions to ports. It also determined all aspects of construction and provisioning. It decided on labor-intensive methods in the construction of railbeds and plate-laying, using cheap labor recruited by contractors, and chose to satisfy the requirements for locomotives primarily with imports from Britain, rather than encouraging the locomotive factories that had developed in India.[17]

Indian railways developed, as a contemporary observer wrote, into "one organic system, a sort of chainwork, well connected in all its links and proceeding upon one definite design,"[18] because they were designed to serve the interests of the colonial state. Lord Dalhousie, championing the cause of railways in India, wrote in 1853 that "a single glance cast upon the map recalling to mind the vast extent of the Empire we hold . . . will suffice to show how immeasurable are the political advantages to be derived from a system of internal communication which would admit of full intelligence of every event being transmitted to the Government under all circumstances, at a speed exceeding five-fold its present rate."[19] The railways were to provide the means for an efficient and speedy exercise of power; they were to render the immense space of India manageable, knitting together its vast and disjointed territory and people "with a network of iron sinew."[20] Indeed, it would be more accurate to say that the vast expansion in the geographical scale enabled by steam power literally created a new space. Compressing time and distance between farflung regions, connecting them in novel ways, establishing links where none existed, the railways brought the geographical space of India within the grasp of its British rulers. It was a truly remarkable achievement, accomplished by deploying political and engineering power on an epic scale, and moving Kipling to pen "The Bridge-Builders" as an unforgettable tribute to the unsung work of empire.

Fig 6. "The Network of Iron Sinew": Bhore Ghat reversing station, GIP Railways, western India, c. 1870. Phot. 406/1(21). Reproduced by permission of the British Library.

Portraying a railway bridge over the Ganges River as a symbol of imperial rationality, Kipling's short story depicts the triumph of reason over India's unruly nature and mythic culture. Through outbreaks of cholera and smallpox, deaths in every manner and shape, riots among "warring castes," despair, and finally even the raging terror of "Mother Gunga" herself, the bridge survives as a beacon of imperial will and rationality. "Behind everything rose the black frame of the Kashi Bridge—plate by plate, girder by girder, span by span."[21] Unlike the sea, which was free to beat against the soft beach, the river is imprisoned. The engineers place her in a dock, run her course between stone sills. Docked and placed in irons, the ancient river goddess's strength fails her against the guard-towers of the bridge. She appeals to higher gods in vain, for they decree that the time has come for her to give

167

Fig. 7. "Mother Gunga—in irons": Solani Aqueduct, Ganges Canal, c. 1866.
Phot. 42/1(193) Reproduced by permission of the British Library.

way to men who build bridges and ride "fire carriages." "Mother
Gunga" has no option but to take her appointed place in the new
imperial geography.

Railroads unified the territory and eased imperial control. If
this secured India with "iron bands,"[22] security did not just mean
the ease of moving troops and exercising military control. The
introduction of railways extended the meaning of security; it implied transforming the landscape and "setting upon" the territory
and people as resources. Although there was a great deal of
inflated rhetoric about its impact, there is little doubt that the
introduction of the railways drove the state into seeking security
in a different order of things. The health and vigor of the empire
was now sought in transforming the territory with technics, in
instilling values of rationality, precision, calculability, speed, and
productivity in the population.[23] In introducing, constructing,
and directing the railways, the state not only gained a new means
of surveillance and control but also committed itself to new
modes and responsibilities of governance. Defining the state's

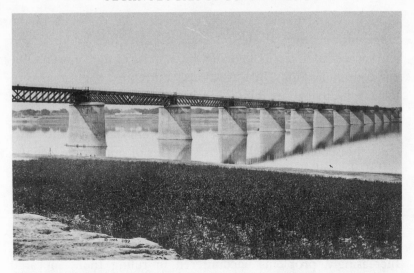

Fig. 8. "Mastering Nature": Jumna railway bridge, Allahabad, c. 1860. Phot. 394 (570). Reproduced by permission of the British Library.

role, G. W. Macgeorge, who had served as a consulting engineer for the railways for the Government of India, wrote in 1894 that state sponsorship and monopoly was particularly suited to India: "In India, the State, occupying a materially different position, will not necessarily be bound to sacrifice great public benefit for the sake of the last anna of profits."[24] The "great public benefit" meant the maintenance of order, development of India's productive capacity, protection against famines, integration of markets, promotion of cotton and grain exports, and exploitation of India to benefit Britain's industries and international trade.

The recasting of the state as an instrument of public benefit was directly related to its growing technological density, to which railways contributed most prominently but not exclusively. No single element matched the scale of the railways, but taken together the state's erection of telegraphs, promotion of geological explorations and mining (most notably for coal), employment of economic botanists and agricultural chemists, foundation of research bodies, and introduction of technical education to supply subordinate staff for irrigation works contributed hugely to the machinery and purposes of government.[25] By the close of the nineteenth century, all these technical institutions and practices had succeeded in technologizing the exercise of state power. Official communications, investigations, and reports about railroads, telegraphs, irrigation, mining, agricultural improvement, and botanical and medical research proliferated. These located India in the technological grid fashioned and administered by the state, and represented colonial rule as a matter of improving technics and their application on the colony.

TECHNICS AND THE SPECIFICATION OF BRITISH INDIA

Increasingly, problems encountered in ruling India appeared suitable for solution through the application of scientific methods. As famines visited the Indian landscape with disconcertingly regular frequency during the late nineteenth century, the colonial rulers looked to science for devising methods to forecast threats to agriculture and to raise productivity. While recognizing that science was primarily concerned with theoretical discoveries, they wished to use it to yield practical knowledge and techniques for placing Indian agriculture on a more secure and productive footing. It is with such an outlook that the Indian government wrote to the Secretary of State for India, in London, in 1898, asking for advice on the appointment of a botanist for the Madras Presidency and stating the belief that "hitherto too much attention had been paid in India to pure or systematic science and too little to applied and economic science."[26] Such a frankly instrumental approach to science could not but meet with the disagreement of Sir William Thisleton-Dyer, Director of Kew Gardens, to whom the Secretary of State turned for advice. Thistleton-Dyer lectured sternly that the development of systematic botanical science was absolutely essential before its insights could be put to use. The Indian government, however, stuck to its opinion, restating its concern that the state had so far primarily supported the "classificatory or systematic stage of science" and had neglected its practical use. It was not against scientific research, but wished it directed toward resolving economic problems.

> [F]ollowing the example of other civilised Governments, notably that of the United States, we should now direct research to fields hitherto unexplored. We are in India face to face with problems arising out of the ever increasing pressure of population on soil. This pressure can only be relieved by increasing the productive capacity of the soil or by providing new employment for the people, and these are objects which in our encouragement of scientific research we must steadily keep in view."[27]

The Indian government was firm in its view that the state ought to utilize scientific knowledge and expertise to resolve practical problems. While wealthy tea planters had the capital to hire their own experts, it was the government's duty to "investigate the main staples of India, which are cultivated by those who are too poor and ignorant to help themselves in the matter." This conception of the government's role and the belief that it required scientific advice in order to perform its role led to the formation of the Indian Advisory Committee (IAC) of the Royal Society in London in 1899. But having triggered the formation of the IAC, the Indian government failed to consult it for over two years. When a complaint from the IAC to this effect reached Lord Curzon, who was then Viceroy, he apologized and reiterated the government's commitment to apply scientific methods. As evidence of its faith in scientific research and expertise, the Indian government sent a list of the steps it had already taken: It had hired two practical mining experts for the geological department, directed the investigation of mineral resources by its scientific staff, appointed a cryptogamic botanist and entrusted another botanist with the task of conducting economic inquiries, enjoined its botanical survey experts to conduct practical inquiries, strengthened the office of the reporter on economic products, employed a bacteriologist to study diseases afflicting the animal stock, and appointed an inspector-general of agriculture to guide and coordinate the work of agricultural improvement. Stating that it remained committed to use science "to promote the industries of the country and investigate its underdeveloped resources," it declared that a central body was needed to coordinate the scientific work carried out by different government departments.

> [I]n view of the fact that the Indian Government own [*sic*] the largest landed estate in the world, that the prosperity of the country is at present mainly dependent on agriculture, that its economic and industrial resources have been very imperfectly explored, and that the funds available for scientific work are limited, the importance of practical research is pre-eminent, and a central authority, which can speak with knowledge upon scientific questions, will be in a position to enforce the repeated declarations of the Government of India on this subject.[28]

In 1902 the Indian government created a Board of Scientific Advice (BSA), composed of the heads of different departments, to review and advise on scientific research.[29] The establishment of this new body marked the triumph of the state's view that science was to serve as a source of knowledge and techniques for the exploration and exploitation of its "landed estate." Equally importantly, its emergence signified the consolidation of the developing constitution of the state in relation to the "standing-reserve." Although it is difficult to gauge the impact of its work over its approximately two decades of existence, the formation of the BSA registered the importance that India as a specific configuration of resources had acquired in the constitution of the state.

The existence of the state in India as an aspect of technological transformation was brought into sharp relief by the BSA's dispute with the IAC in London in 1910 over their respective roles.[30] This dispute was a bureaucratic battle ignited by the IAC's critical comments on the BSA's annual report for 1906–07 and its program for 1908–09. The IAC faulted the work of the BSA and several government departments and threatened to withhold advice unless timely reports were submitted on actions it had recommended. When the IAC's comments reached the BSA's meeting in 1909, they sparked a fiery response. T. H. Holland, director of the Geological Survey of India, whose work had been criticized as "sporadic and fitful," led the charge. He defended himself by arguing that in India, where minerals were largely the property of the government and where there were few nonofficial geologists, the geological survey work could not be confined solely to preparing a geological map; attention also had to be paid to "the subsidiary issues of scientific and economic importance that arise in the course of the survey."[31]

Other officials also referred to the specific situation of India to defend their methods. For example, refuting criticism that the IAC had leveled at the work of the civil veterinary department, officials of that department argued that an accurate knowledge of rinderpest in India could not be obtained from the available scientific literature, which was based on the study of the disease in areas where it was not enzootic; only the study of rinderpest as it existed in India could provide a scientific understanding of the disease. Such a study recommended, contrary to the IAC's opinion, that the anti-rinderpest serum was the only practicable method of dealing with the disease in India. Unbowed by the Royal Society's authority, they declared boldly: "We consider that we should be entirely wanting in our duty to the people of this country if we failed to promote such protective media, etc., as are known to be available."[32] Endorsing such spirited defenses of India-centered scientific work, the Indian government wrote to the Secretary of State for India in 1910 that it could not subordinate its views "based on financial and administrative as well as scientific grounds to any body of scientific men however eminent."[33] The system of seeking advice from the Royal Society, the letter continued, belonged to the time when there were few scientists in the Indian government's service. By the early twentieth century, however, the situation had changed; scientific departments had developed, and there existed a central body in India that was quite competent to advise on most matters, rendering unnecessary the exercise of general control by an advisory body located in London. In any case, local knowledge and experience were essential in dealing with economic science, particularly in dealing with the "habits and prejudices of an ignorant and suspicious population." The Indian government stopped short of recommending severing all ties with the Royal Society, and a compromise was eventually worked out that provided that the BSA would consult the IAC when it considered it necessary, thus freeing it from the Royal Society's control.[34]

We should not let the dust thrown up by the battle over turf obscure what the dispute also brought into view: the restaging of the colonial state as an Indian state. To be sure, the appeal to "our duty to the people of this country" was a clever bit of hyperbole used to silence the critics in London, accompanied as it was by the colonial bureaucracy's time-honored strategy of invoking local conditions to defend its jurisdiction. But it is important to bear in mind that the reference to the authority of local conditions and local knowledge occurred in a context in which colonial governance meant technological transformation. If to rule India was to harness it as a "standing-reserve," then the imperatives of such a governance also specified Indian interests that the state could claim to represent. Such a claim was manifest, for example, in discussions in 1897 over rules for granting prospecting leases for mining. In deciding this issue, the Indian government declared that it was mindful of the special responsibility placed upon it as "the proprietor of all minerals throughout the greater part of India, and as a guardian of the interests of a number of Native States."[35] Moved by this sense of its responsibility, the Indian government proposed that prospecting leases be granted to private syndicates rather than to companies selling unproven shares to the public, for "we should not be justified in leaving the native capitalists, and still less the Native States of India, to the mercy of the European mining market." The state's aim, as an official put it straightforwardly, "should be, not so much to enrich English promoters and capitalists, as to gradually induce the native of India to interest himself in the development of its varied resources."[36] In accordance with this thinking, the Secretary of

State for India approved rule changes proposed by the Indian government that were directed to insure that prospectors for minerals risked their own money rather than publicly raised funds.

Whether the colonial government served English capitalists or not is another matter. It is important, however, to note that the link forged between the state's functions and the existence of India as a configuration of resources positioned the government as the locus for representing and realizing Indian interests. This did not mean that British officials in India did not pay heed to the authorities in London. In fact, the connection between the Secretary of State in London and the Viceroy's administration in India remained strong, and Britain's fiscal and trading interests continued to determine the policies of the colonial government. This was evident in the Indian government's explicit refusal to include the issue of India's fiscal autonomy in the terms of reference of the Indian Industrial Commission it appointed in 1916.[37] India, after all, was a colony, and fiscal autonomy raised the thorny question of the constitutional relationship between Britain and India. It is nevertheless significant that the steadily growing nexus between British rule and technics had brought the state right up against its colonial nature. The imperial connection placed restrictions but did not annul the state's construction of India and Indian interests in terms of mineral deposits, agricultural productivity, industrialization, and scientific and technological reorganization.

The outbreak of the First World War lent an urgency to the question of industrialization. The Indian government declared that "the time has come when the question of the expansion and development of Indian manufactures and industries should be taken up in a more comprehensive manner than has hitherto been apprehended." The Indian Industrial Commission was appointed for this purpose.[38] The commission consisted of ten members, including four Indians, and was headed by T. H. Holland, who had served as the director of the Geological Survey of India and led the defense of the BSA against the Royal Society in 1910.

Beginning its work in 1916, the commission went on inspection tours, circulated questionnaires, and examined witnesses over two years before issuing its report in 1918, accompanied by a separate note penned by Madan Mohan Malaviya, the prominent Indian nationalist. The terms of the commission's appointment were restrictive, and, as it turned out, the government did not follow its recommendations. Yet, the commission's report clearly brings into view the formulation of a powerful discourse that situated the state as the site for defining and acting upon India as a "standing-reserve."

The Indian Industrial Commission's report articulated two central points: first, the state must assume the principal responsibility for industrialization, and second, industrialization was a technical process and could be advanced by a more extensive application of technology. In developing these two points, the report presented a thorough and dispassionate analysis of the state of industrialization in India, beginning with a description of India before British rule. "At a time when the west of Europe, the birthplace of the modern industrial system was inhabited by uncivilised tribes, India was famous for the wealth of her rulers and for the high skill of her craftsmen."[39] The industrial revolution in Britain, however, had produced a wide technological disparity between India and the West. The establishment of Company rule had witnessed some progress in manufacturing in India, and Crown rule had brought a modern communications network to India, but the belief in laissez-faire had impeded a more active state intervention. The report implied that, although India lacked the historical conditions that had produced the industrial revolution in Britain, the colonial state could make up for India's lack of such a history. It fleshed out the state's role by presenting a thorough survey and analysis of manufacturing, agricultural production and efficiency, the generation of energy and power, transport and communications, labor, technical education, and scientific and technical services. Identifying deficiencies in different branches of industry, and agriculture, and in the level of technical education and personnel, it was remarkably candid about the shortcomings in government policies and the inadequacy for scientific and technical guidance for industrialization.

Stating that modern industry depended crucially upon technical knowledge and expertise that private enterprise could not afford to provide—it was "more appropriately the business of the State "[40]—the report recommended a comprehensive program that envisioned the state as the embodiment of the technological imperative. The state was to provide technical help to fledgling industries, facilitate the use of mechanical power in agriculture, improve the technical component of cottage industries, and raise the efficiency of Indian laborers by encouraging the amelioration of their living and working conditions. It was to assume the responsibility for imparting technical education in vocations ranging from artisan to engineer, and for setting up industrial schools, providing scholarships, and strengthening the teaching of mining, metallurgy, and mechanical engineering in existing colleges.

The commission's report also proposed that the state strengthen the connection between science and industry by rationalizing and centralizing its scientific services. For this purpose, it recommended the creation of the Indian Chemical Service, an imperial administrative corps consisting of chemists with different specializations, and a similar reorganization of imperial services in other scientific subjects.[41] Revisiting the issue brought to the fore previously in the dispute between the BSA and the IAC, the commission expressed dissatisfaction with the practice of relying on the Imperial Institute (founded in 1887 to advance the scientific knowledge of colonial territories) and other institutions abroad: "The study of raw materials required for industries can be undertaken only by specialists working on the spot."[42] It called for encouraging local scientific investigation and personnel, and proposed that the union between science and industry be more systematic. To accomplish this, the commission recommended the establishment of imperial and provincial departments of industries charged to coordinate and set policies for different government agencies involved in the promotion of industry, technical education, scientific and technical advice, and legislation.[43]

With dispassionate analysis and cool reasoning, the commission mapped India in technics and placed the state at the center of the topos. Encapsulating the political imperative of technics, the state was to orchestrate the development of India as a configuration of resources and train Indians so that they could be deployed in "setting upon" the "standing-reserve" more efficiently and productively. The report's elaborate and systematic outline for the governmentalization of the state, published in 1918, marked the distance colonialism had traveled since its early-nineteenth-century evangelical "civilizing mission." By the beginning of the twentieth century, colonial power was no longer about bringing the light of Western reason and Christian truths to the dark corners of the globe, but about the scientific and technological reconfiguration of those dark corners. As an incarnation and instrument of the technological will, the colonial state became inseparable from the configuration it had brought into existence. Not surprisingly, it also emerged as the site for the definition and determination of India and Indian interests.

Reinscribing Colonial India

The governmentalization of the colonial state set the background for the cultural imagination of the modern nation. As India surfaced in the territory welded together by colonial governance, the nationalists represented it as a sacred locus—a national home to its religions, communities, languages, traditions, cultures, regions, and castes—as the territory of a people. India was bestowed with an archaic unity and long history, conferred with a philosophical heritage, and armed with its own scientific traditions. The nationalists stretched and displaced the available authoritative idioms, imparting new meanings to the figure of the mother, to the images of Hindu and Muslim communities, to the sacred hymns of the Vedas, and to terms such as *deś, jāti, Hindustān,* and *Bhārat.*[44] Reinterpreting these categories by mobilizing them to represent the space of modernity, the imagination of the nation was anything but straightforward, consistent, and free of contradictions and conflicts, for, the nationalist imagination operated as a form of reinscription. Its ambition was to rewrite India and Indian interests scripted by colonial governmentality, to domesticate and bring within the domain of the nation the space constituted by technics and its political imperative—the state.

In this sense, the struggle for the nation was at once both a product of colonial modernity and an attempt to steer it in a different direction. This meant that the "inner" sphere of the nation—defined by the nationalists as its essential, spiritual domain that the West was to be kept out of—could not be insulated from the inessential "outer" sphere of modern science and technology in which the West was dominant. Nationalism could never concede that the nation existed only in its "inner" recesses, because that would cede the sphere of politics and economics to colonialism altogether.[45] Colonial subjection drove anticolonial nationalism in a more ambitious direction as it simultaneously drew upon and transgressed the inner/outer dichotomy, distinguishing community from the state while seeking to realize the former in the latter. Nationalism spoke in the languages of both kinship and statecraft, it invoked the bonds of community and mobilized for state power. But the two, while distinct, were not separate. Anticolonial nationalism interbraided community and state in the nation-state as it sought a different basis for acting upon the space constituted by technics.

The establishment of the Indian National Congress in 1885 gave an organizational shape to the drive to translate diverse cultural and social conceptions of the nation into the language of politics understood in the arena configured by colonial governmentality. The seventy-two men who met in Bombay to channel and unify the associational politics developing in the major cities and towns into a single organization were overwhelmingly high-caste Hindus, though the gathering included a sprinkling of prominent Parsis and a handful of Muslims. They were primarily Western-educated lawyers, joined by an assortment of journalists, teachers, merchants, and wealthy landowners. The elitist character of the Congress did not change substantially in subsequent decades as its annual meetings drew an ever larger number of delegates. But though they shared an elite status, these men came from a variety of regions, where they participated in different spheres of politics. At local and provincial levels, the Congress politicians were active in municipal politics, district boards, social and cultural reform organizations, Hindu associations, and merchant bodies, and they often championed divisive linguistic and communal mobilizations. Drawing on this diverse group of elite politicians who functioned at different levels and espoused contentious causes to build a single organization, therefore, was an ambitious undertaking.

The true measure of this ambition, contrary to the Cambridge school interpretation,[46] did not lie in the upward push of local and provincial elite interests to the imperial level, but in the Congress's effort to establish the authority of the nation in the space the British had forged as "one organic system, a sort of chainwork." To be sure, the formation of the Congress reflected a desire to match the scale of British power, to mount the claim of the nation at an all-India level. But confronting the British rulers at this level involved more than issues of scale: it entailed seizing and reinscribing India and Indian interests brought into relief by colonial governmentality. This meant the representation of Hindus, Muslims, Sikhs, and Christians, and a multitude of castes and classes as Indians with shared interests as a secular formation; for, in relation to the state and the "standing-reserve" it had brought into being, the nation had to be staged as simultaneously modern and Indian. The Congress claimed to speak for this modern India, insisting that the multitude of local and provincial interests it mobilized shared common political interests as a nation in relation to the state.

In an important sense, the specification of Indian interests in the space of modernity was articulated most fully and effectively by the economic critique of British rule. This became an article of nationalist faith after it was elaborated in great detail by the early nationalists, for whom the demonstration of the destructive effects of British rule formed the enabling basis and substance of their political activity. As the nationalists turned their gaze on the territory constituted by the technologies of the colonial state, India appeared as an underdeveloped "standing-reserve." Production was stagnant, famines stalked the land, and an overwhelming majority of the population was caught in the trap of grinding and growing poverty. The nationalists believed that the fundamental cause of poverty was the insufficient development of productive forces, while British policies, they argued, had aggravated the effects of underdeveloped resources.[47] These ideas underpinned the political mobilization of nationalism. As Congress leaders met year after year, delivering eloquent speeches and formulating closely-reasoned petitions that expressed their deeply felt loyalty to the Crown and gratitude to British rule for having introduced India to modern law and government, a vital sense of the economic interest of the nation authorized their political demands. The betterment of the nation's economic condition, they argued, required the political representation of Indians, which they defined as wider opportunities for the growing Western-educated middle class in civil service and in government bodies.

While these ideas were shared and circulated by nationalist leaders as a whole, their most powerful exponent was Romesh Chunder Dutt (1848–1909). One of the first Indians to enter the coveted Indian Civil Service, Dutt had already acquired at the time something of a reputation for his literary and historical writings, including novels and a history of Bengali literature. After he retired voluntarily in 1896, after twenty-six years of a successful administrative career, he served as the president of the Congress and conducted political work in England on Indian questions. While in England, where he spent most of the period between 1897 and 1904, he wrote and published his immensely influential two-volume *Economic History of India*. A magisterial synthesis of years of nationalist writings and propaganda on the subject, Dutt's study became an immediate classic and the definitive core of the nationalist canon after its publication (1901–03).

Dutt described his book as an effort to recount the "economic story of British India," as an attempt to explain "the deep-seated cause of the poverty of the Indian people."[48] To single out poverty as the defining condition of the people in the context of the recurring famines of the late nineteenth century was to point an accusing finger at British rule; it was to suggest that the government had failed India in some fundamental way. Such an accusation meant identifying the Indian people by accounting for their poverty and specifying the nation by narrating its economic history. To be a nation was to have an economic history of one's own. "The history of India," Dutt wrote, "is not the history of the British and French wars, but of the people of India—their material and moral condition, their trades, industries, and agriculture."[49] India, conceived as an a priori cultural entity, had to be relocated in the arena of modern economy; its history as a nation had to be represented in the arena of production, trade, finance, taxation, and industry brought into existence by colonial government.

This is what Dutt set out to accomplish. Beginning with the inception of British rule in India, devoting a volume each to the pre-Victorian (1757–1837) and Victorian eras (1837–1900), copiously citing official papers, commentaries, and statistics, and moving methodically from the reign of one ruler to the next, the horizon of Dutt's study was set by the colonial government. The economic history of India meant an account of the impact of colonial policies, institutions, and practices. But as Dutt went about assessing the structure and functioning of land taxation, trade and administration, imperial finance and national debt, and irrigation and railways, the nation became visible in its impoverishment by colonial rulers. While Dutt expressed his touching belief in British good faith, he drew an exceedingly bleak picture of the nation under British rule.

The dominant motifs were desolation and ruin. The material and moral condition of the people appeared blighted by the relentlessly growing exactions on land, by the ruin of the handicraft industry through the "deindustrialization" of the country in the interests of British industrialization, and by the ceaseless and crippling drain of economic wealth to Britain. Even the railways appeared as part of the problem: their expansion was too rapid; they were laid down primarily to promote the political interests of rulers and the commercial interests of the British investors; they diverted investments from irrigation and agriculture, where they were much-needed; and as they stimulated the production and trade of raw materials, they held back industrial development and discouraged the cultivation of food grains. The attack on the British record was wide-ranging and sustained, and was carried out with patience and learning. Free of rancor but laced with a passionate sense of the injustice and unfairness of British policies, Dutt's portrait of India's impoverishment and devastation not only indicted British rule but also established Indians as a modern presence in the act of indictment. Conditions of poverty and famine became highly charged images with which Dutt's economic history registered the position of Indians as national subjects in the space of modernity. From this flowed the demand for political representation.

> All British interests, all sections of the British community, have influence on the Indian administration. It is just, and it is expedient that the Indian people should have some voice and some share in that administration which concerns them more than any other class of people. In the absence of this popular element in the Indian administration, all the influences at work make for increased taxation and increased expenditure, and for the sacrifice of Indian revenues on objects which are not purely Indian; no influences are at work which make directly for reduction in expenditure and taxes, and for relieving the burdens of our unrepresented population.[50]

Dutt neither questioned British motives nor demanded a radical dismantling of the colonial structure. Quite the contrary, he saw himself asking for the further evolution of the existing system. His basic point was that the combination of the colonial administration in India, the Parliament in Britain, and the Secretary of State for India, who was a member of the British cabinet and responsible to it, constituted an oligarchy. Notwithstanding the goodwill and generosity of British rulers, an oligarchy could not safeguard and promote Indian interests. "The wit and ingenuity of man could not devise a system of administration for a vast and civilised population, where the people are so absolutely, so completely, so rigorously excluded from all share in the control over the management of their own affairs."[51] Declaring that "[h]istory does not record a single instance of one people ruling another in the interests of the subject nation," Dutt advanced the claims of the educated and influential men to represent the people.[52] The government should enlist, rather than alienate, these men, he suggested; it should appoint them to the highest government councils, share the control of administration with them, and make them responsible for developing industry and agriculture and raising the material standards of the people.

Dutt's elitism was characteristic of Indian nationalism, but we should not view it too narrowly. The educated elite's claim to represent the people was not a wholly self-interested assertion, but was derived from their understanding of how representation was to be achieved in the light of colonial transformations. British rule, Dutt believed, had brought peace to India, but it had also destroyed India's village communities, which had existed since time immemorial. A "simple form of village government," this ancient institution had "survived the wreck of dynasties and the downfall of empires," protecting the people against oppression by landlords and the government.[53] This powerful and deeply romantic representation of India's past had arisen initially during the early-nineteenth-century discussions on land tenure systems. Formulated by such people as Thomas Munro and Charles Metcalfe, made the subject of classic studies by Henry Maine and Baden Henry Baden-Powell, and used famously by Karl Marx to describe "changeless" pre-British India, the elegiac village republic took hold of the nationalist imagination.[54] While it permitted the British to incorporate India in their evolutionary conception of history, enabling them to represent the India of village communities as a stage before the modern state, the Indian nationalists fastened on precisely this symbol of village communities to signify the difference of India as a modern nation.

> National institutions are the results and the outer expressions of national needs. The people of India developed Village Communities, and lived under Polygars and Zemindars, Jagirdars and Talukdars, Sardars and Panchyets, because they needed them. Their social organisation was built up according to their social requirements; they felt secure and happier under their born leaders or within their Rural Communities.[55]

Organically connected to "national needs"and "social requirements," village communities and the social hierarchy consisting of different classes of feudal lords and chieftains were seen as institutions structured to carry out the welfare of the people. Dutt pointed out that the *poligar* chieftains in South India had preserved peace and order in their estates during the wars of the seventeenth and eighteenth centuries, protected cultivators and artisans, and excavated great canals and reservoirs.[56] After the British suppressed the *poligar* chiefs and destroyed the old forms of village self-government—for which Dutt held Thomas Munro's *ryotwari* land tenure settlement primarily responsible—Indians were left with no protection against the government's exactions. "And the villagers, harassed by every petty revenue officer and corrupt policemen, could no longer continue to work together as corporate bodies, as they had done before."[57] As the British administration hollowed out old institutions of real power, it also isolated itself from the people and deprived itself of the opportunity of enlisting popular support. With Indian interests shut out, the administration lurched from one ill-conceived policy to another, producing desolation and ruin. Only the political representation of Indians could counteract the effects of such a ruinous transformation; and, like other elite nationalists, Dutt saw the Western-educated middle class as the natural candidate for performing this task in the context of the modern state.

Village communities expressed India's national existence in some vital manner and authorized the demand for political representation in the modern state. But significantly, Dutt cast village communities themselves unmistakably in the image of the modern state. This was consistent with the wider nationalist effort to indigenize modernity. Just as the nationalists claimed that India's national heritage included scientific knowledge, they also believed that the nation's "inner," organic life embodied the "outer," governmental logic of the modern state; village communities mimicked the modern state at the same time that they expressed the nation's timeless and organic existence. Dutt approvingly cited Mountstuart Elphinstone, governor of Bombay during the early nineteenth century, who had written that village communities "contain in miniature all the materials of a State within themselves, and are almost sufficient to protect their members if all other governments are withdrawn."[58] Dutt returned again and again to this theme, insisting that village communities and traditional chieftains and landlords had shielded people against the ravages of war and natural calamities and provided a framework for the production and distribution of resources. This does not mean that he did not distinguish these institutions from the modern state. Clearly, village communities were irreducibly different from the modern state insofar as they signified the nation as a pre-political formation, representing the organization of the people as an ethical community connected organically through kinship, culture, and social hierarchy. Yet, village communities also adumbrated the structure and functions of the modern state. Such a concept of village communities permitted Dutt to characterize colonial rule as a pure configuration of power that, having destroyed India's "national institutions," possessed no connection to the people. British rule was an oligarchy. Because it kept Indians out of decision-making processes, poverty and deindustrialization were inevitable. The existence of India as a nation demanded political representation.

There was something immensely important at work in Dutt's artful fabrication of a constitutive link between the existence of

India as a nation and its ability to exert control over its resources. Though not alone in promoting this viewpoint, he fashioned it most systematically. After him, the nationalists routinely invoked concepts of village communities, deindustrialization, and economic drain to formulate and press the claims of the nation. The nation came into view as a subject precisely in the sphere where colonialism denied it subjectivity; impoverished, dominated, drained of wealth, deprived of its national institutions, it appeared as a critique of the very ground upon which it stood. Exploited and deindustrialized, how could India not be critical of the colonial domain within which it appeared as an ancient nation?

Nation, Nation-state, and Planning

To enact the inner life of the nation on the outer stage of colonial modernity was an act of profound significance. For to make one's own a field that the alien rulers had brought into being and commanded meant asking how the nation was to reconstitute itself from the ruins of colonial governmentality. The widespread poverty and deindustrialization had demonstrated the truth of the axiom that the nation's vital being could not be secure without institutions connected to its national needs and social requirements. How could the people, whose existence as a nation was evident in the ravages of colonial modernity, exert control over the space of technics? Indeed, what was to be done with this space? It was in answering these questions that the nationalist critiques of colonial modernity also opened the nation to contending definitions.

What quickly acquired dominance in the nationalist critique of colonial modernity and in its search for reconfiguring the nation was the idea of the state. Behind the primacy accorded to the state was the assimilation of technology in the "inner" constitution of the nation. The nationalists agreed that India was not a natural object but a human world governed by artifice and modification.

India as they conceived it was not incompatible with the conscious arrangement of space into agriculture and manufacturing, the rational and efficient application of techniques on nature conceived as a resource, the economic organization of human groups, the division of labor, and the interdependent functioning of different sectors. If these so far had not produced progress and prosperity, the fault lay with the colonial state. British rule had failed India, the nationalists argued, precisely in the sphere where it claimed to have bestowed benefits. Instead of functioning as the center that coordinated and advanced the realization of the potential contained in different peripheries of production, the British had instituted biased and misguided policies that stifled the growth of a technological order. Accumulating and orchestrating evidence with lawyerly skill, the nationalists charged alien rule with prejudice and failure in the court of modernity. This indictment, pronounced initially by Dutt and other early nationalists, eventually escalated into the demand for state power because the state embodied the technological imperative.

The connection between the nation and the state, implicit in Dutt's writings, emerges clearly in Madan Mohan Malaviya's dissenting note in the report of the Indian Industrial Commission in 1916. Malaviya, a prominent nationalist and Congress leader, took issue with the commission majority's report on a number of counts. None was more significant than his disagreement with the majority's seemingly unexceptionable historical explanation for the disparity in industrial progress between Britain and India. He agreed with the report's characterization that at a time when Europe was inhabited by "uncivilised tribes," India was already famous for its wealth and crafts, and that even when European traders first started appearing, Indian industrial development was not inferior to the most advanced European nations. But Malaviya immediately expressed his dissent from the report's view that a disparity in industrial development arose when a combination of certain social and historical conditions produced an industrial revolution in England. "In my opinion this does not give a correct view of the matter," he wrote, "and is calculated to support erroneous ideas about the natural capacity of Indians and Europeans for industrial enterprise, and to stand in the way of right conclusions being reached as to the possibility of industrial development in India with the co-operation of the Government and the people."[59]

Malaviya refused to concede to the often repeated stereotype that Europeans were superior in the "outer" domain of technology. India's history, he argued, demonstrated that Indians had a natural capacity for industry, that industrial enterprise was organically rooted in the nation's life as an ethical community. He substantiated this claim by citing favorable European notices of Indian manufactures existing well into antiquity. India had a history as a manufacturing nation from the time of trade with Babylonia in 3000 B.C.E. Indian muslins had wrapped mummies in Egyptian tombs and had flooded markets in Greece and Rome, provoking the elder Pliny to complain that the Indian trade absorbed vast sums of money. Indian iron manufactures had a worldwide reputation and Indian commodities were in great demand, producing wealth and prosperity that were noted by observers ranging from Alexander the Great to Marco Polo. Though conquests after the eleventh century hampered the state of "Indian industrialists and industries" for a brief period, the foundation of the Mughal empire and "the safety and security of the reign of Akbar seem to have fully revived Indian industries and handicrafts."[60] European travelers, such as François Bernier in the seventeenth century, spoke glowingly of India's immense treasures and proficient manufacturing. Lured by these descriptions, European traders entered India, which led eventually to the conquest of India by the East India Company. After the conquest the picture changed rapidly, as British weavers expressed their deep jealousy of Indian weavers' skill and moved the Company to use its newly-acquired power against the indigenous industry. Malaviya then cited Dutt's *Economic History of India* and William Digby's *"Prosperous" British India* (1901) to lay out the picture of the deindustrialization of India under Company rule. The British destroyed Indian manufacturing and turned India into an agricultural country as they drained India's wealth to finance the industrial revolution in Britain. This, according to Malaviya, was the true explanation for the disparity in industrial development between India and Europe.

Having established that British rule was responsible for wrecking India's existence as a manufacturing nation, Malaviya seized on the state as the instrument for orchestrating its industrial renewal. Here the instructive examples were Germany, Austria, the United States, and Japan—nations that had rapidly left Britain's manufacturing leadership in the dust. The key to their industrial progress, he argued, was the link they had forged between the state and the people through education. He cited testimonies of British observers who noted that Germany, for example, unlike Britain, had devised a national and compulsory education system to create an efficient and productive workforce. But the most impressive example was Japan, where the "Government and the people, working in conjunction," had effected a massive industrial transformation built upon a system of integrated technical and general education."[61] This was responsible both for Japan's remarkable agricultural growth, which it had accomplished without the extensive use of power-driven machinery, and its industrial expansion. Japan's example demonstrated that "the artisan and the labouring population do not stand apart from the rest of the community; and therefore if this *sine qua non* of industrial efficiency and economic progress is to be established, it is necessary that primary education should be made universal."[62]

It was the government's failure in the arena of education rather than its fitful industrial policy, that was more fundamentally responsible for India's backwardness. The remedy lay in the establishment of a system of integrated general and technical education that would enable Indians to catch up with advanced nations. Encapsulated in this proposal was the view that modern technology necessitated the power/knowledge nexus embodied in the state.[63] If Indians were to put to use their natural capacity for industrial enterprise, if they were to achieve nationhood in the arena of modern technology, then the state must act to effect

India's technological transformation. To create a mass industrial society, achieve high levels of economic growth and employment, maintain increasing supplies of goods and services, and attain a high standard of living, the state itself had to be conceived of as a technical institution, as an expression of the nation's will to achieve a quantum leap in its technological capacity.

The conception of the state as the embodiment of the technological imperative earmarked a prominent role for science and scientists. For if the state was to be nothing but a constellation of technical practices, then what could guide its operations more rigorously than science? Acting upon nature in order to develop a complex industrial society demanded the knowledge and application of nature's laws and a systematic understanding and manipulation of modern technics, which science was well-placed to provide. On this point there was little disagreement between the report authored by the British members of the Indian Industrial Commission and Malaviya. While they disagreed over particular organizational forms, there was a general consensus that industrial progress depended upon the use of scientific knowledge and personnel in agriculture and manufacturing. Nationalism took this conception further, identifying the functioning of the nation-state with the application of scientific methods; nationhood was to be realized in a state embodying and applying science.

This view was elaborated tenaciously by the physicist Meghnath Saha (1893–1956), particularly in the journal *Science and Culture* he established for this purpose in 1935. Saha belonged to the distinguished array of Bengali scientists who came to prominence around and after the turn of this century. But unlike most of them, he was born to a humble grocer's family in East Bengal. Spurning the family occupation and working against all odds to excel in academics, he eventually entered Presidency College in Calcutta in 1911 to study science. He was taught by such famous scientists as P. C. Ray and J. C. Bose and became part of an extraordinary group of scientists—S. N. Bose, C. Mahalanobis, C. V. Raman, and J. C. Ghosh—reared by Presidency College. Receiving his Doctor of Science degree in 1919, he published several scientific articles, among which were four papers on thermal ionization published in the *Philosophical Magazine* in 1920. These papers won him entry into the international arena of astrophysics. He spent two years in England and Germany on postdoctoral scholarships, and on his return to India accepted a chair at Allahabad University. In the 1930s, he continued to carry out experiments at the meager laboratory facilities available to him at Allahabad, while at the same time gaining prominence as an important institutional figure in Indian science. After 1933, he became the leading functionary in the Indian Association for the Cultivation of Science, the oldest organization of Indian scientists, established in 1876 by Mahendra Lal Sircar. Saha presided over the Indian Science Congress in 1934 and founded the National Institute of Science, modeled on L'Institut Français, in 1935. The same year, drawing on the British periodical *Nature* and the American periodical *Science* as models, he began publishing *Science and Culture*.[64] In 1948 he founded the Institute of Nuclear Physics.

Saha's extraordinarily active efforts in building institutions in the field of science and in pursuing research were matched by his energetic participation in politics. He vigorously advocated the public roles and responsibilities of science and scientists. He became deeply involved in economic planning and was elected to the Indian parliament in 1952. His pursuit of science and participation in public affairs were inextricably linked, reflecting his conviction that science in India required institutionalization and that the institution of India as a nation demanded the application of science. The inaugural issue of *Science and Culture* outlined this vision. In his editorial he stated that as India passed through a stage in its history when modern structures were built on "the cultural foundations of her ancient and variegated civilisation," it was necessary to pay close attention to "the application of discoveries in modern science to our national and social life."[65] Commenting on Otto Spengler's theory of the rise and decline of civilizations, he wrote that just as the Europeans had developed a modern culture marked by science and technics from the ruins of the Greco-Roman civilization, it was time for India to regenerate itself. It too was emerging from a long dormant state and was facing a challenge thrown by Europe's scientific and technological progress. With Gandhi clearly in mind, the editorial scoffed at national leaders who were "incapable of seeing the great and inevitable part which the new age of technic will play in India's destiny," and who blamed all "our present troubles to the evil effects of science." Only an intensive and proper application of science, Saha proclaimed, could solve India's "bewildering economic, social, and even political problems."[66] There was a certain tautology to this logic, for, when seen through the optic of the "new age of technic," India appeared to have problems—"bewildering economic, social, and even political problems"—that only science could resolve. If what ailed India was the woefully underdeveloped industrial utilization of its productive resources, then science was obviously well placed to direct the development and application of technical apparatus and practices to achieve mastery over nature. Echoing earlier colonial pronouncements on the role of scientific research in India, a later article in *Science and Culture* proclaimed that "'science for science's sake' like the sister adage 'art for art's sake' is fast passing out of the vocabulary of those who have looked out into the genesis, history, and future of both science and art."[67] India could not afford the luxury of pure scientific research; science had to serve industry.

Science could not, however, orchestrate India's industrialization on a systematic basis without organization. Saha's public life and his journal were driven by the desire to organize science for national development, to match scientific means with their ends. India's transformation from a poor agricultural society to an advanced, high-energy-consuming industrial nation demanded planning, because only planned development could orchestrate the growth of a large-scale, complex, and interdependent configuration of technical institutions and practices. In this context, the Soviet Union served as an instructive example: "The success of Russia in developing power, industry and agriculture is entirely due to thoughtful planning extending over years."[68] Lenin's dictum that communism meant Soviet power plus electrification impressed Saha because it provided a model that combined power, large-scale industrialization, and the state. Above all, the Soviet example highlighted the key role of scientists in the planning process; a team of scientists and engineers controlled by the Academy of Sciences—not a committee of bureaucrats—was in charge of planning. This is what impressed Saha the most—communism as an ideology. Noting that there was a great prejudice against everything Russian, and commenting that he was not a politician himself, he said that what nevertheless impressed him "as a scientific man is the extraordinary use they have made of modern scientific knowledge in solving their problems of poverty and want, and the extremely judicious and businesslike fashion in which they proceeded with their schemes and coordinated the labours of economists and technicians."[69]

Saha tried to teach the Soviet lesson of the alliance between the politician and the scientist to the nationalist leaders, whom he found frustratingly naive about industrialization. Though the Congress Working Committee had embraced the idea of planning, Saha found its support for a mixed economy and cottage industry dangerously captive to Gandhian ideas. As the Congress formed provincial governments in 1937 under the Government of India Act and full state power appeared imminent, he believed that planning demanded urgent attention. Fortunately, he found sympathetic ears in two leaders, Subhas Chandra Bose and Jawaharlal Nehru. He invited Bose, who had been elected Congress President in 1938, to address the Indian Science News Association, which published *Science and Culture*. Bose spoke as the leader of a movement on the verge of power. He declared that independence was no longer a dream, and that national reconstruction meant achieving large-scale industrialization.

Whether we like it or not, we have to reconcile ourselves to the fact that the present epoch is the industrial epoch in modern history. There is no escape from the industrial revolution. We can at best determine whether this revolution, that is industrialisation will be a comparatively gradual one, as in Great Britain, or a forced march as in Soviet Russia. *I am afraid that it has to be a forced march in this country* [emphasis original].[70]

Bose said that industrialization did not mean the manufacturing of "umbrella-handles and bell-metal plates," but power supply, metallurgy, machine tools manufacture, chemicals, transport, communications, scientific agriculture; what was needed was a "far-reaching co-operation between Science and Politics." Envisioning planning to encapsulate this alliance between science and politics, Bose invited Saha to attend the meeting of the National Planning Committee in Delhi. Arriving at this meeting in early 1938, Saha discovered that Sir M. Visvesvaraya had been asked to chair the committee. Visvesvaraya, the great engineer, was a kindred soul. Writing in 1920, he had stated that the modern world required a "new type of Indian citizenship" founded in science and industry. India needed to tap its unparalleled potential of energy resources, use science to develop its agriculture, and introduce modern machinery and business methods.[71] An early advocate of planning, he published a book in 1937 explaining the principles of economic planning and addressed to the Congress leaders who had assumed office in seven of the eleven provinces of British India.[72] Given his credentials as a famous Indian engineer and his views on planning, he was an obvious choice to head the planning committee. But the astute Saha convinced Visvevaraya that the committee should be chaired by a powerful nationalist if planning were to have real weight in politics. Accordingly, Saha wrote to Nehru, asking him to head the planning committee instead. "On behalf of the Indian scientists, I would appeal to you to accept the chairmanship and guide the deliberations of the Committee."[73]

Nehru was an apt choice. He was not only the most important nationalist leader after Gandhi, but also the most uncompromisingly modern of all the Congress leaders. He needed no convincing of the central importance of industrialization, science, and planning for the nation. In a message to the Indian Science Congress in January 1938, Nehru wrote:

> Though I have long been a slave driven in the chariot of Indian politics, with little leisure for other thoughts, my mind has often wandered to the days when as a student I haunted the laboratories of that home of science, Cambridge. And though the circumstances made me part company with science, my thoughts turned to it with longing. In later years, through devious processes, I arrived again at science, when I realized that science was not only a pleasant diversion and abstraction, but was the very texture of life, without which our modern world would vanish away. Politics led me to economics and this led me inevitably to science and the scientific approach to all our problems and to life itself. It was science alone that could solve these problems of hunger and poverty, of insanitation [*sic*] and illiteracy, of superstition and deadening custom and tradition, of vast resources turning to waste, of a rich country inhabited by starving people.[74]

These words will come as no surprise to anyone even remotely familiar with Nehru's views. He was, as is well known, an avid advocate of what he called the scientific outlook. What I wish to highlight here, however, is the significance of his statement that through "devious processes" he had come to realize that "science was not only a pleasant diversion and abstraction, but was the very texture of life." Encapsulated here was Nehru's meaningful reappraisal of science as a nationalist. This reassessment cast science not primarily as a body of theoretical knowledge but as a source for powerful applications and techniques for "life itself." A much more expansive view of science than its conception as theoretical discoveries, Nehru's view projected science as a method that could be applied just as easily and effectively to order politics and economics as to understand nature. Such a conception technicized both science and politics as it identified "the scientific approach to all our problems" with the fuller and more efficient use of India's rich but wasted resources. Addressing the National

Academy of Sciences in March 1938 at Allahabad at Saha's request, Nehru elaborated on this vision, saying that the goals of the Indian nation demanded the combination of science with statecraft.

> We have vast problems to face and solve. They will not be solved by the politicians alone, for they may not have the vision or the expert knowledge; they will not be solved by scientists alone, for they will not have the power to do so or the larger outlook which takes everything into its ken.[75]

This must have been music to Saha's ears, for it was in tune with the technicization of both science and politics that he had long championed. The establishment of the National Planning Committee with Nehru at its head was a further realization of his vision of the state as an embodiment of technics. Comprised of fifteen members, the planning committee included Saha and four other scientists, four industrialists and merchants, two economists, an engineer (Visvesvaraya), and three political figures, including Nehru and J. C. Kumarappa, a Gandhian. The committee began its work in December 1938 and set about immediately to quash Gandhian objections to large-scale industrialization. Nehru issued a statement affirming that while the Congress encouraged cottage industry, this was not at the expense of heavy industries and industrialization of the country. "Now that the Congress is, to some extent, identifying itself with the State, it cannot ignore the question of establishing and encouraging large scale industries." The committee followed Nehru's lead and issued a conciliatory statement declaring that there was no conflict between large-scale industrialization and cottage industries, but the Gandhian opposition had been silenced. This was not surprising. The composition of the committee and the contents of its brief were clearly weighted in favor of industrialization, which was perceived as a technical process. As the committee stated in a note to guide subcommittees: "Planning under a democratic system may be defined as the technical co-ordination by disinterested experts, of consumption, production, investment, trade, and

197

income distribution in accordance with social objectives set by bodies representative of the nation."[76] The National Planning Committee stopped its work in 1940 after Nehru's arrest, but resumed functioning after the war. It published a general report along with twenty-six separate volumes of reports by its different subcommittees, and held its last meeting in 1949 under Nehru's chairmanship.[77]

The significance of the institution of planning was that, as Partha Chatterjee points out, it removed the assignment of national priorities from the domain of politics.[78] The definition of planning as "technical co-ordination by disinterested experts" insulated the exercise of state power from the realm of the political process. The state was projected as an essentially technical instrument for planning a modern, industrial society into existence so that the needs of the population could be met. Of course, it was up to the state and its disinterested experts to determine the nature of the population and its needs; and from the perspective of technics, the nation was comprised of secular individuals with secular needs. Be they Hindus or Muslims, workers or capitalists, Brahmins or untouchables, men or women, from the perspective of the state they were Indians with human needs—food, shelter, clothing, medicine, education—that could be satisfied only by the planned development of an appropriate infrastructure and investments in heavy industries, mining and metallurgy, hydroelectric projects, and technical education. Social and material obstacles to economic and technical expansion were to be removed, and the nation was to acquire a growing class of engineers, agronomers, accountants, and scientists committed to raising the productivity and efficiency of India's "standing-reserve."

INDIAN MODERNITY

We have steered far from where we began, namely, the constitution of India as a "standing-reserve" by British rule. But we have done so in order to chart the course set into operation by the technological reconfiguration of British India by the colonial government. What began as an effort to relocate colonial power in technical apparatuses and practices unleashed a political struggle to establish a nation-state that would institute the logic of rational artifice more fully and efficiently. If it appears ironic that the nationalists saw India realized in a political form cast in the image of the colonial state, we should remember that the nation was a hybridized concept. Representing India's coming into being as a timeless community in the time of British rule, the nation was archaic and modern at the same time, which is to say that it was neither one nor the other but formed in the displacement of both. The ancient nation never appeared in itself in its own time, but was summoned in the time and space configured by colonial modernity. It was obligated to articulate itself as *jāti* and *deś*, as mother and home, as an archaic collectivity of kinship and love in the space of modernity. This was not mimicry, for it did not produce the nation as a failed imitation of the colonial modernity, but rather actualized India as a culturally rooted moral community with a rational will to industrialize and achieve technological mastery. The technicist nation-state was the modern repetition of India's ancient national institutions and social needs; it was the nation's coming into being in modernity. If this meant, on the one hand, that India had to express itself in the language of modernity, it was also evident, on the other hand, that its modern articulation was to be irreducibly different from its colonial expression. The Indian nation-state was to "set upon" the "standing-reserve" even more rationally than the colonial state. Planned development and technical experts were to accomplish what the colonial government was unable to undertake because it was captive to narrow British political and commercial interests. Nehru, whose commitment to modernity was deep, pointed to this connection between the nation and its modern realization repeatedly in his *Discovery of India*. He returned again and again to the theme of India as collective memory, history, and traditions coming into being as a nation in modernity. Deeply convinced of this modality of the nation's emergence, he was bitingly critical of Indian communists who, according to him, had "no real roots." In a country as poor as India, communism should have had a wide appeal, but the communists had cut themselves off from the "springs of national sentiment." For them, world history began in November 1917; they failed to realize that the Soviet Union was a national experiment, that it represented the conjoining of national traditions with science and planned economy.[79] India could not imitate the Soviet Union even if the latter offered an example of how India could achieve modernity within a national frame. India had to achieve modernity on its own terms.

CHAPTER SEVEN

A Different Modernity

*If India copies England, it is my firm conviction that she will
be ruined. . . . Civilisation is not an incurable disease, but it
should never be forgotten that the English people are at
present afflicted by it.*
Mahatma Gandhi[1]

INDIA'S ORGANIZATION as a nation-state was implicit in the imagination of India as a nation. This was true even before the nationalists organized for political struggle, because the concept of the national community contained within it the idea of the nation-state as the highest form of organizing a culturally rooted ethical order. Not surprisingly, once Indian nationalists took up political mobilization, their struggle quickly escalated into a demand for state power. With much conviction and determination, they pressed home the point that India's uniqueness as a nation required an independent nation-state, that no alien power could possibly represent and fulfill the aspirations of Indians as a people.

The insistent demand for a nation-state was an urge to establish a modernity of one's own, one that differed from Western modernity. This was a defining feature of Indian nationalism because, being an anticolonial project, it had to articulate its aspirations as a critique of Western modernity and as a desire to institutionalize a culturally specific community. In this context, Partha Chatterjee is entirely correct to point out that Benedict Anderson's enormously influential study, *Imagined Communities*, allows the colonized too little imagination, that there is something deeply flawed in the proposition that the imagined communities in the colonies were nothing but replicas of the modern nation already imagined elsewhere.[2] This, Chatterjee argues, overlooks colonial difference; it ignores the fact that the modern nation in

201

the colonies could not but mark itself as different. This was evident, above all, in the imagination of the nation as a community, that is, in the conception that the nation had an "inner sphere, a "spiritual" domain of culture, in which it was already sovereign. It failed, however, to develop alternatives to the modern state. While successfully projecting the nation as an autonomous community, its imagination was overwhelmed by the history of the modern state. "Here lies the root of our postcolonial misery: not in our inability to think out new forms of the modern community but in our surrender to the old forms of the modern state."[3]

Having correctly observed that the nation had to be imagined differently in India, Chatterjee overlooks the fact that this imperative also applied to the nation-state. The nation-state was not a "surrender to old forms of the modern state": the politics of the state did not simply outmaneuver the logic of community; Nehru the modernizer did not just sideline Gandhi the nonmodernist after having utilized him for mobilizing the masses.[4] The nation-state was immanent in the very hegemonic project of imagining and normalizing a national community. There was no fundamental opposition between the inner sphere of the nation and its outer life as a nation-state; the latter was the former's existence at another, abstract level. The distinction between the two was an internal one opened up by the nationalist discourse as it portrayed the one realized in the other. The state materialized the imagination of India as a pre-political community; it actualized the community's universal life in the political domain. Far from negating India's difference, the nation-state was commensurate with it.

The alignment of the nation-state as the expression of a distinctly Indian modernity was rooted in the nationalist reinscription of the space fabricated by colonial technics. As the nationalists redefined this space as the territory of the nation, they also came to envision a sovereign political order that would enact and express India's being as a free national community in the modern world. This order could not be an imitation of the colonial state.

Insofar as it was anticolonial, Indian nationalism was obliged to define its political struggle in expansive terms, distinguishing its objectives from those of Western modernity.

It was this imperative to represent itself as a critique of the West that brought together Gandhi and Nehru, two men with widely different views on modernity. While Gandhi's opposition to modern science and technology is well known, it is seldom recognized that Nehru was also a critic of Western industrialism. He shared in the running theme of Indian nationalism that class struggle and the horrors of the industrial revolution, conjured up in Manchester, were alien to India, and that India should follow instead a path rooted in the Indian soil.[5] The story of Indian modernity, therefore, cannot be cast in modern/antimodern, inner/outer, state/community oppositions. Instead, it has to be understood as a project that was bound to engage in a critique of Western modernity in the process of founding India as a modern nation. The spectrum of positions, symbolized by Nehru at one end and Gandhi at the other, signified not an elite/subaltern divide, but the scope and limits of the critiques of Western modernity that nationalism articulated in organizing India as a political community. It is essential to grasp the nationalist nature of the critique that anticolonial nationalism was compelled to make if we are to understand both its mobilizing vision and its historical limits. Quite simply, I wish to argue that if India ended up with a modern nation-state, this was because both Nehruvian and Gandhian critiques of Western modernity were articulated in the historical context of nationalism. This was both their strength and their weakness.

NEHRU'S *DISCOVERY OF INDIA* AND THE INDIAN STATE

Of all the Indian nationalists, Nehru reflected and wrote most evocatively about India as a nation. *The Discovery of India*, written over a five-month period in 1944 during Nehru's imprisonment, is an extraordinarily lyrical yet lonely quest for modern India through its history. India, he said, had always been for him an odd mixture of an old story and modern fact.

> India was in my blood and there was much in her that instinctively thrilled me. And yet I approached her almost as an alien critic, full of dislike for the present as well as for many of the relics of the past that I saw. To some extent I came to her via the West, and looked at her as a friendly westerner might have done. I was eager and anxious to change her outlook and appearance and give her the garb of modernity. And yet doubts arose within me. Did I know India?[6]

Though he had read books and seen monuments that spoke of India's past cultural achievements, he wished to discover if there was a real connection between the past and the present. What was the India that was brought into view by the people in the villages and by their cries of "Victory to the Motherland"? Did the present stirring of India as a nation have a basis in the past? Nehru did not wish to live in the past, but he sought in it evidence of the youthful vitality that he discerned in the United States, Russia, China, Canada, Australia, and New Zealand. "Something of that vitality which I saw in China I have sensed at times in Indian people also. . . . I was always in search of this in my wanderings among the Indian people." He looked for "some urge driving the people in a direction not wholly realized," for a restless spirit rooted in the old and yet always seeking fulfillment in the new. Assuming that India had its own history, he found in India a heart that was constantly beating, never incomplete but forever seeking fuller forms, continuous but never completely content. "Astonishing thought: that any culture or civilization should have this continuity for five or six thousand years or more; and not in a static, unchanging sense. For India was changing and progressing all the time."

It was vitally important that Nehru found a continuity over "five or six thousand years" of history, but "not in a static, unchanging sense" so that he could portray the British rule in India as "just one of the unhappy interludes in her long history" from which she would emerge once again as a modern nation. Thus, he delved into the past, writing the biography of the nation as it moved from one period to another: undergoing invasions and conquests, attaining religious and philosophical diversity and depth, achieving scientific accomplishments and literary excellence, encountering both triumphs and tragedies, building powerful states and empires, and giving rise to formalistic thought and rigid social hierarchies. At the end of his masterly but melodic account of India's history from its dawn in the Indus Valley Civilization of 3000 B.C.E. to the evening of British rule in the mid-twentieth century—through the Mauryan and Gupta empires, through Hinduism, Buddhism, and Jainism, through the Vedas, Upanishads, and Islam, through Muslim invasions and Mughal rule, through ancient village republics and modern empires—what did Nehru find?

The discovery of India—what have I discovered? It was presumptuous of me to imagine that I could unveil her and find out what she is to-day and what she was in the long past. To-day she is four hundred million separate individual men and women, each differing from the other, each living in a private universe of thought and feeling. If this is so in the present, how much more difficult it is to grasp that multitudinous past of innumerable successions of human beings. Yet something has bound them together and binds them still. India is a geographical and economic entity, a cultural unity amidst diversity, a bundle of contradictions held together by invisible threads. Overwhelmed again and again, her spirit was never conquered, and to-day when she appears to be the plaything of a proud conqueror, she remains unsubdued and unconquered. About her there is the elusive quality of a legend long ago; some enchantment seems to have held her mind. She is a myth and an idea, a dream and a vision, and yet very real and present and pervasive. There are terrifying glimpses of dark corridors which seem to lead back to the primeval night, but also there is the fullness and warmth of the day about her. Shameful and repellent she is

205

occasionally, perverse and obstinate, sometimes even a little hysteric, this lady with a past. But she is also very lovable, and none of
her children can forget her. . . .[7]

This is a startling gendering of the nation, all the more so because it occurs towards the end of the book, after Nehru has
traced India's existence through centuries, documenting its stoic
existence through the ups and downs of history. After all the
painstaking labor, after asserting that India was a unity amidst
diversity, suddenly everything seems to come apart, an anxiety
surfaces. The nation, when unveiled, turned out to be a woman,
mysterious and wanton, "even a little hysteric." Sure, she was a
mother to her children and tugged at their hearts with "the fullness and warmth of the day," but she also struck fear with "the
terrifying glimpses of dark corridors which seem to lead back to
the primeval night." She was not a figure of devotion and reverence, but a fearsomely powerful and uncomprehendingly enchanting woman who invited intimacy and horror at the same
time. Nehru is bewitched by the image he has composed, by "this
lady with a past," for it is her swing between warmth and wantonness that signifies a pulsating but impure life lived through centuries, unconquered and unsubdued. India's reality was dream-like,
a vision, a legend; it breathed a flawed life.

As sure as Nehru was about its existence, it is difficult not to
read in the image of wantonness a concern that India had fallen
short of full nationhood, an anxiety that it may refuse to obey the
command of modernity. Nehru returned time after time to the
narrow loyalties that stood in the way of Indians acting as a people. The search for modern India was a lonely one, particularly in
view of the growing Hindu-Muslim divide. "What a nation is it is
difficult to define," he admitted, but proposed that its essential
characteristic was a sense of belonging together.[8] How far India
had achieved that was a debatable point. In any case, now was the
time for multinational states, he declared. The Soviet Union and
the United States were multinational states that were developing
a national consciousness. India too, perhaps, had always been a

multinational state that was gradually acquiring a national consciousness. The state, then, was a means of achieving nationality, a modern framework for people of diverse faiths to live together. The Hindu-Muslim conflicts and the demand for Pakistan came in the way of this modern life of India, and seemed "a reversion to some medieval theory." What troubled Nehru even more was his belief that this "reversion" ran counter to India's tradition of "toleration and even encouragement of minorities and different racial groups." The Muslims' fear that they would be overwhelmed by the Hindu majority was unfounded because the real majority were the peasants and workers of all faiths, exploited by alien rule and by their own upper classes. The nation could be divided by class conflicts, but religion could divide only when it served some "vested interest."[9] Unfortunately, this vested interest had taken hold of the people. The deeper cause for the growing communal cleavage, however, was the failure to move with the changing times. Nehru found the Muslim failing in this regard conspicuous, for the Muslim "view of life was even more limited and sterile than the Hindu view."[10] Though Indian Muslims had developed "outstanding figures of the modern type," they still lagged behind.

The answer, then, was modernization. India, he felt, must lessen its religiosity and turn to science. In the doubt and anxiety about the nation's incomplete modernity, then, there was also hope and a call for action. India's unregulated vitality was an insistent appeal to her children to attend to her needs in the modern world. Hadn't she always adapted to changing times while maintaining her irrepressible self? Once again, change she must, for now was the age of science and technology. In achieving mastery over nature with the power of reason and technics, Indians would cast off their narrow outlooks and loyalties and act as a people.

It would be a mistake to conclude that Nehru had defined the nation as feminine, as tradition and home, and opposed it to the masculine, the modern and the world. In fact, the latter were already implicit in the former, the masculinist and the modern already complicit and emergent in the feminization of the nation.

Her mythic and shameful existence was the secret life of the real and the historical; the "lady with a past" was a masculine figure in disguise. Not surprisingly, Nehru followed his discovery of the feminized nation with the injunction: "It is obvious that she has to come out of her shell and take full part in the life and activities of the modern age."[11] At the same time, Nehru was quick to rule out imitation of the West. Quoting Emerson on the value of self-reliance, he reiterated the importance of national roots. India must learn from others, but true internationalism had to "grow out of national cultures and can flourish to-day on a basis of freedom and equality."[12]

Reflecting as it did Nehru's own personality as a cosmopolitan nationalist, the injunction to be national and international at the same time was telling. It recognized that India was a part of the global economy and therefore economic autarky was out of the question. But since the global economy was uneven and dependent for its organization on a system of states, only a nation-state could undertake full-scale modern transformations at the local (national) level. This was the lesson taught by colonization and the expansion of the capitalist global economy, and Nehru had learned it well. He wrote movingly about India's deindustrialization and ruralization carried out in the interest of British capitalists by the colonial state, and poured scorn on the government's professed concern for the fate of the Indian peasant and agriculture as an explanation for its failure to develop industry in India. The real explanation for the lack of industrial development was British rule which, according to Nehru, used the peasant as an alibi in order to exploit India as Britain's economic appendage— so much so that it had created a system of princely states, splitting up India into anachronistic shells of power which could only breed conflicts and impede planned development.[13] In place of the colonial government and its "fifth column" of princely states, India required a nation-state that could coordinate and carry out transformations in the context of the modern global economy. India was to be a nation so that it could operate internationally.

Nehru wrote the inevitability of the modern nation-state into his rendering of the nation as an untamed woman. Openness to change was sculpted into the figuration of India as an exuberant woman who had adapted to the turn of events through the centuries without losing her vital national force. The gendering of India as a woman, therefore, was a way of instituting the logic of modernity within the constitutive body of the nation; it was a way to inject the imperative for scientific and technological transformation into the inner being of the nation. The male and the modern were immanent in her.

The emergence of a modernity anchored in the feminized nation was not a violation of India's inner being but was consistent with her history as a spirit anchored in the old but restlessly seeking fulfillment in the new. The nation as mother and as woman provided a nurturing home to modernity. Nehru frankly acknowledged that India had a great distance to travel in modernizing itself, but he saw modernity as something more than applications of science. For him, the achievement of modern nationhood meant facing life with "the temper and approach of science, allied to philosophy, and with reverence for all that lies beyond."[14] The West had made great strides in science, but it still had a long way to go in developing science as a method, an approach, a critical temper in the search for truth. Science's advance as positive knowledge had shrunk the sphere of religion in the narrow sense, but science still had little to say about the purpose of life, which was the traditional concern of religion in the widest sense. In spite of the great progress achieved by the modern world, we knew little about the lonely and tragic business of the soul. The knowledge of external events provided by science were useful, for these events affected the soul, but we still had much to learn about the mind's inner fears and conflicts. Science must bring the spirit and the flesh into creative harmony; it must extend its horizon to include the totality of our being. India was the appropriate place to develop such a science because the fearless search for truth in all aspects of our being was consistent with the essential features of Indian thought.

The struggle for national freedom was inseparable from this magnanimous ambition to expand science's horizon, to render it as a search for truth. Nehru grounded the source of this ambition in India's cultural heritage. This was the creative energy that animated Indian nationalism, the energy that British rule choked, leaving the people no option but to mount a negative, single-track opposition to alien domination. Indians were reduced to mouthing slogans and developing phobias and prejudices instead of inquiring into real problems.[15] In this sense, British power was doubly injurious; it exploited Indians economically and it impoverished them morally. The fight for political independence, then, though necessary, was not the ultimate purpose of India's desire for nationhood; India demanded freedom in order to face life with a scientific temper.

Here was a philosophy of Indian nationalism that internalized modernity and distinguished it from the West. Nehru freely conceded that India had much to learn from the West, which had achieved immense technical advances. Yet, he argued, "The modern West, with all its great and manifold achievements, does not appear to have been a conspicuous success or to have solved the basic problems of life."[16] Conflict and self-destruction appeared to be inherent in this civilization. There was something counterfeit about it. "We eat ersatz foods produced with the help of ersatz fertilizers; we indulge in ersatz emotions and our human relations seldom go beyond the superficial plane."[17] Sterility, falling birth-rates, and racial decadence had set in because modern industrialism and capitalism caused people to lose touch with the soil; they lacked a sense of purpose of life. Science had made great progress, and the world seemed to be on the verge of epochal discoveries and enormous increases in its control over resources. Yet the pursuit of science without a sense of purpose may come back to haunt the world. As a solution Nehru proposed a synthesis of science and humanism, in a "kind of scientific humanism" that reconciled the concern with the phenomenal life of the world with the inner spiritual life of the individual. This concurred with

Einstein's view that the fate of the human race was evermore dependent on moral strength. "He takes us back suddenly from the proud age of science to the old philosophers, from the lust of power and the profit motive to the spirit of renunciation with which India has been so familiar."[18]

Nehru's critique of modern civilization was neither novel nor deep; Europeans also, including European scientists such as Einstein, had expressed worries about science and technology running amok and had called for the restraining and guiding vision of human needs and moral purpose. Nehru, however, located the source of his critique in the Indian fiber. India's spirit of renunciation, according to him, was naturally suited to redirect science and fashion a true scientific temper that would impart a moral intent to scientific and technical progress. The bitter conflict between science and religion that tore apart nineteenth-century Europe would not occur in India because it had always seen the two as inseparable. Of course religion in the narrow sense, which came in the way of the relationship between the people and the world, would have to be abandoned, for such was the spirit of the age, a spirit fully in conformity with India's own traditions. When some Hindus spoke of going back to the Vedas and some Muslims talked of establishing an Islamic theocracy, they went against this spirit and indulged in idle fancies.

"There is only one-way traffic in Time."[19] India had to march with it, discarding old religious and social orthodoxies and hierarchies, and adopting science and the principle of equality, along with an economic system to match them. The profit motive would have to be subdued, but this would not upset most Indians because they had never championed acquisitiveness. They had always valued the common good, and the long existence of self-governing villages stood testimony to their commitment to collective life. The Indian value for the common good could be harnessed to fashion a new universality amidst particular interests and identities. Modern technics called for the expression of such a universality. The progress of science and technology was knit-

211

ting the world together more tightly than ever before, demanding that particularist loyalties and identities expand their perspectives and find a common horizon.

Writing against the background of growing Hindu-Muslim conflicts and the demand for the establishment of Pakistan, Nehru was all too aware that India was yet to achieve this common horizon, that its religious communities, castes, linguistic groups, and local loyalties were yet to constitute themselves as a people. The territory was marked by economic unevenness and social inequalities, which further complicated the representation of Indians as subjects in the framework of modernity. It was against the background of the failure of Indians to articulate themselves as a modern community that Nehru saw the state as an expression and the means of instituting the ever-elusive nation. To the extent that the Indian values of collective good provided a basis for it, the modern nation-state was not a Western import. Not only was it rooted in the Indian soil; it also contained principles of ethical conduct for the common good that the modern West sorely lacked.

What added depth and complexity to Nehru's invocation of a national ethos to chart a different course for Indian modernity was the remarkable candor with which he approached the past. Though he shared with other nationalists the belief that India had pioneered many achievements commonly thought of as European, he did not believe that India's history or its social and cultural heritage were without blemishes. There is something disarming in the openness with which he looked India's history in the eye, identifying failures and shortcomings, noting tragedies and ironies. Underpinning this honest appraisal, however, was the quiet confidence that India had a history, that the events of five or six thousand years belonged to one determinate nation. For Nehru, India first stirred in the composition of the Vedas and the Upanishads; India was present in the high and low points of philosophy, science, and literature through the ages, evident as much in warfare and conquests as in economic progress and prosperity.

This nation's past was at once enabling and disabling. If its philosophical and scientific heritage and its traditions of renunciation and collective life poised India to advance the spirit of the present age, the widespread inequality, poverty, undeveloped resources, and religious divisions hobbled its progress. But the one could be the source of overcoming the other. The nation's ethos, developed through history, could become the basis for its self-renewal, for the eradication of poverty and the dissolution of social inequalities. It was this critical nationalist purpose to constitute India as a modern community that animated Nehru's turn to history and made his account richly resonant. The past was not dead but alive, open to the modern age and ready to give moral direction to science and technology. The beauty of this formulation was that it located the nation as a space for the critique of Western modernity while internalizing the program of modernization.

The profound ideological significance of this vision is undeniable. It gave Indian nationalism an irresistible elan; it cast the struggle for the modern nation not as a narrowly conceived nativist affair but as an expansive moral campaign to unlock the nation's creative energy to live according to the ideals of a scientific temper. India demanded a state and desired planned development not to imitate the West but to establish an existence consistent with its national ethos, one that more fully embodied the scientific approach than the West. At the heart of this thought was a conception of the nation in which the immanence of the state was scripted so as to nationalize the society, producing Indians as a people in the space of modernity. Faced with particular interests and identities that refused to articulate themselves into a people, the state was to bring about what Etienne Balibar calls the *"delayed nationalization of society."*[20] The state was to accomplish what the nationalist discourse had failed to achieve so far—that is, successfully institute Indians as a "fictive ethnicity," to use Balibar's term. Questions of difference—caste, class, gender, religion, ethnicity—were to be handled at the level of law and economy. Rapid modernization and the functioning of law and democracy were to eventually confer full nationhood on those who could not yet be fully Indian because of economic backwardness and social inequality. There was much imaginative depth and dexterity in the ideological work of producing Indians as a people.

GANDHI AND MODERNITY

The concept of Indians as a people also underpinned Gandhi's all-out denunciation of modern civilization. As he penned a stinging critique of industrial civilization in *Hind Swaraj* (1909), Gandhi singled out the railways as one of the most glaring examples of the evil and incestous relationship between modernity and colonialism. He did not single out the railways because of a blind opposition to machinery, though this is how his attitude is commonly portrayed. Rather for him the railways stood for modern civilization and signified a new, oppressive reorganization of India's territory, people, society, culture, and politics by British rule. He believed that machinery had assembled a different kind of India, a new space constructed by a network of social practices, ideas, values, and a dark desire for a civilization that was at odds with what he believed to be the life and traditions of the authentic nation.[21] Yet while Gandhi invoked and drew upon the romantic critique of modern science and technology, we should not be too quick to absorb him wholly within it. For even as he shared and drew upon the romantic critique, his opposition to modern technology was not based on the belief that it objectified human beings, depriving them of their human essence. What he objected to, as he put it, was "the craze for machinery, not machinery as such,"[22] suggesting that he believed that modern technology produced a certain kind of human subject. Technology did not signify machines alone, but signified as well a complex web of social, economic, cultural, and political practices aimed at accumulating capital and fabricating possessive individuals.

Yet Gandhi was a nationalist, and the nation was the secure foundation for his critique of modernity. Machinery and the modern civilization represented the negation of India's being as a nation, as an ethical community. To project modern technology and industrialization as India's future, therefore, was a gross perversion of Indian ideals. Indians must constitute their nation according to their *dharma*, the body of ethical principles drawn from their tradition and updated to suit the modern world. Gandhi elaborated and practiced these ethical principles—the pursuit of *brahmacharya*, *satya* (truth), and freedom from possessiveness and greed—during the course of his struggles in both South Africa and India. Together, these concepts defined India in terms sharply opposed to the modern West. But the perspective of the nation also left Gandhi's ideology vulnerable to the idea of the modern nation-state, to which he was opposed. And thus as Indian nationalism moved inexorably toward the state and the program for planned industrialization, Gandhi stood alone and helpless. The source of his marginalization lay in the concept of the nation as a community.

Gandhi arrived at his critique of modernity during the course of his struggle with racism on behalf of Indians in South Africa. Leading Indians in a campaign against various discriminatory laws aimed at them, Gandhi came to see them as a national community and modern civilization as their enemy. The differences among Indians—between traders and laborers, Hindus and Muslims, Tamils and Gujaratis, educated and illiterate—were insignificant to the British and the Boers, in whose eyes they were all the same: "coolies." Gandhi found, much to his dismay, that he was none the better for having trained as a barrister in England. For the whites, he was just another coolie. This encounter with racism led him to conclude that Indians constituted a community whose values as a national group were despised by a modern civilization blinded by the power of material accumulation. Racism was an expression of brute force, and its roots lay in the modern West's desire to accumulate wealth at any cost. Its protagonists believed that might was right and that nations were doomed to either accumulate economic resources or self-destruct: "It is in pursuance of these principles that Western nations have settled in

South Africa and subdued the numerically overwhelmingly superior races of South Africa."[23] Behind the discrimination practiced against Indians was the West's fear of Indian simplicity and otherworldliness; their existence as a national community called into question the West's blind ambition for power and wealth.

While Nehru believed that colonialism was a perversion of modernity, Gandhi drew a natural connection between the two, arguing that colonialism was a consequence of the modern West's insatiable acquisitiveness. Elaborating this theme in detail in *Hind Swaraj*, he insisted that India could fully overcome colonial domination only when it returned to its national roots. The railways, he believed, epitomized modern civilization's intrinsic relationship with colonialism, for they were the means by which the British held India. In a famous line, he wrote: "The English have not taken India; we have given it to them."[24] Indians were responsible for the British conquest, for they had assisted the East India Company; it is they who had been charmed by pieces of silver to welcome the Company government. When Indian princes fought among themselves, they embraced a force that knew only war and greed. British power continued to prevail in India because it satisfied India's "base interest." If India wished to end its miserable slavery to Britain, the answer was not industrialization: "In this connection, I remind you that it is the British flag which is waving in Japan."[25] If India wished to avoid British rule without the British, then it must recognize that the source of its bondage was modernity's voracious appetite for material wealth.

> When I read Mr. Dutt's Economic History of India, I wept; and as I think of it again my heart sickens. It is machinery that has impoverished India. It is difficult to measure the harm that Manchester has done to us. It is due to Manchester that Indian handicraft has all but disappeared. . . . Machinery has begun to desolate Europe. Ruination is now knocking at the English gates. Machinery is the chief symbol of modern civilization; it represents a great sin.[26]

What impelled modern civilization toward global domination, according to Gandhi, was not technology itself but what Ashis

Nandy calls "technicism." In one of the ablest recent interpretations of Gandhi's thought, highlighting its critical edge, Nandy suggests that Gandhi was not opposed to science or technology, but espoused plural concepts of science and technology. Gandhi believed, he argues, that modern technology was not the last word in technology, and that there were other traditions of its use that better supported the liberation of humanity. Modern technology, on the other hand, was instrumental and bent upon global mastery through the rule of technocracy.[27]

The theme of the loss of human control to technology was Gandhi's constant refrain. Asked in 1936 by a Japanese correspondent if he was opposed to the machine age, Gandhi responded: "To say that is to caricature my views. I am not against machinery as such, but I am totally opposed to it when it masters us."[28] Mastery by machine, however, referred to the substitution of the value for human welfare with the value for profit. This is important to bear in mind if we are to grasp that Gandhi's critique did not see technology as a deranged creature spinning out of the control of its creator. Though he appears to be a romantic critic, Gandhi counterposed human ends to the machine in order to decry the acquisitive spirit, not to oppose technology as such. Commenting on the craze for labor-saving machinery, he remarked that it helped a few to ride on the backs of millions: "The impetus behind it all is not the philanthropy to save labour, but greed."[29] He wanted the "mad rush for wealth" to stop, for it was this that accounted for the West's encroachment on the globe.

Gandhi bore testimony as a nationalist witness to modernity's world domination. Indebted as he was to such Western thinkers as Leo Tolstoy, Edward Carpenter, John Ruskin, Henry Maine, Henry David Thoreau, and Ralph Waldo Emerson, Gandhi's impeachment of modern civilization was a political project on behalf of India as a nation. The critique of modernity was not a nativist rejection of the West, but an ideological work of profound significance, for it was in formulating his opposition to the modern West that he outlined his vision of the nation. India, for him, meant its villages, not its cities and factories. Villages signified peasants and a mode of living outside modernity. It is important to note that Gandhi did not endorse village life as it existed, but projected it as a sign of an alternative to modern civilization. In this regard, the mention of Henry Maine's book on village communities in *Hind Swaraj*'s appendix is significant. Like many other nationalists, Gandhi used the idea of village communities to signify cooperation and harmony as key symbols of India's nationhood. The world of the modern state, industry, railways, doctors, and lawyers represented conflicts and competition, and was alien to India's tradition. The village communities, on the other hand, stood for harmony and love. Clearly, for Gandhi village life meant more than its empirical present. It was not the actual space lived in by the peasants. Though he spoken frequently of the miserable poverty of the peasantry and the exploitation of the countryside by towns, he was no peasant revolutionary. The village stood for the warmth of the home: it evoked the intimacy of face-to-face relationships; it was an order that settled disputes and conflicts in the manner of a family. The identification of India in such an image of the village highlighted kinship and affect, and slid easily into the metaphor of the family that Gandhi often used. India was a family, he claimed, and he repeatedly invoked blood and brotherhood to characterize Hindu-Muslim relations.[30]

Kinship and territoriality were bound together to constitute India as a radically different ethical order from the modern West. Rejecting the brute force, machinery, greed, and violence associated with Western modernity, Gandhi envisioned India as a family bound by love. Just as brothers may quarrel from time to time in any family, so the diversity of faiths in India did not run against the unity of the nation, which was bound by bonds of kinship. He combined this idea of the nation as a family with concepts of *swaraj* (self-rule), *satyagraha* ("truth force," or nonviolent resistance), and *brahmacharya* (continence) to construct an elaborate political and moral basis for the nation. Together, these concepts rendered the achievement of freedom dependent on a strict pursuit of truth, the renunciation of desire for material possession and sexual gratification, the disavowal of violence, the ability to overcome fear, and the practice of self-discipline. Viewed against the background of colonial governmentality, Gandhi's program was a far-reaching project to achieve self-governance. Indians were to attain their freedom and become national subjects by discarding Western disciplines and returning to indigenous sources of self-subjectification.

Undoubtedly, these ideas were far removed from Western images of the nation, as was his conception of India as a civilization, a configuration of cultures and communities, not only a territorial unit. But far from suggesting that Gandhi's discourse stood outside the parameters of nationalism, these ideas bear testimony to the magnitude of the ideological challenge he posed as a nationalist.[31] His was an attempt to seize the space brought into view by colonial modernity and provide it with an alternative ethical significance. The distance of the alternative from the Western discourse enhanced the moral claim of the nation. For, from the standpoint of this ethical order, Western modernity appeared violent, materialistic, and immoral, while the nation, on the other hand, was committed to truth and love. Individuals were to achieve freedom as an inner experience through self-discipline, but the individual pursuit of truth was vitally connected to their life as a community, as a nation. No arena of life was outside the search for individual realization. Indeed, individuals could experience freedom only in community life. Politics and economy, then, were securely within the domain of the individual's disciplined search for truth. In this respect, Gandhi's agenda differed crucially from both the traditional ideology of renunciation and the romantic longing for a lost way of life.[32] His was a philosophy of action based on the notion that individual self-rule and community self-rule were deeply intertwined: one was incomplete without the other. Such a perspective imparted to anticolonial nationalism the sense of a great moral struggle. Indians were fighting not just for power but for their souls, for their vision of an order based on *dharma* and truth. Gandhi was equally insistent that the capture of state power without the practice of self-rule at the individual level would amount to having "English rule without Englishmen"; then "it will be called not Hindustan but Englishstan."[33]

Opposed to the modern state, Gandhi did not wish the independent Indian political order to imitate colonial rule. His utopia was modeled on the *rāmrājya* of the epics, an updated patriarchy in which the ruler expressed the collective will and moral laws of the community. "In an ideal State," he wrote, "there would be no political institution and therefore no political power."[34] In 1946, when the modern nation-state appeared imminent, he posed an alternative political structure, outlining it as a constellation of villages organized in "ever-widening, never ending circles." It would not be "a pyramid with the apex sustained by the bottom," but an oceanic circle "whose centre will be the individual always ready to perish for the village, the latter ready to perish for the circle of villages, till at last the whole becomes one life composed of individuals." The outermost circumference of this circle would not possess power to crush the inner circle, but would strengthen it and derive strength from it. Recognizing that this might be dismissed as utopian, he wrote that if "Euclid's point, though incapable of being drawn by human agency, has an imperishable value, my picture has its own for mankind to live." India should live for this picture, he recommended, even if it might be unrealizable in its completeness. In this picture, every village would be a republic. No one was to be first or last; everyone would be equal.[35]

Clearly, Gandhi's conception of politics did not envision a bourgeois civil society and a modern state with a representational form of government. Still, it would be a mistake to see him, as is customary, as an outsider to modernity, an anomalous figure who stood completely apart from other nationalists. Nor would it be adequate to trace his connection to modern nationalism primarily via the imperative for nationalism to come to terms with the practical aspects of organizing a movement and dealing with the bourgeois legal and political structures set up by the colonial state.[36] To think of India as a nation, quite apart from reckoning with colonial institutions in the course of political struggle, was to locate it in the force field of modernity. As a national claim on the territory configured by modern technics, swaraj was at once an intervention into modernity and an attempt to steer it in a different direction. The concept of swaraj rejected the colonial state as a model, but it also envisioned that a national political authority would fill the place vacated by alien rulers; another ethical order would arise and exercise sovereignty over the territory ruled by the British. India was to be a nation in a world of nations. To be sure, it would be different from every other nation, but this was not exceptional to nationalist thought.

Try as he might, Gandhi could not escape the logic of his nationalist thought. The state, as an expression of the collective life of the community, was immanent in the concept of the nation even as the association of modernity with colonialism demanded that the nation-state be different. Nationalism could not wish away the modern state; instead, it subjected the state to the pressures of the nation, demanding that it shed its character as an embodiment of technics. Swaraj was not a negation of the modern state, but its reinscription; it represented an effort to create something new and authentic from the available and alien.

In this context, *Hind Swaraj* is a revealing text.[37] Published first in Gujarati in *Indian Opinion* in two installments in 1909, and then translated into English by Gandhi himself and published in 1910, this most utopian of Gandhi's writings was intended as an intervention in nationalist politics. Published several years before his active involvement in Indian nationalism, this text already signaled Gandhi's idea that the time of utopia was here and now. India was to be seized from the grip of modern civilization embodied in British rule and developed according to its own distinctly national genius through the politics of nationalism. Central to this effort was the claim that India existed independent of British rule. Gandhi denied that the unification of the territory brought about by railroads was responsible for national consciousness. India had been a nation, a singular entity, even before the introduction of railways. "We were one nation before they [the British] came to India. One thought inspired us. . . . It was because we were one nation that they were able to establish one kingdom."[38] Explaining this further, he said that awareness of this unity was not new. In the times before the railways, "our leading men" traveled throughout India, learned one another's languages, established pilgrimage sites in different parts of the territory, and saw that India was undivided by nature. The introduction of foreigners did not unmake this unity, for India, like any other true nation, had the capacity for assimilating foreigners and their religions: Muslims, Christians, and Parsis. Religion could not divide Hindus and Muslims, for they shared the blood of the same ancestors; they were brothers. Above all, India was defined by a civilizational unity that has remained mostly intact in spite of the inroads made by the modern West.

The idea of India's timeless singularity was significant, for it was an attempt to establish the authority of the nation over the space constituted by modern technics. This unity was to reconfirm itself in the form of swaraj, a form of home rule that would assume control by displacing the world of railways, machinery, lawyers, doctors, and parliamentary government. Home rule did not mean India's fragmentation into its constituent communities and villages, because Gandhi viewed these as parts of a whole that symbolized India's singularity. For all his traditionalism and the glorification of India's ancient virtues, Gandhi's home rule called for the rule of the modern nation. In concluding *Hind Swaraj* Gandhi declared that real home rule was self-rule of the Indian nation, accomplished through passive resistance directed at British rule in all its manifestations—machinery, European goods, the desire for wealth, law courts, and modern education and medicine. India was to resist colonial modernity as a nation; swaraj was to mean a nation-state forged in the undoing of the colonial state.

The concept of swaraj empowered the struggle for the nation-state, but was ill-suited to achieve the non-modern state that Gandhi outlined on the eve of India's independence. His ideal of the independent political order as an oceanic circle sat uneasily with his vision of India as a nation and as a singular unity. It is true

that Gandhi's view of India was far more open-ended and plural-
ist than that of many of his contemporaries. But so long as the
subcontinent's plurality was used to identify the oneness of its
history and civilization and to deny unassimilable differences, the
imagined oceanic circle lacked an adequate ideological basis. To
define the nation as a family was to impose the stifling organic
unity of love and kinship on difference. If Muslims were brothers
or were foreigners who had been assimilated into the family, and
if India's civilizational ethos was fundamentally Hindu, as it was
in Gandhi's thought, then how could the political structure be
anything but unitary? The formula of unity in diversity, shared by
both Gandhi and Nehru acknowledged multiplicity only in order
to extract from it an essential singularity. Nehru clearly recognized that difference—dramatized by Hindu-Muslim conflicts—
posed a problem for India's nationhood. But he thought that the
nation-state would bring about a fuller nationalization of society
by educating and transforming those, such as the Muslims, whose
insistence on cultural difference he read as a reflection of their
economic backwardness and incomplete modernization. Gandhi
refused to confer such a commanding power to the nation-state,
but he failed to adequately acknowledge difference. Village, family, love, truth, and nonviolence signified India's irreducibly different civilization, but the civilization itself remained one, notwithstanding the existence of divergent cultures and histories.
Without a conception of India rooted in social and cultural differences, without the vision of a polity that genuinely acknowledged and negotiated plurality, his idea of the political order as an
oceanic circle could only remain a dream.

NATIONALISM AND MODERNITY

In 1945 Gandhi wrote to Nehru, noting differences in outlook
between them and reaffirming the views expressed in *Hind
Swaraj*.[39] He reiterated that his experiences since writing it had
reconfirmed all his views about the evils of machinery. True

freedom would come when people realized that Indians must live in villages and huts, not in cities and palaces. The village he had in mind was not one in which the villager lived "like an animal in filth and darkness," but an ideal village inhabited by intelligent human beings. There would be no diseases—"no plague, no cholera, and no small pox." He acknowledged that such a village "exists only in my imagination," but added that human beings live in the world of their imagination. In this imagined world, there was room even for railways and other modern institutions, so long as the basic ideals of swaraj remained supreme.

Nehru was firm in stating his disagreement.[40] Villages were places of backward and narrow outlook; industries were inevitable and even necessary if India was to achieve progress and relieve the poverty of its millions. Even more brutally, Nehru added that *Hind Swaraj* had seemed "completely unreal" to him even two decades earlier when he first read it. Now the world had changed even more, rendering it ever more irrelevant. In any case, he added, the Congress had never been asked to adopt the program outlined in *Hind Swaraj*, "except for certain relatively minor aspects of it." Nehru's response was a cutting blow. Gandhi wrote later, referring to a conversation he and Nehru had had on following up this exchange, that they had agreed on much.[41] He agreed with Nehru that the real question was how to bring about the highest moral, intellectual, political, and moral development; that there should be equal opportunity for all in both town and the countryside; and that human beings could not live in isolation but required both independence and interdependence. But Gandhi cited these "agreements" desperately to cover over the deep chasm that had opened between his and Nehru's views, and one cannot help but detect something profoundly sad in this effort.

This exchange on the eve of India's independence confirms the customary view of Gandhi and Nehru as standing poles apart— one a trenchant critic of modernity, the other its ardent proponent; one a visionary for a non-modern India of villages and decentralized politics, the other an architect of a statist modernization. From this point of view, the moment of Indian independence and partition in 1947 emerges as a time of great betrayal and tragedy. While Nehru appears eager to set the state on the path to modernize a carved-up India, Gandhi emerges as a lonely figure, cast aside by the forces of modernity, who alone heroically confronts the carnage of partition caused by the drive to create modern nation-states. So common is this understanding that it would be unfair to attribute it to any single writer. And of course, there is no denying the difference between the two men. Undoubtedly, Nehru set great faith in the power of modern science and technology, while Gandhi did not. But their views have to be placed in the ideological context of anticolonial nationalism. When located in this context, it becomes clear that the production of a people under colonial domination obliged nationalism to position itself as a critique of Western modernity. This was as true for Nehru as it was for Gandhi, even if the two men articulated different critiques. Producing a modern nation under colonial modernity required the latter's relocation and revision so that it expressed and advanced national concerns. Thus, both Nehru and Gandhi contended that India's modern nationhood would be the fulfillment of its timeless unity as a community; India would be at once modern and not modern, at once represented and not represented in a state.

Such was the divided ideological logic produced by India's integration into the uneven global economy by means of the colonial state. To be a nation in an international system of states meant that the nationalists had to both constitute a modern nation and claim that it was irreducibly Indian. This was not a split imposed by the division between elite and subaltern politics, or between the language of community and the rhetoric of capital, but one that constituted the very conditions of the possibility of the modern nation. From this point of view, Gandhi and Nehru represented two different stances *within* the historical production of Indians as a people. Both formulated powerful critiques of colonial modernity while seeking to seize control of its territory and institutions and establish over it the authority of the nation.

Immanent in this idea of India as a timeless and singular unity was the concept of the state that both expressed and guaranteed the community's universal existence. Thus, if Gandhi found himself sidelined by the nation-state and its program of modernization, this was not due to Nehru's clever machination; the commitment to nationalism left him with no ideological resources to contest what he opposed but had in fact helped to bring about. He was fated by his own ideological discourse of the modern nation to cut a tragic figure.

CHAPTER EIGHT

Divided Love

> Before the nation came to rule over us we had other
> governments which were foreign, and these, like other
> governments, had some element of the machine in them.
> But the difference between them and the government by
> the Nation is like the difference between the hand-loom
> and the power-loom. In the products of the hand-loom
> the magic of man's living fingers finds its expression, and
> its hum harmonises with the music of life. But the power-
> loom is relentlessly lifeless and accurate and monotonous
> in its production. . . . The truth is that the spirit of conflict
> and conquest is at the origin and in the centre of Western
> nationalism; its basis is not social co-operation. It has
> evolved a perfect organisation of power, but not spiritual
> idealism. It is like the pack of predatory creatures
> that must have its victims.
> *Rabindranath Tagore*[1]

LATE-COMERS and newcomers have an alarming affinity to positivism," Adorno wrote in the 1950s, referring to the enthusiasm
for this philosophy among the contemporary Indian intellectuals.[2] He added: "It would be poor psychology to assume that ex-
clusion arouses only hate and resentment; it arouses too a possessive, intolerant kind of love, and those whom repressive culture
has held at a distance can easily become its most diehard defenders."[3] A century before Adorno wrote these lines, the Western-
educated intelligentsia in Calcutta had greeted positivism with
precisely this "possessive, intolerant kind of love." Positivism
glowed in the aura of power and universality that Western rationality had come to enjoy by the midnineteenth century, following
the East India Company's eager reinvention of its despotic power
as the rule of reason. Formed in the shadow of this power, the

new intelligentsia took to positivism and other such ideas because these drew their force from the representation of Western science as a sign of modernity and progress. These ideas captivated Western-educated intellectuals, awakening an obsessive enthusiasm for Western knowledge and an irrepressible desire to expand the cultural power of science. But it was a love not without an acute sense of pain and division; the untimely love of "late-comers and newcomers" was also divided love. The stronger the aura of science, the more unavoidable was the question: How could the West alone claim to possess universal knowledge? This question drove intellectuals to increasingly reexamine and reinterpret traditions. Keen as they were to embrace and disseminate Western science, no less intent were they to identify scientific thought in indigenous knowledge and advance its universal claim. They sincerely wished to learn from the achievements of Western science manifested in Western power, but they also wanted to recover and create a place for traditions of indigenous rational thought, mathematics, astronomy, alchemy, and medicine. Desire for the one did not exclude but rather strengthened the love for the other.

The passionate belief in the existence of an indigenous tradition of science was no mere fantasy. As Indian intellectuals demonstrated with patient and persuasive scholarly studies and argued with passion and conviction, scientific thought was not alien to the subcontinent's traditions. This was not nativism, but a carefully formulated proposition, arguing that the concept of science was culturally located. This may be a truism today, but intellectuals in the colonies functioned under the dominant view that science was universal and that its particular history of emergence and application had little to do with the status of its epistemology. Although Max Weber was to formulate his thesis about the "disenchantment of the world" by the rational order of science only in this century, the idea that the West had fashioned a universal epistemology that stood in conflict with religious and magical understanding and authority was already common in the nineteenth century. In the colonies, this Whiggish history of science was taught with single-minded conviction because it served the ideals of the "civilizing mission." Nowhere was the singularity and the scientific genealogy of the West's identity scripted with greater determination than outside its borders. In the non-Western world the Christian background and motivations of Galileo, Pascal, Boyle, and Newton were tucked away in the background, and what was highlighted was the undermining of religious and traditional authority by science. If the West had found it necessary to break from the religious dogmas of Christianity, the argument went, this was all the more imperative in the non-Western world. This was because the beliefs and practices of the colonized—which were read as religions even if they did not have a concept of a Supreme Being, a creed, or a holy book like the Bible—were full of falsehoods and myths. Hinduism, for example, could be considered a religion, but because it was undeniably inferior to Christianity, it could not possibly coexist with science, let alone act as its founding source. Science had to be totally free from religion in India; it had to be a completely secular knowledge, more so than in Europe.

To argue against this representation of science was no mean endeavor, and Indian intellectuals approached this task with great imagination and learning. Shuttling between the alien and the indigenous, translating one into the language of the other, they sought to identify a body of indigenous scientific tradition and develop an Indian science. No one exemplified this better than P. C. Ray, the chemist, who divided his love between experimental work in chemistry and historical research on "Hindu chemistry." His research on mercury's place in the periodic table went hand in hand with his historical reconstruction of the vital place mercury occupied in Hindu alchemy. Together, his scientific and historical researches outlined an "Indian school of chemistry."

Somewhat different was the career of J. C. Bose (1858–1937) who turned from research on electrical waves to an exploration of consciousness in plants in an effort to demonstrate the monism of Vedantic Hinduism. His research on the relationship between animate and inanimate matter did not seek to define an "Indian science," but it was a bold and influential effort to locate science in indigenous cultural resources. Indians were well positioned by Vedic Hinduism's non-dualism, he argued, to make the world of science more integrated and humane. Such claims for Indian universalism, whether made by positing an indigenous science or by identifying indigenous cultural resources for science, challenged the dominant view that Western science's epistemology transcended its cultural location. They were also crucial in forging the relationship between science and the nation-state by situating the latter as the locus for India's claim to universality, which was defined in terms of Hindu traditions.

To possess a scientific tradition of one's own not only meant that one had existed as a people long before the British set foot in India, but also that one's existence as a community was irreducibly different. This was of vital significance, for embedded in it was the claim that what defined India was not the modern apparatus introduced by colonial government; rather, what made India unique was its culture—its learned texts, traditions, and ancient history. This was an article of faith with the nationalists, embraced by people ranging from Swami Dayananda, the fiery religious reformer, to Jawaharlal Nehru, the secular nationalist. It was also a profoundly contestatory proposition that enabled the nationalists to construct a different image of modernity—one that indigenized it. Thus, while accepting the Orientalist image of India as spiritual, the nationalists claimed that science was not alien or marginal to the nation's culture and history. India, the argument went, was the original home of science, though, unlike the West, it had never separated science from religious life and the philosophy of daily living. Such a conception of indigenous culture permitted the nationalists to intervene in the field of governmentality and offer indigenous medicine and *brahma-charya* as disciplines of the body. Combining material and spiritual concerns, these disciplines were seen as more appropriate for India than Western medicine because they conceived the body to be more than a sum total of organs, functions, symptoms, and diseases. Through such nationalist reinterpretations, Hindu science became an estranged form in which Western modernity was normalized, appropriated, and made part of the internal structure of the nation.

With the vital sign of modernity—science—lodged in the "inner" fiber of the nation, India could be modern without being Western. Even the modern state was surreptitiously incorporated in the inner domain without undermining the claim that India was unique. The idea of the village community, for example, which was held up as a compelling sign of India's nationhood, was nothing but a refracted image of the modern state. The village was structured as a patriarchy, but its primary function was not the maintenance of the hierarchical order. The ancient village communities now were said to have performed duties associated with the modern state—maintaining peace and providing protection, settling disputes, and carrying out numerous welfare functions. Unlike the modern state, however, these institutions were not distant and impersonal, but closely woven into the fabric of society; they offered the love and comfort of home while performing governmental functions.

Concepts of kinship, love, family, patriarchy, and community figured prominently in the nationalist discourse, but there is no reason why we should consider them as necessarily opposed to the capitalist order that colonialism sought to establish. To imagine the nation in British India as an inner domain of culture, as a community based on kinship and love, was not to reject modernity but to signify a different form of it. The nationalists wished to rework the arrangements under which India was organized as a space by colonial technics. Even Gandhi was willing to accept some presence of railroads and telegraphs in independent India. Other nationalists were willing to go further. For all the biting critiques that the nationalists made of British industrial and economic policies, they never proposed dismantling the infrastructure of colonial rule. Rather, they believed that the transfer of power would introduce a different form of governance. Under a national government, the profit motive would not guide technology and industry; instead, a distinctly Indian ethos of collective welfare would transform how modern industry functioned. The language of family and love served to signify this principle of collective welfare, suggesting that India was to be organized as if it were a family—but this did not mean that the space of the nation would be run by families. The point was to formulate alternative principles of governance, not to undo modern governmentality altogether and replace it with the rule of patriarchal heads. When the nationalists spoke of "Mother India," it was to indicate their reverence for the nation *as if* she were a mother. In that role, it was not the mother herself who appeared, but a figure cross-hatched with modernity; she embodied the desire for a political community at once inside and outside Western modernity. Such an imagination permitted the nationalists to represent their struggle for the modern nation as the rejection of colonial modernity and as an effort to restore the ancient community based on kinship.

It is vital that we do not overlook the location of the ancient community as a "before" of the modern nation. In philosopher's language, it was "always already" a construct of modernity. Community was set up as a prefiguration of the nation-state, as its nonidentical earlier form. Encapsulating the logic of the nation-state without being identical with it, community institutionalized modernity in another guise: the nation-state could be represented as the "return" of the ancient community, and not as a modern invention. The relationship of encapsulation and non-identity between the nation and the nation-state, then, was a productive one that enabled the emergence and authorization of Indian modernity. But the fact that the nation-state was instituted and authorized by the image of a community meant that the latter contained the possibility of an immanent critique of modernity. Both Nehru and Gandhi utilized this possibility, in different ways, to mount critiques of the West. Tagore's bitter critique can also be situated in this history of modernity, for what he denounced was "the government by the Nation," distinguishing it from the spirit of cooperation he identified in the nation as a community. He worried that Indian nationalism had abandoned the idea of the nation as a community and become like Western nationalism, which was nothing but "a perfect organisation of power," a machine. Of course the nationalists, most famously Gandhi, disagreed with Tagore's reading of Indian nationalism, but not with the distinction he made between India as a national community and Western nationalism. The beauty of this concept of community was that it permitted the nationalists to imagine the modern Indian nation as a critique of Western modernity. India could incorporate machines into the national community without becoming a machine because its relationship with modernity was mediated by cultural difference.

Indian modernity exists in its own time. It came into existence as a form of belated enlightenment, separated from the time of Europe and addressed to those who lived in other times. Not just peasants, women, and the uneducated and illiterate subalterns, but the indigenous society as a whole appeared trapped in another time. Colonial rule saw itself as an agent of bringing the timeless "native" into the present, into the time of History. Nationalism shared this agenda. It, too, thought that India had to be awakened from its slumber and live a full life in the modern world; and science and technology were alluring because they would help India catch up with the West. Sharing an intimate relationship, colonialism and nationalism constituted India in a time that is at once different from that of the West and from that of India's traditions. From this arises the specific trajectory of Indian modernity; its history cannot be conceived of as a seamless narrative of progress along a trajectory of successive stages: colonial, national, postnational (or postmodern). In the time of Indian modernity, neither "Indian" nor "modernity" exists separate and whole, for other times and other subjects explode their self-representations of wholeness and finality. Like colonial rule, the nationalist imagination was never able to purge its others; rather, it was in the impossible effort to appropriate nonnational forms of knowledges and subjects, and relativize them as minor, backward, and traditional that the nation-state instituted itself as the realization of community.

Indian modernity has always existed as an internally divided process. An aura of dislocation and disorientation has always accompanied Indian modernity's existence. I do not mean this in a negative sense; uncertainties and estrangements point to its sources of creativity and to possibilities of new arrangements and new accommodations. There is simply no way to tidy up this messy history of India and narrate it as the victory of capital over community, modernity over tradition, West over non-West. These neat oppositions exist side by side with the history of their untidy complicities and intermixtures. One does not negate the other—difference does not cancel identity, hybridity does not dissolve opposition, capital does not erase community—but rather, one enables the other's reformulation. It is thus that Indian modernity emerges as Janus-faced; crafted in the image of Europe, it is also ineluctably different; founded in the capital community opposition, it is also the undoing of that polarity.

It was with this kind of divided love and logic that Nehru, independent India's first prime minister, approached the "delayed nationalization of society" after the achievement of Indian independence. He saw his blueprint for modern India as a plan consistent with India's spirit. His commitment to science, industry, and the modern state was no slavish imitation of the West. Contrary to what has now become orthodox opinion, Nehru was a critic of Western modernity and thought that India's modernization would be the realization of its promise as a community. Neither an imitation of the West nor a return to the mythic past, Indian modernity, he thought, would be of its own kind, incorporating an undefinable nationness that Indians had evolved over centuries. This conviction underpinned his program of industrialization, his patronage of science and scientists, and his adoption of planning as a scientific instrument of social change. Planned development had set its sights on achieving a massive industrial transformation of the country. Viewing nature as a resource to be developed and exploited, the regime unleashed intrusive and aggressive technologies on the environment. Mineral-rich regions were mined ever more intensively, and the pace of industrialization was quickened. Unruly rivers met with the disapproving eyes of planners who set about twisting and turning the rivers' courses, erecting walls and embankments to check and channel their ferocity, and building dams to generate electricity and irrigate the land. Fertilizers and pesticides followed, and combined with heavy industries to pollute and poison the land, water, and air.

As a result of these measures, industry and agriculture have registered growth, and the number of technical and scientific personnel, trained in the proliferating engineering and medical colleges and universities, is impressive. The Indian middle class has also come a long way since its beginnings in colonial India. Schooled in modern educational institutions, running the bureaucracy, employed in modern professions, and powering capitalist enterprise, they function as the leading proponents of modernization. Even as they recognize the circulation of new technologies, commodities, and media as threats to indigenous culture, their enthusiasm for liberalization is unmistakable. But as the nation acquires a global look with the circulation of international capital and commodities, the latest phase of globalization—now carried out without colonial and imperial domination—widens the proverbial gap between the rich and the poor. As India transforms and expands its horizon and brings under its purview hitherto isolated regions and peoples, the elitism of modern India is brought to the surface ever more clearly. All this occurs in the name of securing national progress, with security measured in terms of a national-security state endowed with state science and nuclear warfare capabilities.

The nation-state is in a hurry to keep the nation's appointment with History. An uncanny likeness to colonialism characterizes its assumption of a commanding role and its desperate desire to function as a "civilizing" agent of its own, under whose watchful care and guiding agency Indians are to be lifted out of their backwardness, ignorance, hidebound traditions, and fatalism. But a significant difference from British rule also distinguishes the nation-state. Whereas the colonial rulers had determined that the price of modernizing the colonized was despotic government, the nationalists instituted democracy and entrusted it with the function of articulating the modern state with the population. Over time, electoral politics and representative government have expanded and the social composition of elected representatives and bureaucracy has broadened, extending the reach and dominance of the modern state. But the more deeply rooted democracy becomes, the more it doubles as something other than its professed ideals. I do not mean here the distressing criminalization of politics, the rampant corruption, the disturbingly frequent use of the state's coercive apparatus. Instead, I refer to the fact that the broadening of the social composition of the state and the deepening of democracy's functioning have been achieved through the politics of caste and religion—something that alienates democracy's self-representation as a system composed of secular individuals.

In a certain sense, the Indian political system has never been insulated from caste and religion—one has to only think of the Sanskritic and Brahminical Hinduism that underlay the cultural imagination of the nation. In recent decades, however, the politicization of subaltern castes, on the one hand, and the mobilization of Hindu majoritarianism, on the other, have forced the political system to acknowledge the presence of caste and religion. It would be a mistake to think that all these appeals to caste, ethnicity, and religion represent the assertion of the language of community over the narrative of capital. As was the case earlier with Indian nationalism, the politics of caste and religion are thoroughly worked over by the language of modernity. Communities speak of themselves as enumerated groups, and claims for representation in administration and other modern institutions are couched in terms of measurements and proportions. We are witnessing, once again, the contradictory functioning of modernity. What is new is that the current masquerade of modernity as community strains against the earlier conception of the national community; it questions the idea that the "fictive ethnicity" instituted by the nation-state is the horizon of politics and offers enumerated communities—majority and minority groups—as a more authentic foundation of modernity. It brings Indian modernity face to face with its own difference, forcing it to negotiate the polarities of secular and religious, community and state, science and culture, whose hybridizations have formed the stuff of its historical existence.

Hybridization means that ideologies that organize themselves along polarities of community and state, tradition and modernity, cannot possibly be true to their representations. The choices presented as one or the other are false choices, for there are no pure positions. Neither community nor modernity appear in themselves, nor have they ever done so. If Hindu majoritarianism cannot pass as the resurgence of the authentic tradition, neither can the secular nation be defended as the pure domain of rationality and modernity. These are familiar masquerades. To make one's way through their obfuscations requires something both more delicate and more difficult than the comfortable make-believe that there exists a critical position outside the historical configuration of Indian modernity. Criticism means identifying new arrangements out of the complicities and interpenetrations of community and state, tradition and modernity. If the modern nation has never lived an undivided and complete life, then criticism cannot adopt a panoptic distance; it must be located in immanent criticism—in the authorization of those forms that have lived subaltern, minor lives in the constitution of modernity.

Friedrich Nietzsche wrote that critical history is "an attempt to gain a past *a posteriori* from which we might spring, as against that from which we do spring."[4] It is in this sense that the heterogenous and disjunctive history of Indian modernity offers possibilities for gaining a past from which postcolonial India might spring.

Notes

CHAPTER ONE
THE SIGN OF SCIENCE

1. Words of an Indian engineer, cited in Alexander Stille, "The Ganges' Next Life," *The New Yorker*, January 19, 1998, 67.

2. Ashis Nandy's *The Intimate Enemy: The Loss and Recovery of Self under Colonialism* (Delhi: Oxford University Press, 1983) is a powerful statement on modern science's association with power in the colonial and postcolonial world. See also his "Introduction: Science as a Reason of State," in *Science, Hegemony and Violence: A Requiem for Modernity*, ed. Ashis Nandy (Delhi: Oxford University Press, 1988). For similar critiques, see Ziauddin Sardar, ed., *The Revenge of Athena: Science, Exploitation and the Third World* (London and New York: Mansell Publishing, 1988), and Claude Alvares, *Science, Development and Violence: The Twilight of Modernity* (Delhi: Oxford University Press, 1992).

3. Joseph Conrad, *The Heart of Darkness*, 3rd ed. (New York: W. W. Norton, 1988), 10. For a recent general account of science as the ideology of Western domination, see Michael Adas, *Machines as the Measure of Men: Science, Technology, and Ideologies of Western Dominance* (Ithaca and London: Cornell University Press, 1989).

4. Max Horkheimer and Theodor Adorno, *Dialectic of Enlightenment*, trans. John Cumming (New York: Herder and Herder, 1972), 4.

5. Rudyard Kipling, "The Bridge Builders," in *The Day's Work* (New York: Doubleday & McClure, 1898), 3–47.

6. Ranajit Guha, "Dominance without Hegemony and Its Historiography," in *Subaltern Studies VI*, ed. Ranajit Guha (Delhi: Oxford University Press, 1989), 274.

7. Michel Foucault, "Governmentality," in *The Foucault Effect: Studies in Governmentality*, ed. Graham Burchell et al. (Chicago: University of Chicago Press, 1991), 87–104.

8. Bruno Latour, *We Have Never Been Modern* (Cambridge, Mass.: Harvard University Press, 1993).

9. Ibid., 97.

10. Edward Said, *Culture and Imperialism* (New York: Alfred A. Knopf, 1993), 58.

CHAPTER TWO
STAGING SCIENCE

1. John Stuart Mill, *On Liberty* (London, 1859; reprint. Northbrook, Ill.: AHM Publishing, 1947), 10.

2. All quotations pertaining to *Kim* appear in Rudyard Kipling, *Kim* (London, 1901; reprint, Harmondsworth: Puffin Classics, 1987), 7–9. For a history of the Zam-Zammah and a description of the Lahore Museum, see T. H. Thornton and J. L. Kipling, *Lahore* (Lahore: Government Civil Secretariat Press, 1876), 59–60, 62–77.

3. On ambivalence and hybridity as a source and site of colonial power, see Homi K. Bhabha's essays "Of Mimicry and Man: The Ambivalence of Colonial Discourse," and "Signs Taken for Wonders," in his *The Location of Culture* (London and New York: Routledge, 1994), 85–92, 102–22, respectively.

4. For the centrality of colonies in nineteenth-century exhibitions, see Carol Breckenridge, "The Aesthetics and Politics of Colonial Collecting: India at World Fairs," *Comparative Studies in Society and History* 32:2 (1989), 195–215; R.W. Rydell, *All the World's a Fair* (Chicago: University of Chicago Press, 1988); and Paul Greenhalgh, *Ephemeral Vistas: The Expositions Universelles, Great Exhibitions and World's Fairs, 1851–1939* (Manchester: Manchester University Press, 1988).

5. For a recent general account of science's use as an instrument of Western dominance, see Michael Adas, *Machines as the Measure of Men: Science, Technology, and Ideologies of Western Dominance* (Ithaca and London: Cornell University Press, 1989).

6. Speaking of the opportunity that India offered for scientific inquiry, George Campbell, the governor of Bengal and a noted colonial ethnologist, remarked in 1866: "In fact, it is now evident, that as this country, in a far greater degree than any other in the world, offers an unlimited field for ethnological observation and enquiry, and presents an infinity of varieties of almost every one of the great divisions of the human race, so also there is no lack of able and qualified men to reap this abundant harvest." Asiatic Society, *Proceedings of the Asiatic Society of Bengal, January to December, 1866* (Calcutta: Baptist Mission Press, 1867), 46.

7. As one British official put it, museums in India could be better organized to perform these scientific functions, it was believed, than in Europe "where museums had grown up by accretion of legacies and bequests generally tied up with special conditions." Government of India, *Report on the Conference as regards Museums in India Held at Calcutta on Dec. 27th to 31st, 1907* (Calcutta: Superintendent, Government Printing, 1908), 16.

8. India Office Library and Records, London: P/186, Government of Bengal, Financial Department (Industry and Science) Proceedings No: 2–1, May 1874 (hereafter cited as IOLR).

9. Foucault writes in *The Order of Things* (New York: Vintage, 1973): "Natural history in the Classical age is not merely the discovery of a new object of curiosity; it covers a series of complex operations that introduce the possibility of a constant order into a totality of representations. It constitutes a whole do-

main of empiricity as at the same time *describable* and *orderable*" (158). He attributes this possibility for an order, a language, to a gap that opened up between things and words when things seemed to be things in themselves. It was in this gap, arranged in the juxtaposition of objects, that a language murmured, and the taxonomic order of natural history made its appearance (129–32). Ken Arnold's "Cabinet for the Curious: Practicing Science in Early Modern English Museums," (Ph.D. diss., Princeton University, 1991), particularly chapters 6 and 7, chart this shift.

10. *Indian Museum, The Indian Museum 1814–1914* (Calcutta: Baptist Mission Press, 1914), 1–9 passim.; see also S. F. Markham and H. Hargreaves, *The Museums of India* (London: The Museums Association, 1936), 123. See O. P. Kejariwal, *The Asiatic Society of Bengal and the Discovery of India's Past 1784–1838* (Delhi: Oxford University Press, 1988), 85, 102–123 passim., for an account of struggles to establish and improve the museum.

11. National Archives of India (NAI), New Delhi: Government of India, Home (Public), Proceedings No. 49, October 7, 1859, letter from the Secretary, Asiatic Society, dated October 8, 1858.

12. The results of Thurston's anthropometric research and ethnographic tours are contained in his monumental *Castes and Tribes of Southern India*, 7 vols. (Madras: Government Press, 1909), a classic of its genre in Victorian anthropology.

13. Ibid., 13–18. By 1911, there were thirty-nine museums spread all over India. For a list of these, see Government of India, *The Conference of Orientalists including Museums and Archaeology Conference held at Simla, July 1911* (Simla: Government Central Branch Press, 1911), 99–115. This figure rose to 105 by 1936, (Markham and Hargreaves, *The Museums of India*, 13).

14. The stress on natural history and classification emerges clearly in records. See Government of Madras, *Administration Report of the Government Central Museum for the year 1895–96* (Madras, 1896) Appendix E, 15. See also IOLR: P/687, Government of India, Department of Agriculture, Revenue and Commerce (Industrial Arts, Museums, Exhibitions), Proceedings No: 6, April 1872, "Précis of the history of the Government Central Museum, Bombay."

15. See Carol Breckenridge, "The Aesthetics and Politics of Colonial Collecting: India at World Fairs."

16. Government of Bengal, *Indian Industrial and Agricultural Exhibition, 1906–07. Catalogue of Exhibits of the Bengal Agricultural Department* (Calcutta: Bengal Secretariat Press, 1907), iii. On the role of Indian officials and landed gentry in organizing exhibitions, see Government of Madras, *Selections from the Records of the Madras Government*, no. 32 A, *Report on the Agricultural Exhibition in the Provinces in the Year 1856* (Madras: Asylum Press, 1856), 41; Moulvi Arshad Ali, ed., *A Report on Pagla Mian's Mela with Agricultural and Industrial Exhibition* (Feni, Noakhali: published by the editor, 1915), 2; and IOLR: P/

186, Government of Bengal, Statistical Department (Industry and Science) Proceedings No: 17–1, May 1873.

17. A complete description of the exhibition and the statement of its aims, demonstrating the stress on function, is provided in Satya Chandra Mukerji, *Allahabad in Pictures* (Allahabad: Indian Press, 1910), 44–50.

18. For the difference between classification and function, see Foucault, *The Order of Things*, 217–21, 226–32.

19. Accounts and references to these appear in Government of Madras, *Report on the Agricultural Exhibitions in the Provinces in the Year 1856*; Abdool Luteef Khan Bahadoor, *A Discourse on the Nature, Objects, and Advantages of a Periodical Census, read at a meeting of the Bethune Society, held on the 5th of April, 1865* (Calcutta: Hurkaru Press, 1865), vi–vii; and Government of India, *Report of the Nagpore Exhibition of Arts, Manufactures and Produce, December 1865* (Nagpore: Central Provinces' Printing Press, n.d.).

20. Letter from G. S. Forbes, Secretary, Board of Revenue, dated July 10, 1856, in Government of Madras, *Selections from the Records*, no. 32 A, mentioning exhibitions held in previous year, 1.

21. IOLR: P/186, Government of Bengal, Statistical Department (Industry and Science), Proceedings No: 17–1, May 1873. In Bengal, an annual local fair named after a Muslim saint and miracle worker (the Pagla Mian Mela or the "mad saint's fair") and established by the famous Bengali poet and an official in British administration, Nabin Chandra Sen, was turned into an agricultural and industrial exhibition. See Moulvi Arshad Ali, ed., *A Report on Pagla Mian's Mela with Agricultural and Industrial Exhibition*, 1–2. See also Nabin Chandra Sen, *Āmār-Jīban* [Bengali], vol. 4. (Calcutta, 1912), reprinted in *Nabin Chandra Rachnabali*, ed. Sajanikant Das (Calcutta: Bangiya Sahitya Parishad, 1959), 2:428–37.

22. "The Calcutta International Exhibition," *Hindoo Patriot*, December 10, 1883.

23. We can gauge some sense of the success that even a local exhibition could enjoy from the following report on the agricultural exhibition in South Arcot in 1856. It states that, after the registration of exhibited articles, at midday on February 20, "the Exhibition was formally thrown open to the public, the signal for doing so being the firing of a salute, on the Collector and the Committee taking their places on a platform raised for the purpose. Upon this the crowds who had been waiting outside for some hours streamed in in such numbers that it was no easy matter for the Peons assisted by a Guard of Sepoys to preserve order. The visitors continued to pour through the building until shortly after 4 p.m., when further admissions were ordered to cease. It had been announced publicly that the place would be lighted up in the evening and thrown open to Native females only. A considerable number availed themselves of this opportunity, as the immense crowds during the day had for the

most part deterred all but those who had the courage to fight their way in. These evening visitors were not numbered, but those during the day amounted to upwards of 30,000." See Government of Madras, *Selections from the Records* no. 32 A, 41–42.

24. IOLR: P/186, Government of Bengal, Statistical Department (Industry and Science) Proceedings No: 17–1, May 1873. For attendance at the Calcutta exhibition, see the *Bengalee*, March 15, 1884.

25. Indian Museum, *The Indian Museum 1814–1914*, xliii–xlviii. By 1936, the annual number of visitors to the Indian Museum, Calcutta and the Victoria and Albert Museum, Bombay was reported to be a million each. (Markham and Hargreaves, *Museums of India*, 69).

26. Government of Madras, *Administration Report of the Government Central Museum for the year 1894–95*, 2. For equally impressive numbers at smaller museums, see Central Museum, Lahore, *Report on the Working of the Lahore Museum for 1892–93*, 1; and Provincial Museum Committee Lucknow, *Letter from the President, Provincial Museum Committee, Lucknow, dated 5th June, 1886*, 4.

27. Asiatic Society, *Proceedings of the Asiatic Society of Bengal, January to December, 1866*, 5.

28. Ibid., 71.

29. Ibid., 82.

30. Ibid., 71.

31. Ibid., 83–85.

32. Ibid., 90.

33. Ibid., 90.

34. Ibid., 91.

35. Ibid., 188–89.

36. Ibid., 190; *Proceedings of the Asiatic Society of Bengal for November, 1867* (Calcutta: Baptist Mission Press, 1868), 157–62.

37. *Proceedings of the Asiatic Society of Bengal, January to December, 1868* (Calcutta: Baptist Mission Press, 1869), 29–31.

38. On labeling and exhibiting, see Markham and Hargreaves, *The Museums of India*, 62–66.

39. Government of Bombay, *Selections from the Records of the Bombay Government*, n.s., no. 83, *Report on the Government Central Museum and on the Agricultural and Horticultural Society of Western India for 1863. With Appendices, being the History of the Establishment of the Victoria and Albert Museum and of the Victoria Gardens, Bombay* (Bombay: Education Society's Press, 1864) Appendix A, 17.

40. Government of India, *Report on the Nagpore Exhibition of Arts, Manufactures and Produce*, 27.

41. Government of Bengal, *Record of Cases Treated in the Mesmeric Hospital, From June to December 1847: With Reports of the Official Visitors* (Calcutta: Military Orphan Press, 1847), xxi–xxxii passim.

42. James Esdaile, *Mesmerism in India and its Practical Application in Surgery and Medicine* (London: Longman, Brown, Green, and Longmans, 1846), 49.

43. The following quotations and account are taken from Esdaile, *Mesmerism in India*, 251–52.

44. Letter to *The Englishman*, July 30th, 1845, reprinted in Esdaile, *Mesmerism in India*, 253. The following account is taken from 253–62 passim.

45. *Hindoo Patriot*, December 10, 1883.

46. *Englishman*, December 6, 1883.

47. "Prayag ki Pradurshini," *Saraswati* [Hindi] 1:12 (January 1911): 33–36.

48. *Pioneer*, December 3, 1910.

49. R. B. Sanyal, *Hours with Nature* (Calcutta: S.K. Lahiri & Co., 1896), 84–121. He was superintendent of the Zoological Garden, Calcutta, when he published this book.

50. Ibid., 86–88.

51. Ibid., 98.

52. Ibid., 84, 87.

53. The annual reports of most museums report these visits. See, for example, Government of Madras, *Administration Report of the Government Central Museum for the year 1896–97*, 2.

54. The following account is taken from Central Museum, Lahore, *Report on the Working of the Lahore Museum* (Lahore: Government Printing), 1892–93 to 1915–16 of the annual series.

55. IOLR: Mss.Eur.178/72, Monorama Bose, "Notes on Various Subjects."

56. IOLR: Mss.Eur.178/69, "Diary of Monorama Bose, 1884–1905," entries for 18 April and 26 May 1884, 25 July and 30 Dec. 1884 and 23 May 1885.

57. In the 1930s, the Lahore Museum began screening such films as "Automobile (Making a Motor Car)" and "Surfing, the Famous Sport of Waikiki" to attract the uneducated. Central Museum, Lahore, *Report* for years 1922–23 to 1936–37.

58. IOLR: P/186, Government of Bengal, Statistical Department (Industry and Science) Proceedings No: 17–1, May 1873. This reply was reinvoked later, see P/894, Government of Bengal, Financial Department (Industry and Science) Proceedings No: 3–3/5, March 1876.

59. Moulvi Arshad Ali, ed., *A Report on Pagla Mian's Mela with Agricultural and Industrial Exhibition*, 2. The report also notes that "circus and bioscope performances were given under the denomination of scientific instructive amusement" (12).

60. *Saraswati* 11:1 (January 1910): 26–27 (my translation).

61. *Bengalee*, November 17, 1883.

62. Asiatic Society, *Proceedings of the Asiatic Society of Bengal, January to December, 1866*, 88–89.

63. Government of Madras, *Selections from the Records of the Madras Government*, no. 32 A, 41, 59; and *Selections from the Records of the Madras Government*, no. 45, *Report on the Agricultural Exhibitions in the Provinces in the Year 1856* (Madras: Fort St. George Gazette Press, 1858), 2:29, 63.

64. Ibid., 151.

65. Edgar Thurston, "Anthropology in Madras," *Nature*, May 26, 1898, reprinted in Government of Madras, *Administration Report of the Government Central Museum for the Year 1898–99*, Appendix F.

66. Government of Madras, *Selections from the Records of the Madras Government*, no. 45, 2:121.

67. Ibid., 121.

68. Abdool Luteef Khan Bahadoor, *Discourse on the Nature, Objects, and Advantages of a Periodical Census*, vi–vii.

69. Government of India, *Conference of Orientalists including Museums and Archaeology Conference held at Simla, July 1911*, 117–18.

70. Government of Madras, *Administration Report of the Government Central Museum for the Year 1894–95*, 1.

71. Ibid.

72. Government of Madras, *Administration Report of the Government Central Museum for the year 1895–96*, Appendix E, 14. A very similar description appears in Markham and Hargreaves, *The Museums of India*, 61.

73. Edgar Thurston, "Anthropology in Madras," 26.

74. For the politics of disciplinary regimes and class politics, see Tony Bennett, "The Exhibitionary Complex," *New Formations*, 4 (Spring 1988): 73–102; and Eilean Hooper-Greenhill, *Museums and the Shaping of Knowledge* (London: Routledge, 1992), 167–90. Though these studies do not describe them, it is reasonable to suppose that twists and turns must have also characterized the functioning of European museums as instruments of class and disciplinary power.

75. Jacques Derrida, *Of Grammatology*, trans. Giayatri Chakvavorty Spivak (Baltimore and London: Johns Hopkins University Press, 1976) 141–164. Derrida defines the supplement as an addition that also substitutes. He writes: "It [the supplement] adds only to replace. It intervenes or insinuates itself *in-the-place-of. . . .* Compensatory (suppléant) and vicarious, the supplement is an adjunct, subaltern instance which *takes-(the)-place (tient-lieu)*" (145).

76. Colonial science, from this point of view, emerges as a bad imitation of science born and developed in Europe. See George Basalla, "The Spread of Western Science," *Science*, 156 (1967): 611–22.

77. For the importance of foreign exotic objects in Renaissance England and for their place in the development of museums, see Ken Arnold's "Cabinets for the Curious: Practicing Science in Early Modern English Museums." Also rele-

vant is Steven Mullaney, "Strange Things, Gross Terms, Curious Customs: The Rehearsal of Cultures in the Late Renaissance," in *Representing the English Renaissance*, Stephen Greenblatt ed. (Berkeley: University of California Press, 1988), 65–92.

78. For persuasive arguments against such binarisms, see Sara Suleri, *The Rhetoric of English India* (Chicago: University of Chicago Press, 1992).

CHAPTER THREE

TRANSLATION AND POWER

1. Walter Benjamin, *Illuminations*, ed. Hanna Arendt (New York: Schocken Books, 1969), 75.

2. *Calcutta Monthly* 1:4 (October 1896): 37.

3. Rajendralal Mitra, *A Scheme for the Rendering of European Scientific Terms in India* (Calcutta: Thacker, Spink & Co. 1877), 18. Mitra wrote this originally as a submission to a committee established by the Bengal government to study and develop proposals on vernacular textbooks for the medical college.

4. Ibid., 3–4.

5. I draw this point from Partha Chatterjee, "The Disciplines of Colonial Bengal," in *Texts of Power: Emerging Disciplines in Colonial Bengal*, ed. Partha Chatterjee (Minneapolis and London: University of Minnesota Press, 1995), 21–22.

6. Mitra, *A Scheme for the Rendering*, 5.

7. Benjamin, *Illuminations*, 82.

8. David Kopf, *British Orientalism and the Bengal Renaissance: The Dynamics of Indian Modernization, 1773–1835* (Berkeley: University of California Press, 1969), 45–107; and O. P. Kejariwal, *The Asiatic Society of Bengal and the Discovery of India's Past 1784–1838* (Delhi: Oxford University Press, 1988).

9. See Kopf, *British Orientalism*, 178–213, and his *The Brahmo Samaj and the Shaping of the Modern Indian Mind* (Princeton: Princeton University Press, 1988), particularly 42–85; and Arabinda Poddar, *Renaissance in Bengal: Quests and Confrontations* (Simla: Indian Institute of Advanced Study, 1970), 148–71 passim. For more general accounts, see Atulchandra Gupta, ed., *Studies in the Bengal Renaissance* (Jadavpur: The National Council of Education, Bengal, 1958); and Nemai Sadhan Bose, *The Indian Awakening and Bengal* (Calcutta: Firma K. L. Mukhopadhyaya, 1969).

10. Kopf, *The Brahmo Samaj*, 49–59.

11. On the history of the middle class, see B. B. Misra, *The Indian Middle Classes* (London: Oxford University Press, 1961); and P. Sinha, *Nineteenth Century Bengal: Aspects of Social History* (Calcutta: Firma K. L. Mukhopadhyaya, 1965).

12. Sumit Sarkar, "Calcutta and the 'Bengal Renaissance'," in *Calcutta: The Living City*, ed. Sukanta Chaudhuri (Calcutta: Oxford University Press, 1990), 1:95–105.

13. A comprehensive list and description of such organizations appears in Rajat Sanyal, *Voluntary Associations and the Urban Public Life in Bengal 1815– 1876* (Calcutta: Rddhi-India, 1980).

14. Society for the Acquisition of General Knowledge, *Selection of Discourses Read at the Meetings of the Society for the Acquisition of General Knowledge*, (Calcutta: Bishop's College Press, 1843), 3: iii–iv.

15. Ibid., 3: 75–91; 2: iii–iv.

16. The list of members, which includes once again the Tagores, the Mitras, the Boses, the Dutts, and Mullicks, appears in Bethune Society, *Selections from the Bethune Society Papers* (Calcutta: Stanhope Press, 1857), 3: Appendix, iv–xii.

17. Nemai Sadhan Bose, *The Indian Awakening and Bengal*, 302–04. Arabinda Poddar, *Renaissance in Bengal*, 101–03. See also Bethune Society, *Minutes of Proceedings of the Bethune Society For the Session Ending April 21st 1870* (Calcutta: Stanhope Press, 1870), 14–18.

18. For a brief account of the organization and the patronage it received from the Bengali literati, see Burra Bazar Family Literary Club, *The Seventeenth Anniversary Report of the Burra Bazar Family Literary Club, Established in 1857, with the Abstracts of Anniversary Address and other Lectures* (Calcutta: Calcutta Press, 1874).

19. Mahomedan Literary Society, *A Quarter Century of the Mahomedan Literary Society of Calcutta: A Resumé of its Work from 1863 to 1889 for the Jubilee of the Twenty-Fifth Year* (Calcutta: Stanhope Press, 1889), 7–8.

20. The following description is based on *Abdul Luteef Khan's* autobiography, *A Short Account of My Public Life* (Calcutta: W. Newman & Co., 1885).

21. Abdool Luteef Khan Bahadoor, *A Discourse on the Nature, Objects, and Advantages of a Periodical Census, read at a meeting of the Bethune Society, held on the 5th of April, 1865* (Calcutta: Hurkaru Press, 1865), 28.

22. Colly Coomar Doss, *The Address Delivered before the meeting held at the School Society's School on 7th June, 1845 for the purpose of establishing the Calcutta Phrenological Society* (Calcutta: n.p., n.d.).

23. *Friend of India*, April 25, 1850 noted that this organization published a Bengali periodical on phrenology, which I have been unable to find. The organization, however, was still in existence in 1856 (see *The New Calcutta Directory* (Calcutta: Military Orphan Press, 1856), part 6, 75). On the formation of a society to promote phrenology in 1825, see *The Asiatic Journal* 20 (1825): 223, 337–40.

24. Mahrendralal Sircar, *On the Physiological Basis of Psychology* (Calcutta: Anglo-Sanskrit Press, 1870), ii.

247

25. Recounting the outcry that followed his experience of conversion to homeopathy, Sircar wrote: "I declared my convictions (Feb. 1867) at the Fourth Annual Meeting of the Bengal Branch of the British Medical Association, of which I was then the vice-president. I advocated as worthy of trial by the profession a system of medicine which four years ago, at the inauguration of the Association, I had in utter ignorance denounced as a baseless quackery! What the result of this open confession of faith was is not unknown to my colleagues in England. It was of course no other than professional excommunication. . . . To the honour of the lay press of India, it must be said, that they, both European and Native, one and all denounced the conduct of medical men in Calcutta towards me as the most intolerant and bigotted that could be imagined, unworthy of men who belong to a noble and sacred profession, and pretended to be men of science." "Dr Mohendra Lal Sirkar's Conversion to Homeopathy," in Ram Gopal Sanyal, *Reminiscences and Anecdotes of Great Men of India* (Calcutta: Wooma Churn Chukerbutty, 1894), 55–56.

26. M. N. Sircar, *Life of Peary Churn Sircar* (Calcutta: published by the author, 1914), 1–15, 20–52, 71–78.

27. Not surprisingly, there is a vast amount of writings on Bankim in both Bengali and English. Two of the most insightful recent studies on which my account is based are Partha Chatterjee, *Nationalist Thought and the Colonial World—A Derivative Discourse?* (London: Zed Books, 1986), 54–84; and Tapan Raychaudhuri, *Europe Reconsidered: Perceptions of the West in Nineteenth Century Bengal* (Delhi: Oxford University Press, 1988), 103–218.

28. Bankim Chandra Chattopadhyaya, "Mill, Darwin, and Hinduism," in *Sociological Essays*, trans. and ed. S. N. Mukherjee and Marian Maddern (Calcutta: Rddhi-India, 1986), 60–70. See the discussion of this essay also in Partha Chatterjee, *Nationalist Thought*, 67–69.

29. Ibid., 70.

30. Geraldine Forbes's *Positivism in Bengal: A Case Study in the Transmission and Assimilation of an Ideology* (Calcutta: Minerva, 1975) describes the widespread influence of positivism among the *bhadralok* elite and their close association with Positivists in Britain. For the influence of positivism in the rise of sociology as a discipline, see Bela Dutt Gupta, *Sociology in India* (Calcutta: Centre for Sociological Research, 1972).

31. See Bengal Social Science Association, *Transactions of the Bengal Social Science Association*, 6 vols. (1867–78). Aside from Bengal, the members were drawn from Bihar and from Benaras, Bombay, and several other cities. There was a branch in Muzaffarpur (Bihar), run by Sayyid Imdad Ali, the founder of the Behar Scientific Society.

32. A list of Bengali publications, with authors, between 1818 and 1855 appears in Rev. J. Long, "A Return on the Names and Writings of 515 Persons Connected With Bengali Literature either as Authors or Translators of Printed

Works," *Selection from the Records of the Bengal Government*, no. 22 (Calcutta: Calcutta Gazette, 1855), 124–48. An authoritative history of the development of Bengali literature is S. K. De, *Bengali Literature in the Nineteenth Century, 1757–1857*, 2nd rev. ed. (Calcutta: Firma K. L. Mukhopadhyaya, 1962). For the growing reference to science in Bengali publications, see Binaybhushan Ray, *Unnis Shataker Banglaya Vigyan Sadhana* [Bengali] (Calcutta: Subarnarekha, 1987), 227–77.

33. Mahendralal Sircar, "On the Necessity of National Support to an Institution for the Cultivation of the Physical Sciences by the Natives of India," in *The Projected Science Association for the Natives of India* (Calcutta: Anglo-Sanskrit Press, 1872), xi–xiv. See also the essay "On the Desirability of A National Institution for the Cultivation of the Sciences by the Natives of India" included in the same volume. For a brief sketch of Sircar's career, see Santimay Chatterjee and Enakshi Chatterjee, "Mahendra Lal Sircar: Darkness before Dawn," in *The Urban Experience: Calcutta*, ed. Pradip Sinha (Calcutta: Riddhi-India, 1987), 122–33. For a description of Father Lafont's role as a popularizer of science, see "The Late Reved. Father E. Lafont, S.J., C.I.E.," *The Empress* 22: 2 (May 1908), 2–3; and "Annals of St. Xavier's College, Calcutta, 1835–1935," typescript compiled by A. Verstreten (St. Xavier's College Library, Calcutta).

34. Indian Association for the Cultivation of Science, *Report of the Indian Association for the Cultivation of Science and Proceedings of the Science Convention for the year 1918*, 38–40.

35. Benaras Institute, *The Transactions of the Benaras Institute for the Session 1864–65* (Benaras: Medical Hall Press, 1865), 5–6.

36. The following information is drawn from British Indian Association, *The British Indian Association, Behar* (n.p., n.d.); and from the series, Behar Scientific Society, *Proceedings of the Behar Scientific Society* (Calcutta: Thacker, Spink, & Co., 1868–71).

37. Aligarh Scientific Society, *Proceedings of the Scientific Society* (Ghazeepore: printed at Syed Ahmud's private press, 1864). On the formation and the history of this organization, see David Lelyveld, *Aligarh's First Generation* (Princeton: Princeton University Press, 1978), 77–81. Lelyveld provides a wonderfully evocative description of the *sharīf* culture in chapter 2.

38. Lelyveld, *Aligarh's First Generation*, 79. On Zakaullah and the milieu of the "Delhi renaissance", see C. F. Andrews, *Zaka Ullah of Delhi* (London, 1929; reprint, Lahore: Universal Books, 1976), particularly vii–xvi, 34–46, 57–66. On Zakaullah, Sayyid Ahmad Khan, and other Muslim enthusiasts of science, see S. Irfan Habib, "Institutional Efforts: Popularization of Science in the Mid 19th Century," *Fundamenta Scientiae* 6:4 (1985), 299–312.

39. Gail Minault, "Sayyid Ahmad Dehlavi and the 'Delhi Renaissance'," in *Delhi through the Ages*, ed. Robert E. Frykenberg (Delhi: Oxford University Press, 1986), 287–98.

40. S. Irfan Habib and Dhruv Raina, "The Introduction of Scientific Rationality into India: A Study of Master Ramchandra—Urdu Journalist, Mathematician and Educationalist," *Annals of Science* 46 (1989), 597–610.

41. See C. A. Bayly, *The Local Roots of Indian Politics: Allahabad 1880–1920* (Cambridge: Cambridge University Press, 1975) for a rich description of the social composition of the newly-ascendant urban elite composed of service and professional families, landholders, and merchants (57–87), and for an account of how the culture of Hindi and Hindu reform eclipsed the public presence of the Bengali elite (104–21).

42. Thus *Satya Prakash* 1:1 (1883), 1–2, a journal published from a small district town, Bareilly, called itself a journal of Oriental literature and science, and its publisher declared himself a person accomplished in both *"purviya"* (Eastern) and *"paschimiya"* (Western) knowledge, well-versed in Sanskrit, Persian, and Arabic as also in mesmerism and Theosophy.

43. R. S. Mcgregor, *Hindi Literature of the Nineteenth and Early Twentieth Centuries* (Wiesbaden: Otto Harrossowitz, 1974), 69–89.

44. See *Hindi Pradeep* [Hindi] 1:1 (1877), 1:4 (1877), 1:5 (1878), 1:6 (1878), 13–14 for articles on chemistry, natural philosophy, food and digestion. Similar columns appeared in *Nagari Pracharini Patrika* 1:1 (1897), 3:1 (1898), 3:3 (1898). The most prestigious of all literary journals, *Saraswati*, 1:1 (1900), also began with an article on photography by the editor, Shyam Sundar Das, and established a regular column on science. For further details on the development of science journalism, see Manoj Kumar Patairiya, *Hindi Vigyan Patrakarita* [Hindi] (Delhi: Takhshila Prakashan, 1990), 27–39.

45. For the scheme for a scientific dictionary, see *Nagari Pracharini Patrika* [Hindi] 10:3 (1906).

46. Premchandra Srivastava, *Amrit Jayanti Samaroh Smarika* (Prayag: Vigyan Parishad, 1988), 1–2, 9–12. See also *Vigyan* 1:1 (1915) for information on the organization's history and activities.

47. Omkar Bhatt, *Bhugolsār* [Hindi] (Agra: Agra School Book Society, 1841).

48. "Note," in Government of India, *Minute by the Right Honourable the Governor-General* [Lord Auckland] ([Delhi]:n.p. 1840), lxx–lxxii.

49. Bhatt, *Bhugolsār*, 2–3.

50. Ibid., 85–86.

51. Ibid., 20.

52. Ibid., 101–02.

53. Ibid., 103.

54. Sumit Sarkar, "Rammohun Roy and the Break with the Past," in *Rammohun Roy and the Process of Modernization in India*, ed. V. C. Joshi (Delhi: Vikas, 1975), 46–68.

55. Mahendralal Sircar, "On the Desirability of a National Institution for the Cultivation of the Science," in *The Projected Science Association for the Natives of India*, 4–7.

56. Burra Bazar Family Literary Club, *The Seventeenth Anniversary Report*, 17–18.

57. Mahomedan Literary Society, *A Quarter Century of the Mahomedan Literary Society of Calcutta*, 12.

58. Burra Bazar Family Literary Club, *The Seventeenth Anniversary Report*, 11.

59. Mahendralal Sircar, "On the Necessity of National Support to an Institution for the Cultivation of the Physical Sciences," in *The Projected Science Association for the Natives of India*, iv–ix.

60. Homi K. Bhabha, "Signs Taken for Wonders: Questions of Ambivalence and Authority under a Tree outside Delhi, May 1817," in *The Location of Culture* (London and New York: Routledge, 1994), 112.

61. Bhatt, *Bhugolsār*, 104.

62. Ibid., 121–22.

63. David C. Lindberg, *The Beginnings of Western Science: The European Scientific Tradition in Philosophical, Religious, and Institutional Context, 600 B.C. to A.D. 1450* (Chicago and London: University of Chicago Press, 1992), 197–201.

64. Bhatt, *Bhugolsār*. 121.

65. Rev. K. M. Banerjea, *A Lecture Read Before the Bethune Society on February 13, 1868* (Calcutta: Thacker, Spink and Co., 1868), 6, 23.

66. Bethune Society, *Minutes of Proceedings of the Bethune Society*, 17–18.

67. Burra Bazar Family Literary Club, *The Seventeenth Anniversary*, 19–20.

68. Jogendra Chandra Ghosh, *The Hindu Theocracy: How to Further its Ends* (Calcutta, S. K. Lahiri & Co., 1897), 1. This was the text of speech before the meeting of the Indo-Positivists held on the anniversary of Auguste Comte's death.

69. See, for example, Lala Ruchi Ram Sahni, *Science and Religion: Being the Substance of a Lecture Given at the 32nd Anniversary of the Punjab Brahmo Samaj, Lahore* (Lahore: n.p., 1895), 1–3, 9–14.

70. For a history of the Arya Samaj, see Kenneth W. Jones, *Arya Dharm: Hindu Consciousness in 19th-Century Punjab* (Berkeley and Los Angeles, University of California Press, 1976); and J. F. T. Jordens, *Dayananda Sarasvati: His Life and Ideas* (Delhi: Oxford University Press, 1978).

71. Shriman Amar Singh, *The Advent of a Science-Grounded Religion for All Mankind* (Lahore: Dev Ashram, 1913), 1. See also Dev Samaj, *Religion of the Age* (Lahore: Dev Samaj, 1914), reprinted from the journal *Science-Grounded Religion*, for the philosophy of the Dev Samaj.

72. The most comprehensive statement of Theosophy is contained in H. P. Blavatsky, *The Secret Doctrine: The Synthesis of Science, Religion, and Philosophy*, 5th ed., 6 vols. (Wheaton, Ill.: Theosophical Press, 1945). Originally published in 1893–97, this magnum opus became the canonical text of Theosophy.

73. J. N. Farquhar, *Modern Religious Movements in India*, (New York: Macmillan, 1915), 208–91 gives an account of Theosophy in India. See also

Kenneth W. Jones, *Socio-Religious Reform Movements in India*, vol. 3, part 1 of *The New Cambridge History of India* (Cambridge: Cambridge University Press, 1989), 167–79.

74. H. P. Blavatsky, "Occult or Exact Science?" *Theosophist* (April-May, 1886), reprinted in H. P. Blavatsky, *Occult or Exact Science*, H. P. Blavatsky Series, no. 19 (Bangalore: Theosophical Company, 1984), 11.

75. Henry Steel Olcott, *Old Diary Leaves: The History of the Theosophical Society* (1900; reprint, Madras: The Theosophical Publishing House, 1974), 2:395–404.

76. Ibid., 453–61.

77. Ibid., 453.

78. R. Suntharalingam, *Politics and Nationalist Awakening in South India, 1852–1891* (Tucson: University of Arizona Press, 1974), 2: 301–02, 304–08.

79. D. A. Washbrook, *The Emergence of Provincial Politics: The Madras Presidency 1870–1920* (Cambridge: Cambridge University Press, 1976), 288–90.

80. N. K. Ramaswami Aiya, *The Strange Story of My Spiritual Evolution* (Madras: Theosophist Office, 1910).

81. Ibid., 2.

82. N. K. Ramaswami Aiya *Multum in Parvo or Morality, Religion, Sociology and Science* (Chingleput and Trichinopoly: Indian Press & South Indian Times, 1894). The author is described as a "Bachelor of Arts and Laws (Madras)."

83. N. K. Ramaswami Aiya, *The Strange Story*, 3.

84. Olcott also mentions the incident, writing that "Among the questioners was a blatant, coarse-voiced infidel who roared at my companion, until he had driven her into a state of nervous agitation." The editor's footnote identifies this "infidel" as N. K. Ramasami Aiya "who later joined our Society and did some good work." Olcott, *Old Diary Leaves* (1935; reprint, Madras: The Theosophical Publishing House, 1975), 6: 378.

85. The other writings by Aiya that I have been able to locate are the following: *Vedanta—The Philosophy of Science* (Chittur: Victoria Jubilee Press, 1903), argued for the truth of the Advaita Vedanta philosophy, that is, of strict Vendantic monism. Aiya says in the text that the study of Sankara convinced him of the accuracy of the monism he had learned from Western philosophy (5–6). *Godward Ho!* (Tanjore: V. Govindan & Brothers, 1909), was "a comparative study of Science, Philosophy and Religion," drawn from the writings of Herbert Spencer and Annie Besant. Aiya mentions here that he had sent a pamphlet, *Religion of Science*, to Herbert Spencer, who wrote in reply that he was pleased to know that Indian philosophy resembled his ideas (iii). Perhaps this pamphlet was *Religio-Scientific Philosophy or Religion of Science and Science of Religion* (Tanjore: Kalyansundaran Powr Press, 1910), a tract arguing that both science and religion teach the unity of nature.

86. N. K. Ramaswami Aiya, *The Strange Story*, 3–13 passim.

87. This is laid out in Swami Dayananda's seminal text, *Satyārth Prakāsh* [Hindi] (1882, 2nd ed.; reprint, Delhi: Govindram Hasananda, 1963). According to Kenneth W. Jones (*Arya Dharm*, 35), "First published in 1875, this book, more than any other, was to influence Hindu thinking in Punjab and much of northwestern India" (*Arya Dharm*, 35).

88. Guru Datta Vidyarthi, *Wisdom of the Rishis or Complete Works of Pandita Guru Datta Vidyarthi*, ed. Swami Vedananda Tirtha (Lahore: Arya Pustakalaya, n.d.), 243. The chapter entitled "Evidences of the Human Spirit" is an argument against the designation of the human spirit as a delusion. It develops its argument by first citing Western scientists and philosophers (Thomas Henry Huxley, among others), and then Vedic texts.

89. Ibid., 259.

90. "Poor India! O thou self-lost soul, why seekest thou an astrologer, when Nature is the greatest and the most sapient astrologer?" Babulji Sadashiv Sangit, *An Essay in English read at the Pāthāre Prabhū Social Samaj Hall on Sunday 20th August 1905, Mr. Balaram Krishnanath Dhurandhar B.A., L.L.B., being in the chair* (Bombay: published by the author, 1906).

91. Mahendralal Sircar, *On the Physiological Basis of Psychology*, 4.

92. Jagadish Chandra Bose, *Literature and Science: The Substance of the Presidential Address Given in Bengali by Prof. J. C. Bose to the Literary Conference at Mymensing, April 14, 1911* (Calcutta: n.p., 1911).

93. U. P. Krishnamachari, *The Tribunal of Science Over Reformation Vs. Orthodoxy* (Benaras: published by the author, 1916).

94. Ibid., vi.

95. Ibid., 57–61. A somewhat similar defense of idol worship, arguing that the ignorance of the masses dictated that Positive Science could only be communicated through a religion that involved the senses, was offered by V. Mutukumaraswami, *Symbolic Worship in India* (Rangoon: Mercantile Press, 1904), 7.

96. "On the Health of the Body," *Calcutta Monthly* 1:4 (October 1896), 33–36.

CHAPTER FOUR
THE IMAGE OF THE ARCHAIC

1. T. S. Eliot, "Burnt Norton," in *Four Quartets* (London: Faber and Faber, 1944), 14.

2. *Śāstrārtha beech Ārya Samāj aur Pandit Ganesh Datta Śāstri* [Hindi] (Lahore: Punjab Economical Press, 1896), 1–16, provides details of the events leading up to the disputation and of the personalities involved.

3. Cited in *Śāstrārtha*, 19.

4. Ibid., 20.

5. The authoritative study of the Lokāyata philosophy is Debiprasad Chatto-padhyaya, *Lokayata: A Study in Ancient Indian Materialism* (Delhi: People's Publishing House, 1968). Although the original Lokāyata texts have not survived, the vital presence of this philosophy is reflected in texts of rival philosophies which refer to Lokāyata writings and offer detailed refutations. According to Eli Franco, one original text that survives is the eighth-century philosopher Jayarāśi's *Tattvopaplavasiṃha*, available in a Sanskrit manuscript dating from the end of the thirteenth century. See Franco's *Perception, Knowledge and Disbelief: A Study of Jayarāśi's Scepticism* (Weisbaden: Steiner, 1987), which includes an English translation of the text. Chattopadhyaya, however, argues that *Jayarāśi's* radical skepticism, captured in the text's title (which means "the lion that throws overboard all categories") disqualifies him as a member of the Lokāyata school. See Chattopadhyaya's *Indian Philosophy: A Popular Introduction* (Delhi: People's Publishing House, 1964), 186–88.

6. Madhava Acharya, *Sarva-Darśana-Saṃgraha*, trans. E. B. Cowell and A. E. Gough (London: K. Paul, Trench, Trubner, 1914), 10. This is a translation of a fourteenth-century Telugu text that, in the course of presenting and reviewing different philosophical systems, quotes from *Bṛhaspatisutra*, the original and founding Lokāyata text attributed to the legendary Bṛhaspati. Jayarāśi also invokes *Bṛhaspatisutra* to refute the conception of soul and transmigration. See Eli Franco, *Perception, Knowledge, and Disbelief*, 46. I am grateful to Sheldon Pollock for referring me to these two texts.

7. Benedict Anderson, *Imagined Communities* (London: Verso, 1983), 19.

8. Drawing on Walter Benjamin, Anderson calls this sense of cohesion and simultaneity "homogenous empty-time"—a form of temporality that replaces the medieval conception of simultaneity-along-time. It permits people who do not know each other to imagine that they and their actions are linked together by synchronicity, that they form a nation because they are temporally coincident—they occupy the "homogenous empty-time." Ibid., 30–31.

9. On these questions, see Homi K. Bhabha's insightful "DissemiNation: Time, Narrative, and the Margins of the Modern Nation," in Homi Bhabha, ed., *Nation and Narration* (London and New York: Routledge, 1990), 291–322.

10. Kenneth W. Jones, *Arya Dharm: Hindu Consciousness in 19th-Century Punjab* (Berkeley and Los Angeles, University of California Press, 1976), 13–29, 36–66.

11. See Brian K. Smith, *Reflections on Resemblance, Ritual, and Religion* (New York: Oxford University Press, 1989), 17–18.

12. Sheldon Pollock, "From Discourse of Ritual to Discourse of Power in Sanskrit Culture," *Journal of Ritual Studies* 4:2 (Summer 1990): 330.

13. For an account of some of these debates, see Durga Prasad, *A Triumph of Truth* (Lahore: Virajanand Press, 1889), 29–33; 36–41, 70–78.

14. A verbatim account of the debate and Dayananda's written supplement

on questions that could not be discussed appears in Prasad, *A Triumph of Truth*, 158–244.

15. See Prasad, *A Triumph of Truth*, 168–71 for the statements by Rev. Scott and Mohammad Kasim.

16. Ibid., 171. This debate was cut short as, according to the text, the Christian and Muslim representatives were unwilling to pursue it to its completion, prompting Dayananda to say that he was denied consideration of the remaining questions by "the shifts and subterfuges of paid priestcraft" (209).

17. Sheldon Pollock, "The Theory of Practice and the Practice of Theory in Indian Intellectual History," *Journal of American Oriental Society* 105:3 (1985): 515.

18. Prasad, *A Triumph of Truth*, 171.

19. Swami Dayananda Sarasvati, *Satyārtha Prakāsh*, 55–56. So firm was the belief in the efficacy of the sacrificial fire that, when an editor of a newspaper suggested that McDuggall's powder, instead of butter, be used as a disinfectant, the Arya Samaj responded: "We pity this knowledge of the Editor with respect to the *Hom* philosophy of the Aryas. . . . we will simply ask the learned Editor to state what obnoxious *gases* there are in the atmosphere and how does McDuggall's powder clean the atmosphere of them. The truth is that he believes this powder to be a disinfectant at the most because it is so regarded by English Science. The ancient Scientific world with him has no existence." *Arya Patrika*, 2:25 (December 7, 1886), 6.

20. Jones, *Arya Dharm*, 72, 162–64.

21. The militant wing's argument that the nationalization of education demanded a Vedic curriculum and the description of the curriculum of the Gurukul school appear in Arya Pratinidhi Sabha, *The Rules and the Scheme of Studies of the Proposed Gurukula Sanctioned by the Arya Pratinidhi Sabha* (Lahore: Mufid-'i'-am Press, 1899). See also Jones, *Arya Dharm*, 90–93 for details on the dissension in Arya Samaj.

22. Guru Datta Vidyarthi, *Wisdom of the Rishis or Complete Works of Pandita Guru Datta Vidyarthi*, ed. Swami Vedananda Tirtha (Lahore: Arya Pustakalaya, n.d.), 5–25.

23. This argument is developed in a chapter entitled "The Terminology of the Vedas," in ibid., 26–91.

24. Cited in ibid., 60.

25. Ibid., 59–60.

26. Ibid., 92–93.

27. Ibid., 98.

28. Ibid., 102.

29. Ibid., 105.

30. Pollock, "The Theory of Practice and the Practice of Theory in Indian Intellectual History," 515.

31. It was in the 1780s that H. T. Colebrooke and other members of the Asiatic Society began publishing inquiries into Hindu mathematics, astronomy, and medicine. See S. N. Sen, "Survey of Studies in European Languages, " in *History of Astronomy in India*, ed. S. N. Sen and K. S. Shukla (New Delhi: Indian National Science Academy, 1985), 50–67; and Michael Adas, *Machines as the Measure of Men: Science, Technology, and Ideologies of Western Dominance* (Ithaca and London: Cornell University Press, 1989), 103–05.

32. Kissory Chandra Mitra, *Hindu Medicine and Medical Education* (Calcutta: R. C. Lepage & Co., Metropolitan Press, 1865), 1.

33. Ibid., 1.

34. Ibid., 6.

35. One among many examples ridiculing Hindu science in comparison to modern Western science and classical Greek knowledge is Allan Webb, *The Historical Relations of the Ancient Hindu with Greek Medicine in connection with the Study of Modern Medical Science in India: Being a General Introductory Lecture Delivered June 1850 at the Calcutta Medical College* (Calcutta: Military Orphan Press, 1850). Webb, who was a professor of medicine and surgical anatomy at the Calcutta Medical College, granted little to the Hindus. He was most generous when it came to some of the traditional practices of healing that resembled mesmerism (26–27).

36. Poonam Bala, *Imperialism and Medicine in Bengal* (New Delhi: Sage, 1991), 41–64, 71–87; B. Gupta, "Indigenous Medicine in Nineteenth-Century and Twentieth-Century Bengal," in *Asian Medical Systems: A Comparative Study*, ed. C. Leslie (Berkeley and London: University of California Press, 1976), 368–78; C. Leslie, "The Professionalization of Indigenous Medicine," in *Entrepreneurship and Modernization of Occupational Cultures in South Asia* (Durham: DUPCSSA, 1973), 216–42; and David Arnold, "Medical Priorities and Practice in Nineteenth-Century British India," *South Asia Research* 5:2 (1985), 167–83.

37. Noting the efforts that the Ayurvedic practitioners had undertaken, Kaviraj Gananath Sen in his *Hindu Medicine: An Address Delivered at the Hindu University Foundation Ceremony at Benaras* (Madras: Ayurvedic Printing Works, 1916), recounted the following measures taken by 1916: The All India Ayurvedic Conference had come into existence, drawing the practioners of Ayurveda to the seven annual sessions it had held so far; the All India Board of Ayurvedic Education had come into existence along with Ayurvedic schools and colleges; and no less than fifty Ayurvedic journals were being published in different Indian languages (21–22). See also P. Brass, "The Politics of Ayurvedic Education in India," in *Education and Politics in India*, ed. S. H. Rudolph and L. I. Rudolph (Cambridge, Mass.: Harvard University Press, 1972) 356–67.

38. For example, *Arogya-Jiwan*, a Hindi journal was launched in 1893 to advance Ayurveda's claims, offering translations of Sanskrit texts, and medical

advice on pregnancy and child-rearing. A compelling example among the many defenses of the scientific claims of traditional medicine is Shaukat Rai Chaudhary, *Ayurveda Ka Vaigyanik Swaroop* [Hindi] (Kangri: Gurukul Yantralaya, 1918), which concluded that Ayurvedic pathology and physiology were far superior to the knowledge offered by modern Western medicine.

39. *Nagari Pracharini Patrika* [Hindi] 3:1 (1898), 3–11.

40. The biographical details on Seal are based on David Kopf, *The Brahmo Samaj and the Shaping of the Modern Indian Mind* (Princeton: Princeton University Press, 1998) 60–63.

41. Brajendranath Seal, *The Positive Sciences of the Hindus* (London, 1915; reprint, Delhi: Motilal Banarasidas, 1991), v–vi.

42. P. C. Ray, *Life and Experiences of a Bengali Chemist* (Calcutta: Chuckervertty, Chatterjee & Co., 1932), 62.

43. For the early history and nationalist motivations in the establishment of the Bengal Chemical and Pharmaceutical Works, see Ibid., 92–111 passim.

44. P. C. Ray, *A History of Hindu Chemistry*, rev. ed., 2 vols. (Calcutta: Chuckervertty, Chatterjee & Co., 1904–25). On the connection between Ray's scientific work and historical study, I have learned much from Dhruv Raina's fascinating manuscript, "The Early Years of P. C. Ray: The Inauguration of the School of Chemistry and the Social History of Science (1885–1907)."

45. Ray, *A History of Hindu Chemistry*, 1, xxxix–xlvii; 2, lxxxiii–xciii.

46. Ibid., 1, ii.

47. Manindranath Banerjea, "On the Ancient Hindu Conception of Ether," *Proceedings of the Indian Association for the Cultivation of Science* 1 (1915), 62.

48. *Kayastha Samachar*, 6:5 (November 1902), 431.

49. P. C. Ray, *Antiquity of Hindu Chemistry* (Calcutta: published by the printer, 1918), 3.

50. Ibid., 12.

51. P. C. Ray, *Pursuit of Chemistry in Ancient India* (Calcutta: published by the Printer, 1918), 15.

52. Accounts of these attacks and a vigorous defense of *ayurveda* appears in Kaviraj T. S. Ram. Bhishagratna, *In Defense of Ayurveda (An Answer to the Attack of Ayurveda by Dr. T. M. Nadir, M.D.)* (Cachinnate: Manoranjini Press, 1909). The author was a senior physician at the Vivekananda Ayurvedic Hospital, Cachinnate. See also Shaukat Rai Chaudhary, *Ayurveda Ka Vaigyanik Swaroop* (Kangni: Gurukula Yantralaya, 1918), 2–3 for an account of criticisms leveled against *ayurveda*.

53. Srinivasa Murti went on head the Government School of Indian Medicine established in 1925 and served in that capacity until 1942. For biographical details on Murti, see "Dr. G. Srinivasamurti—A Memoir," in Dr. G. Srinivasamurti Foundation, *The Doctor G. Srinivasamurti Birth Centenary* (Madras and Bangalore: Dr. G. Srinivasamurti Foundation, 1987), 2–4.

54. G. Srinivasa Murti, "Secretary's Minute," *Report of the Committee on Indigenous Systems of Medicine* (Madras: Government Printing Press, 1923). This was resubmitted, in a slightly revised form as a report to the Government of India Committee on Indigenous Medicine, and published as *Memorandum on "Science and the Art of Indian Medicine"* (Delhi: Government of India (Delhi, 1948). I have used the latter version.

55. Ibid., 12–13.

56. Ibid., 24.

57. Speaking of the people in whose name the American Declaration of Independence was signed, Jacques Derrida writes that this people did not exist prior to the Declaration. "The signature invents the signer. The signer can only authorize him or herself to sign once he or she has come to the end (*parvenu au vout*), if one can say this, of his or her own signature, in a sort of fabulous retroactivity." "Declarations of Independence," *New Political Science* 15 (Summer 1986), 10.

58. "Āryāvarta kā Prāchin aur Vartamān," *Satyaprakāsh* [Hindi] 1:1 (January 1883), 4.

59. Ibid., 6.

60. Homi K. Bhabha identifies this tension as one produced by what he calls pedagogical and performative representations of the nation. See his "Dissemi-Nation: Time, Narrative, and the Margins of the Modern Nation," in Homi K. Bhabha, ed., *Nation and Narration* (London and New York, Routledge, 1990) 298–99. Derrida evokes something similar in writing of the undecidability between the constative and performative structures of utterance. See his "Declarations of Independence," 8–12.

61. *Arya Patrika*, 2:46 (May 3, 1887), 3.

62. Swami Dayananda, *Satyārtha Prakāsh*, 368–69.

63. Ibid., 369–406, passim.

64. Prasad, *A Triumph of Truth*, 235.

65. Guru Datta Vidyarthi, *Wisdom of the Rishis*, 99.

66. Swami Dayananda, *Satyārtha Prakāsh*, 23–24.

67. "Sakhi Samvād," *Pānchāl Panditā*, 4:7 (May 1900 [1901]), 10–11.

68. Guru Datta Vidyarthi, *Wisdom of the Rishis*, 103.

69. *Mritak Śrāddha Khandan* (Lahore: Virajanand Yantralaya, 1893), 3.

70. Ibid., 3–4.

71. *Swarg Men Subject Committee* (Dinapore: Aryavarta Patra, 1895).

72. Ibid., 12–15.

73. Ibid., 19.

74. Ray, *A History of Hindu Chemistry*, 1:195.

75. Ray, *Pursuit of Chemistry in Ancient India*, 4.

76. P. C. Ray, *Pursuit of Chemistry in Bengal* [Calcutta University Extension Lecture, delivered on 10 January 1916] (Calcutta: B. M. Gupta, 1916), 4.

77. Here, Ray drew on ideas that were well established. James Mill was only the most eminent exponent of the view espoused by many intellectuals at the close of the nineteenth century that Hindu philosophy, particularly Vedanta, was inimical to the investigation of the physical world. "The Vedantist was most imperatively enjoined to abstract his attention from the delusive appearances that were around him, and to concentrate on the reality that underlay them," wrote an anonymous author, adding that a "school of philosophy so obnoxious to material prosperity, so repressive of the habit of observation, took away at once the motive and means for the growth of physical science." "Hindu Mind in Its Relation to Science and Religion," *Calcutta Review* 98:195 (1894), 71–72.

78. Ray, *Pursuit of Chemistry in Bengal*, 9.

79. Ibid., 14.

80. Ray, *Pursuit of Chemistry in Ancient India*, 1.

81. Ibid., 15–16.

82. Murti, *Memorandum*, 45.

83. Ibid., 23.

84. Ibid., 18.

85. Jawaharlal Nehru, *The Discovery of India* (New York: 1946; reprint, Delhi: Oxford University Press, 1989), 223. Nehru writes: "During the first thousand years of the Christian era, there are many ups and downs in India, many conflicts with invading elements and internal troubles. Yet it is a period of vigorous national life, bubbling over with energy and spreading out in all directions. . . . Yet even before that Golden Age [the period of the Gupta empire, 500–800 A.D.], signs of weakness and decay become visible. . . . In the south there was still vitality and vigour and this lasted for some centuries more; in the Indian colonies abroad there was aggressive and full-blooded life right up to the middle of the next millennium. But the heart seems to petrify, its beats are slower, and gradually this petrification and decay spread to the limbs" (221–23 passim).

CHAPTER FIVE
BODY AND GOVERNMENTALITY

1. Michel Foucault, "Governmentality," in Graham Burchell, Colin Gordon, and Peter Miller, ed., *The Foucault Effect: Studies in Governmentality* (Chicago: University of Chicago Press, 1991), 100.

2. Cited in David Arnold, *Colonizing the Body: State Medicine and Epidemic Disease in Nineteenth-Century India* (Delhi: Oxford University Press, 1993), 6.

3. M. K. Gandhi, *Collected Works of Mahatma Gandhi* (Delhi: Publications Division, 1958), 62: 428f.

4. M. K. Gandhi, *A Guide to Health*, trans. A. Rama Iyer (Madras: S. Ganesan, 1930), 64–65.

5. M. K. Gandhi, *Hind Swaraj or Indian Home Rule* (Natal, South Africa, 1910; reprint, Ahmedabad: Navjivan Publishing House, 1938), 59.

6. Foucault, "Governmentality," 92.

7. Ibid., 99.

8. Ibid., 93.

9. Ann Laura Stoler, *Race and the Education of Desire: Foucault's* "History of Sexuality" *and the Colonial Order of Things* (Durham: Duke University Press, 1995).

10. Michel Foucault, *The History of Sexuality Volume I: An Introduction* (New York: Vintage, 1980), 142.

11. Partha Chatterjee has called this displacement of liberal principles "the rule of colonial difference." See his *The Nation and Its Fragments: Colonial and Postcolonial Histories* (Princeton: Princeton University Press, 1993), 18. David Scott's otherwise fine essay, "Colonial Governmentality," *Social Text* 43 (Fall 1995) 191–220, ignores this peculiarity of colonial governmentality, viewing the latter merely as a mode of universalizing the political forms of modernity.

12. Arnold, *Colonizing the Body*, 9.

13. During the early part of the nineteenth century, the British treated Indians as part of the landscape, as creatures of its soil, drainage, water, climate, and diseases, which they surveyed and distributed into distinct medico-topographical regions. Animated by the idea that India represented a unique environment, the colonial medical establishment concentrated its focus on identifying distinct health and disease regimes. For further details, see Arnold, *Colonizing the Body*, 24–43.

14. Beginning with the late-eighteenth-century Orientalist researches, the British studied and translated classical texts, and investigated indigenous medical practices in an effort to incorporate both indigenous medical knowledge and indigenous materia medica into Western medicine. Although these were never considered equal to Western medicine, the British believed that the examination of indigenous medical ideas, practices, and drugs, conducted under their superior eyes, could yield elements useful for the development of a therapeutic system suitable for India. See Arnold, *Colonizing the Body*, 43–50.

15. Mark Harrison, *Public Health in British India: Anglo-Indian Preventive Medicine 1859–1914* (Cambridge: Cambridge University Press, 1994), 61.

16. House of Commons, "Report of the Commissioners Appointed to Inquire into the Sanitary State of the Army in India," *Parliamentary Papers*, 1863, vol. 19, part 1. On the appointment and the work of this Royal Commission, see Arnold, *Colonizing the Body*, 67–98; and Harrison, *Public Health in British India*, 60–66.

17. House of Commons, "Report of the Commissioners Appointed to Inquire into the Sanitary State of the Army in India," xxx, xxxii.

18. Typical in this respect was James Ranald Martin, a surgeon who became the president of the East India Company's Medical Board and served as a member of the Royal Commission on army sanitation. A proponent of climatological determinism, he wrote bitingly about the sanitary habits of Indians and poured scorn on their medical practices. See his *Notes on the Medical Topography of Calcutta* (Calcutta: Huttman, 1837), 24–28, 60; and *The Influence of Tropical Climates on European Constitutions, Including Practical Observations on the Nature and Treatment of the Diseases of Europeans on their Return from Tropical Climates* (London: Churchill, 1856).

19. Cited in Great Britain, *Report on Measures Adopted for Sanitary Improvements in India, from June 1869 to June 1870; together with abstracts of Sanitary Reports for 1868 forwarded from Bengal, Madras, and Bombay* (London: HMSO, 1870), 40.

20. Initially, Sanitary Commissioners were responsible for the army and the civilian population, but they were relieved of the charge for military hygiene after 1867. For further details, see Harrison, *Public Health in British India*, 9, 23–29, 76–82; and Radhika Ramasubban, "Imperial Health in British India, 1857–1900," in Roy Macleod and Milton Lewis, ed. *Disease, Medicine, and Empire: Perspectives on Western Medicine and the Experience of European Expansion* (London and New York: Routledge, 1988), 38–60.

21. "Abstract of Report of Sanitary Commissioner for 1864," in Great Britain, *Memorandum on Measures Adopted for Sanitary Improvements in India upto the end of 1867; together with Abstracts of the Sanitary Reports hitherto forwarded from Bengal, Madras, and Bombay* (London: HMSO, 1868), 42.

22. J. A. Turner and B. K. Goldsmith, *Sanitation in India*, 2nd ed. (Bombay: Times of India, 1917), 985–87.

23. Quoted in "Report of the Commissioners Appointed to Inquire into the Sanitary State of the Army in India," 370.

24. H. R. Tinker, *The Foundations of Local Self-Government in India, Pakistan and Burma* (London: The Athlone Press, 1954), 50–51.

25. Ibid., 334.

26. Cited in Edmund A. Parkes, *A Manual of Practical Hygiene* (London: Churchill, 1864), 563.

27. The Calcutta Fever Hospital and Municipal Enquiry Committee, 1836–47, for example, had drawn a grim picture of the sanitary state of Calcutta. The disposal of night soil, for instance, involved its collection from private privies by *mehtars*, who were responsible for conveying it to depots, from where it was taken to boats and carried downstream before being thrown into the river. An educated Bengali complained to the committee that the *mehtars* "walk through the streets and high roads with baskets full of stink on their heads" and that "when it happens to the lot of a person, who has just made a hearty meal, to face

before any one of these mehtars, it is needless to say how it is felt by him." Cited in S. W. Goode, *Municipal Calcutta: Its Institutions in their Origin and Growth* (Edinburgh: T. and A. Constable, 1916), 169. In fact, only a small proportion of the city's night soil was ever transported to boats; ninety percent was thrown into public drains.

28. See W. F. Bynum, *Science and the Practice of Medicine in the Nineteenth Century* (Cambridge: Cambridge University Press, 1994), 72–77.

29. Margaret Pelling, *Cholera, Fever and English Medicine 1825–1865* (Oxford: Oxford University Press, 1978), 24.

30. "Abstract of the Report of Sanitary Commissioner for 1864," in Great Britain, *Memorandum on Measures Adopted for Sanitary Improvements in India upto the end of 1867*, 41.

31. Following the commission's recommendation and the prevailing medical opinion, nearly a sixth of the British troops were relocated to the hill stations by the 1870s, and barracks were reconstructed to protect them from the effects of India's weather. Arnold, *Colonizing the Body*, 78–79. The government followed these steps to isolate and protect the troops from the supposedly diseased environment with other measures such as rationing the consumption of alcohol and enacting the Contagious Diseases Act in 1868 to permit the medical inspection, detention, and treatment of prostitutes. See Harrison, *Public Health in British India*, 72–76; and K. Ballhatchet, *Race, Sex, and Class under the Raj: Imperial Attitudes and Policies and Their Critics* (London: Weidenfield and Nicolson, 1980), chaps. 2 and 3.

32. House of Commons, "Report of the Commissioners Appointed to Inquire into the Sanitary State of the Army in India," p. 371; Great Britain, *Memorandum on Measures Adopted for Sanitary Improvements in India upto the end of 1867; together with Abstracts of the Sanitary Reports hitherto forwarded from Bengal, Madras, and Bombay* (London: HMSO, 1868), 2.

33. Veena Oldenberg's *The Making of Colonial Lucknow* (Princeton: Princeton University Press, 1984), chap. 4 contains a persuasive account of the application of sanitary measures as an instrument of colonial control. She argues that unlike Britain, where pauperism and squalor were viewed as the root cause of disease, the municipal authorities in India paid scant attention to poverty; afflicted by a "curious myopia," the British were never able to develop "a comprehensive long-range plan to drain and cleanse the city" (142–43). Cf. J. B. Harrison, "Allahabad: A Sanitary History," in Kenneth Ballhatchet and John Harrison, ed., *The City in South Asia: Pre-Modern and Modern* (London: Curzon Press, 1980), 167–95.

34. Ian Hacking, *The Taming of Chance* (Cambridge: Cambridge University Press, 1990).

35. John M. Eyler, *Victorian Social Medicine: The Ideas and Methods of William*

Farr (Baltimore and London: Johns Hopkins Press, 1979), 161. See 159–89 for the description of the collaboration between Farr and Nightingale.

36. Parkes, *A Manual of Practical Hygiene*, xviii.

37. Joseph Ewart, *A Digest of Vital Statistics of the European and Native Armies in India* (London: Smith, Elder and Co., 1859), v.

38. Ibid., 19–41.

39. See Ira Klein, "Death in India," *Journal of Asian Studies* 32 (1973): 632–59; and Klein, "Urban Development and Death: Bombay City, 1870–1914," *Modern Asian Studies* 20 (1986): 725–54.

40. The use of statistics is too widely present in colonial records to single out any particular set. But for some examples, see Government of India, *Report of the Commissioners appointed to Inquire into the Cholera Epidemic of 1861 in North India.* (Calcutta, Government Printing, 1862); "Abstract of Bengal Sanitary Report for 1865," in Great Britain, *Memorandum of Measures Adopted for the Sanitary Improvements in India upto* 1867; Government of Bengal, *Report on the Calcutta Medical Institutions* 1871–1900 and Government of Bengal, *Report of the Commissioner Appointed under Section 28 of Act IV (B.C.) of 1876 to Enquire into Certain Matters connected with the Sanitation of the Town of Calcutta* (Calcutta: Bengal Secretariat Press, 1885).

41. Government of India, *Proceedings of the First All-India Sanitary Conference* (Calcutta: Government Printing, 1912), Appendices 11–13.

42. For example, see James L. Bryden's *Epidemic Cholera in the Bengal Presidency: A Report on the Cholera of 1866–68, and its relation to the Cholera of Previous Epidemics* (Calcutta: Superintendent of Government Printing, 1869). Bryden, a surgeon in the army, served in the office of the sanitary commissioner. See also T. R. Lewis and D. D. Cunningham, *Cholera in relation to Certain Physical Phenomena* (Calcutta: Superintendent of Government Printing, 1878).

43. The *Report of the Commissioners appointed to Inquire into the Cholera Epidemic of 1861 in North India* used figures on meteorology, topography, and cholera epidemics to argue that, while there was an undeniable relationship between the disease and the season of the year, cholera was neither caused nor communicated by the atmosphere; rather, human intercourse, it suggested, was responsible for the transmission of the disease (199–205). For details on the struggle between miasma and contagion theories, see Harrison, *Public Health in British India*, 52–62, 99–116; Arnold, *Colonizing the Body*, 189–98.

44. What follows is a brutally condensed version of Harish Naraindas's detailed, careful, and insightful article, "Poisons, Putrescence and the Weather: A Genealogy of the Advent of Tropical Medicine," *Contributions to Indian Sociology*, n.s., 30:1 (1996): 1–35.

45. Arnold, *Colonizing the Body*, 195. Thus Leonard Rogers wrote two monographs that traced the connection between climate and epidemics, using the

accumulated records on meteorology and diseases to formulate a system for predicting the outbreak of diseases. See his *Small-Pox and Climate in India* (London: HMSO, 1926); and *The Incidence and Spread of Cholera in India; Forecasting and Control of Epidemics* (Calcutta: Thacker, Spink & Co., 1928).

46. Katherine Prior, "The Angry *Pandas*: Hindu Priests and the Colonial Government in the Dispersal of the Hardwar Mela in 1892," *South Asia* 16:1 (1993): 40.

47. "Abstract of the Fourth Annual Report of the Sanitary Commissioner with the Government of India, 1867," in Government of India, *Report on Measures Adopted for Sanitary Improvements in India during the year 1868, and upto the month of June 1869; together with Abstracts of Sanitary Reports for 1867 forwarded from Bengal, Madras, and Bombay* (London: HMSO, 1869), 11–30.

48. Prior, "The Angry *Pandas*" 40–42. Prior argues that this intervention was part of a larger transformation of religious fairs that occurred as a result of the British conquest. The British disarmed the warrior ascetics, took over the policing duties of the fair, and assumed responsibility for its government, so that by the 1830s and the 1840s the fair was "a shadow of its eighteenth-century self." Ironically, such measures eliminated the cultural and political aspects of the Hardwar fair and rendered it into a purely religious event (26–32).

49. For more on the British confrontation with indigenous treatments of smallpox, see Arnold, *Colonizing the Body*, chap. 3.

50. Government of Bengal, *Report of the Smallpox Commissioners* (Calcutta: Military Orphan Press, 1850), 5, 18, 31.

51. Ibid., 28–30, Appendix, xxii.

52. Ibid., 54–55.

53. Arnold, *Colonizing the Body*, 141.

54. Ibid., 202–03.

55. M. E. Couchman, *Account of Plague Administration in the Bombay Presidency from September 1896 until May 1897* (Bombay: Government Central Press, 1897), 15–16.

56. Ibid., 5.

57. Government of Bombay, *Supplement to the Account of Plague Administration in the Bombay Presidency from September 1896 till May 1897*, 5–9.

58. Aside from the famous Arthur Road Hospital incident in 1896, when nearly a thousand mill workers attacked the hospital, "street tumults" were frequent because Indians viewed quarantine and hospitalization with suspicion. P. C. H. Snow, *Report on the Outbreak of Bubonic Plague in Bombay, 1896–97* (Bombay: Times of India, 1897), 18. See also Arnold, *Colonizing the Body*, chap. 5; and I. J. Catanach, "Plague and the Tensions of Empire: India, 1896–1918," in *Imperial Medicine and Indigenous Societies*, ed. David Arnold (Delhi: Oxford University Press, 1989), 149–71.

59. P. C. H. Snow, *Report on the Outbreak of Bubonic Plague*, 18–19.

60. Ibid., 213.

61. Partha Chatterjee, "Two Poets and Death: On Civil and Political Society in the Non-Christian World," in *Questions of Modernity*, ed. Timothy Mitchell (Minneapolis: University of Minnesota Press), forthcoming.

62. "A Discourse on the Sanitary Improvement of Calcutta, By Dr. Chuckerbutty," in Bethune Society, *Selections from the Bethune Society's Papers* (Calcutta: P. S. O'Rozario and Co., 1854), 52–53. Kanny Loll Dey (Kanai Lal Dey), also a doctor and a teacher at the Calcutta Medical College, struck a similar theme in describing the Hindu body housed in dwellings that were not far from being "little black holes"—crowded, unclean, and full of noxious air. See his *Hindu Social Laws and Habits viewed in Relation to Health* (Calcutta: R. C. Lepage & Co., 1866).

63. Gobind Chunder Dhur in his *The Plague: Being a Reprint of Letters Published in the Indian Mirror for Allaying Popular Alarm and Conciliating the People to the Action of the Authorities* (Calcutta: Sanyal & Co., 1898), for example, advised the government to practice moderation in its policies of segregating and hospitalizing plague victims while asking "my own countrymen" to follow the advice of the health officer (2).

64. Thus, M. A. Mulraj's *A Sanitary Primer. Being an Elementary Treatise on Personal Hygiene, For the use of Indian Schools and General Public* (Allahabad: Victoria Press, 1879), one of several pamphlets of its kind, extolled the virtues of a science of hygiene based on facts about the population derived from the registration of births and deaths (2).

65. M. L. Dhingra, *The Science of Health for the Public in India showing how health may be preserved, disease prevented, and life prolonged* (Allahabad: The Pioneer Press, 1900), ii.

66. Arnold, *Colonizing the Body*, 9.

67. U. N. Mukerji, *Medical Practice in Bengal* (Calcutta: S. Lahiri & Co., 1907), 2–7.

68. Ibid., 38.

69. Jadu Nath Ganguli, *A National System of Medicine for India* (Calcutta: Beni Madhav Ganguli, 1911), 2–3.

70. Mahendralal Sircar, *A Sketch of the Treatment of Cholera* (Calcutta: Anglo-Sanskrit Press, 1870), iv. On Sircar's account of his conversion to homeopathy and the controversy it generated, see Ramogopal Sanyal, ed., *Reminiscences and Anecdotes of Great Men of India* (Calcutta, 1894, reprint, Calcutta: Riddhi-India, 1984), 55–56.

71. For example, Prem Bihari Mathur's *Plague-Panacea or a Pamphlet on Plague and its Remedies* (Agra: Damodar Printing Works, 1907) recounts how the author established a dispensary to treat plague victims, using "Greek, Indian, and Homeopathic systems of treatment" (46–56). Unlike state-sponsored sanitary primers, such as J. M. Cunningham's *A Sanitary Primer for Indian Schools*

(Lahore: Arya Press, 1882), Indians commonly invoked homeopathy, *ayurveda*, and *yunani*. See B. B. Biswas, *Half-Hour with Plague* (Calcutta: n.p., 1907): and Rai Bahadur Lala Baijnath, *The Plague in India: Its Causes, Prevention and Cure* (Meerut: Vaishya Hitkari Office, 1905).

72. See, for examples, *Pānchāl Panditā*, [Bilingual] 4:1 (November 15, 1900), 4:3 (January 15, 1901), and 4:4 (February 15, 1901), 4:6 (April 15, 1901), and 4:7 (May 15, 1901).

73. These are noted in Shaligram Srivastava, *Prayāg Pradeep* [Hindi], (Allahabad: Hindustani Academy, 1937), 161.

74. Yashoda Devi, *Grihini Kartayvashāstra, Ārogyashāstra arthāt Pākshāstra* [Hindi] 3rd ed. (Allahabad: Hitaishi Yantrālaya, 1924).

75. Ibid., 47–66 passim.

76. Pandit Jwala Prasad Jha, *Chromopathy or the Science of Healing Diseases by Colours* (Madras: Theosophical Book-Depot, 1912).

77. Milind Wakankar, "Body, Crowd, Identity: Genealogy of a Hindu Nationalist Ascetics," *Social Text* 45 (Winter 1995), 46.

78. See chapter 3.

79. M. K. Gandhi, *Autobiography: The Story of My Experiments with Truth*, trans. Mahadev Desai (New York: Dover, 1983), 16–20.

80. John Roseselli, "The Self-Image of Effeteness: Physical Education and Nationalism in Nineteenth-Century Bengal," *Past and Present* 86 (February, 1980): 121–48. Milind Wakankar's "Body, Crowd, Identity," contains an insightful discussion of this physical culture in the context of governmentality.

81. Swami Dayananda Sarasvati, *Satyārth Prakāsh*, 44–45, 58–68.

82. Yashoda Devi, *Ārogya Vidhān: Vidyārthi Jīvan* [Hindi] (Allahabad: Stree Aushadhālaya Press, 1929), 2–4.

83. Ibid., 17–18, 21–23.

84. For a concise description of the history of "masturbatory hypothesis," see E. H. Hare, "Masturbatory Insanity: The History of an Idea," *The Journal of Mental Science* 108:452 (January 1962), 2–25. I owe this reference to Elizabeth Lunbeck.

85. Ibid., 43–47.

86. On the medicalization of *brahmacharya*, cf. Joseph S. Alter, "Celibacy, Sexuality, and the Transformation of Gender into Nationalism in North India," *Journal of Asian Studies* 53:1 (February 1994), 45–66.

87. Gandhi, *A Guide to Health*, 64.

88. Ibid., 70.

89. M. K. Gandhi, *Self-Restraint Versus Self-Indulgence* (Navjivan: Ahmedabad, 1933), 83–85. This quotation comes from Gandhi's article in Gujarati published originally in 1924 and translated and republished in this collection.

90. Bhikhu Parekh, *Colonialism, Tradition and Reform: An Analysis of Gandhi's Political Discourse* (New Delhi: Sage, 1989), 183.

91. Gandhi, *A Guide to Health*, 65.

92. Parekh, *Colonialism, Tradition and Reform*, 179–80, 182.

93. Partha Chatterjee, *The Nation and its Fragments: Colonial and Postcolonial Histories* (Princeton: Princeton University Press, 1993), 6, 9–10, 120–21.

CHAPTER SIX
TECHNOLOGIES OF GOVERNMENT

1. Jawaharlal Nehru, *The Discovery of India* (New York, 1946. reprint, Delhi: Oxford University Press, 1987), 396. Here Nehru described the work of the National Planning Committee established by the Congress in 1938.

2. M. Heidegger, "The Question Concerning Technology," in *Martin Heidegger: Basic Writings*, ed., David Farrell Krell (New York: Harper, 1993), 320, 322.

3. Ibid., 323.

4. Langdon Winner's concept of technological politics captures something of my notion of the encoding of power in technology. See his *Autonomous Technology: Technics-out-of-Control as a Theme in Political Thought* (Cambridge, Mass.: MIT Press, 1977), particularly chapters 5 and 6. See also his "Do Artifacts have Politics?" *Daedalus* 109:1 (Winter 1980): 121–36. I am grateful to my colleague Michael S. Mahoney for drawing my attention to Winner's work and for helping me to think through the question of technology and politics.

5. Minute by Dalhousie, February 28, 1856, cited in Ramsay Muir, *The Making of British India, 1756–1858* (Manchester: Manchester University Press, 1915), 365.

6. Unless stated otherwise, the information on irrigation is drawn from the following studies: E. W. C. Sandes, *The Military Engineer in India*, 2 vols. (Chatham: Institution of Royal Engineers, 1935), 2:5–26; Daniel R. Headrick, *The Tentacles of Progress: Technology Transfer in the Age of Imperialism, 1850–1940* (New York: Oxford University Press, 1988), 176–96; Elizabeth Whitcombe, "Irrigation," in *The Cambridge Economic History of India* (Cambridge: Cambridge University Press, 1982), 2:677–737; and Ian Stone, *Canal Irrigation in India: Perspectives on Technological Change in a Peasant Economy* (Cambridge: Cambridge University Press, 1984), 13–67.

7. This debate can be followed in Major-General Sir Arthur Cotton and Colonel Sir Proby T. Cautley, *The Ganges Canal: A Discussion Regarding the Projection and Present State of the Ganges Canal* (London: printed for private circulation, 1864); Major-General Sir Arthur Cotton, *Reply, by Major-General Sir Arthur Cotton to Colonel Sir Proby T. Cautley's "Disquisition" on the Ganges Canal* (London: printed for private circulation, 1864); Colonel Sir Proby T. Cautley, *Ganges Canal. A Valedictory Note to Major-General Sir Arthur Cotton, respecting the Ganges Canal* (London: printed for private circulation, 1864); and Major-

General Sir Arthur Cotton, *Reply to Sir Proby Cautley's Valedictory Note on the Ganges Canal* (London: printed for private circulation, 1865). An account of the debate is also found in Ian Stone, *Canal Irrigation in India*, 45–56.

8. David Gilmartin sketches the close connection between military security and the settling of the "wasteland" on the frontier through canal projects in the Indus basin in his "Scientific Empire and Imperial Science: Colonialism and Irrigation Technology in the Indus Basin," *Journal of Asian Studies* 53:4 (November 1994), 1127–49.

9. Government of India, *Report of the Indian Irrigation Commission 1901–03* (London: HMSO, 1903), 1:11.

10. Gilmartin, "Scientific Empire and Imperial Science," 1135. What follows is drawn from this study (1135–43).

11. Government of India, *Report of the Indian Irrigation Commission*, 1:102–03.

12. Ian J. Kerr, *Building the Railways of the Raj, 1850–1900* (Delhi: Oxford University Press, 1995), 4. Although scholars disagree on the amount, there is a general agreement that it was the largest single investment within the British Empire (4, 17–18).

13. See Kerr, *Building the Railways of the Raj*, for the information on railroad construction (30–31, 38), and its cost (19).

14. Daniel R. Headrick, *Tentacles of Progress: Technology Transfer in the Age of Imperialism, 1840–1940* (New York: Oxford University Press, 1988), 55.

15. Although the promoters had envisioned the railways primarily for transporting freight, the transportation of passengers became most of its business. Headrick, *Tentacles of Progress*, 55–58. See also, Edward Davidson, *The Railways of India: With an Account of their Rise, Progress, and Construction* (London: E & F. N. Spon, 1868), 40. For a recent account of the tunneling and bridge-building entailed by the railways, see Ian Derbyshire, "The Building of India's Railways: The Application of Western Technology in the Colonial Periphery, 1850–1920," in *Technology and the Raj: Western Technology and Technical Transfers to India*, ed. Roy Macleod and Deepak Kumar (Delhi and London: Sage, 1995), 177–215, particularly 190–200.

16. Davidson, *The Railways of India*, 96.

17. The information on the state's decisive role in the construction of railways is taken from John Hurd, "Railways," in *The Cambridge Economic History of India*, ed., Dharma Kumar (Cambridge: Cambridge University Press, 1982), 2: 741–43; Headrick, *Tentacles of Progress*, 62, 81–85; Derbyshire, "The Building of India's Railways," 185–90; and Kerr, *Building the Railways of the Raj*, chaps. 2 & 3.

18. Framjee R. Vicajee, *Political and Social Effects of Railways in India* (London: R. Clay & Sons, 1875), 15.

19. House of Commons, "Correspondence Lately Received from India on

Railway Undertaking in that Country," *Parliamentary Papers*, 1852–53, vol. 76, 481, paper 787, 114–15.

20. Davidson, *The Railway of India*, 369.

21. Rudyard Kipling, "The Bridge-Builders," in *The Day's Work* (New York: Doubleday & McClure, 1898), 7.

22. Vicajee, *Political and Social Effects of Railways in India*, 21.

23. See Michael Adas's *Machines as Measures of Men: Science, Technology, and Ideologies of Western Dominance* (Ithaca and London: Cornell University Press, 1989), 221–36 for a succinct discussion of railways as a representation of Western dominance.

24. G. W. Macgeorge, *Ways and Works in India: Being an Account of the Public Works in that Country from the Earliest Times up to the Present Day* (Westminster: Archibald Constable and Co., 1894), 10.

25. For telegraphs, see Saroj Ghose, "Commercial Needs and Military Necessities: The Telegraph in India," in *Technology and the Raj*, ed. Macleod and Kumar, 153–176; and Headrick, *Tentacles of Progress*, 119–22. Deepak Kumar's *Science and the Raj, 1857–1905* (Delhi: Oxford University Press, 1995), chaps. 3 and 4, provides an account of the state's sponsorship of and institutional role in geology, botany, forestry, agricultural research, and technical education.

26. IOLR: L/E/7/403, file 345, Revenue and Statistics Department, letter from the Government of India to Lord Hamilton, Secretary of State for India, January 27, 1898.

27. IOLR: L/E/7/413, File 85, Revenue and Statistics Department, letter from the Government of India to Lord Hamilton, Secretary of State for India, December 22, 1898.

28. Ibid., Resolution of the Government of India, dated August 28, 1902.

29. The history of the IAC and the BSA is treated more fully in Roy M. Macleod, "Scientific Advice for British India: Imperial Perceptions and Administrative Goals, 1898–1923," *Modern Asian Studies* 9:3 (1975), 343–84.

30. Unless noted otherwise, the information on this dispute is taken from Macleod, "Scientific Advice for British India," 365–71.

31. IOLR: L/E/7/669, File 684, enclosure no. 1.

32. Ibid., enclosure no. 4.

33. Ibid., letter from the Government of India, dated March 3, 1910.

34. Macleod, "Scientific Advice for British India," 370–71.

35. IOLR: L/E/7/412, file 2939, letter from the Government of India to the Secretary of State, dated October 21, 1897.

36. Ibid., letter from Denzil Ibbetson, Secretary, Government of India, dated October 13, 1897.

37. IOLR: L/E/7/855, file 8417, "Proceedings of the Indian Legislative Council," March 21, 1916.

38. Ibid., Resolution of Government of India, no. 3403, May 20, 1916.

39. East India (Industrial Commission), *Report of the Indian Industrial Commission, 1916–18* (London, HMSO, 1919) 1:1 (hereafter cited as IIC). For a detailed and insightful reading of the Industrial Commission's report and its proceedings, see Shiv Visvanathan, *Organizing for Science: The Making of an Industrial Research Laboratory in India* (Delhi: Oxford University Press, 1985), chap. 3.

40. *IIC*, 1: 77.

41. For the Commission's recommendations, see *IIC*, 1:229–42.

42. Ibid., 90.

43. Ibid., 75–91 on scientific services and 195–223 on imperial and provincial departments of industries.

44. Sudipta Kaviraj's *The Unhappy Consciousness: Bankimchandra Chattopadhyaya and the Formation of Nationalist Discourse in India* (Delhi: Oxford University Press, 1996), particularly chapter 4, tracks the ambivalent production of the nation in Bengal with remarkable acuity.

45. In this context, it is significant that Sudipta Kaviraj notes a complementary relationship between R. C. Dutt's *Economic History of India*, a canonical nationalist text of political economy, and his romantic novels that invoke and extend the image of the community. See Kaviraj, *The Unhappy Consciousness*, 113.

46. For the Cambridge school interpretation, see John Gallagher, Gordon Johnson, and Anil Seal, ed., *Locality, Province and Nation: Essays on Indian Politics* (Cambridge: Cambridge University Press, 1973).

47. Cf. Bipan Chandra, *The Rise and Growth of Economic Nationalism in India* (Delhi: People's Publishing House, 1966), chap. 1.

48. R. C. Dutt, *The Economic History of India under Early British Rule*, 2nd ed., vol. 1 of *The Economic History of India* (London: Kegan Paul, Trench, Trübner & Co., 1906), xiii (hereafter cited as *EHI*, I).

49. Dutt, *EHI*, I, 97.

50. Dutt, *The Economic History of India in the Victorian Age*, 2nd ed., vol. 2. of *The Economic History of India* (London: Kegan Paul, Trench, Trübner & Co., 1906), 600–01). (hereafter cited as *EHI*, II).

51. Ibid., 615.

52. *EHI*, I, xvi, xviii.

53. Ibid., 117–18.

54. For a discussion of the concept of village communities in colonial thought, see Bernard Cohn, "Notes on the History of the Study of Indian Society and Culture," in *Structure and Change in Indian Society*, ed. Milton Singer and Bernard Cohn (Chicago: Aldine, 1968); and Louis Dumont, "The 'village community' from Munro to Maine," *Contributions to Indian Sociology* 9 (1965), 67–89.

55. *EHI*, II, 89.

56. *EHI*, I, 131–32.

57. Ibid., 151.

58. *EHI*, II, 50.

59. *IIC*, 1: 247.

60. Ibid., 1: 248–49.

61. Ibid., 1: 261–62. See pages 264–75 for Malaviya's discussion of the role of education and industrialization in different European countries, United States, and Japan in comparison to India.

62. Ibid., 1:275.

63. Here I am indebted to Shiv Visvanathan's detailed examination of Malaviya's dissenting note to the report of the Commission. He identifies the following as its implicit arguments: "First, modern technology necessitates as a discipline a new linking of power and knowledge. It is the logic of technology which eventually reconstitutes in a new fashion the state and the school. Both exist in order to ensure an economy in the reproduction of industrial norms. The intersection of knowledge and power is further embodied in the isomorphy between the pedagogic state and the compulsory school. The link between knowledge and power is also revealed in the special status given to the notion of intelligence. It is no longer hereditary but an input to be fed in by the agency of the state. Intelligence becomes industrialized, standardized and productivity-linked in the new notion of personnel. It is the state which assumes responsibility for it through the school." Visvanathan, *Organizing for Science*, 48.

64. This compressed summary of Saha's career is based on Robert S. Anderson, *Building Scientific Institutions in India: Saha and Bhabha* (Montreal: Centre for Developing Area Studies, McGill University, 1975); and Santimay Chatterjee and Enakshi Chatterjee, *Meghnath Saha* (Delhi: National Book Trust, 1984). The latter also contains a full bibliography of Saha's writings.

65. "Science and Culture," *Science and Culture* 1:1 (June 1935), 1.

66. Ibid., 3–4.

67. "Problems of Industrial Development in India," *Science and Culture* 2:11 (May 1937), 529.

68. "Indian National Reconstruction and the Soviet Example," *Science and Culture*, 3:4 (October 1937), 188.

69. M. N. Saha, *Annual Address to the National Institute of Sciences in India* (Calcutta: National Institute of Sciences, 1938), 24. Another example that impressed Saha a great deal was the Tennessee Valley Authority (TVA). However, he believed that the TVA experiment could not be made use of just by hiring engineers to study it and then replicate it, because the TVA represented "a complete revolution in the attitude of the Government towards Regional Planning and the setting up of a form of Government almost quite unknown in this country." "Principles of Regional Planning," *Science and Culture* 10:5 (November 1944), 177. Drawing on the TVA model, Saha proposed a regional plan of

flood control, power generation, and navigation for the Damodar Valley in eastern India, and it was largely due to his efforts that the experiment of the Damodar Valley Corporation (DVC) was carried out. See M. N. Saha and K. Ray, "Planning for the Damodar Valley," *Science and Culture* 10:1 (July 1944), 20–33.

70. "Address of the Congress President—Mr. Subhas Chandra Bose," *Science and Culture* 4:3 (September 1938), 139.

71. M. Visvesvaraya, *Reconstructing India* (London: S. King & Son Ltd., 1920), v, 10–14, 17–32, 57–94.

72. M. Visvesvaraya, *Nation Building: A Five-Year Plan for the Provinces* (Bangalore: Bangalore Press, 1937).

73. Letter dated October 7, 1938, "Correspondence with Jawaharlal Nehru," M. N. Saha Papers, Nehru Memorial Museum and Library, New Delhi.

74. "The Indian Science Congress—Message from Pandit Jawaharlal Nehru," *Science and Culture* 3:7 (January 1938), 349.

75. Jawaharlal Nehru, "The Progress of Science" (Address to the National Academy of Sciences, at their Seventh Annual Meeting at Allahabad on March 5, 1938) in *Jawaharlal Nehru on Science and Society: A Collection of His Writings and Speeches*, ed. Baldev Singh (New Delhi: Nehru Memorial Museum and Library, 1988), 23–24.

76. For Nehru's statement, see National Planning Committee, *National Planning Committee: Being an Abstract of Proceedings and other particulars relating to the National Planning Committee* (Bombay: National Planning Committee, 1939), 66. The note of guidance for subcommittees appears on 77. For more on the silencing of the Gandhian opposition to industrialization, see Chatterjee, *The Nation and Its Fragments: Colonial and Postcolonial Histories* (Princeton: Princeton University Press, 1993) 201–02.

77. K. T. Shah, ed., *Report. National Planning Committee* (Bombay: Vora & Co., 1949). The twenty-six reports by subcommittees were published during 1947–49.

78. Chatterjee, *The Nation and Its Fragments*, 202. Nehru described the experience of working in the planning committee as "soothing and gratifying," and in "pleasant contrast to the squabbles and conflicts of politics." Nehru, *The Discovery of India*, 399.

79. Nehru, *The Discovery of India*, 515–17.

CHAPTER SEVEN
A DIFFERENT MODERNITY

1. M. K. Gandhi, *Hind Swaraj or Indian Home Rule* (Natal, South Africa, 1910; reprint, Ahmedabad: Navjivan Publishing House, 1938), 34, 38.

2. Partha Chatterjee, *The Nation and Its Fragments: Colonial and Postcolonial Histories* (Princeton: Princeton University Press, 1993) 4–6.

3. Ibid., 11.

4. This is argued at length in Chatterjee's *Nationalist Thought and the Colonial World: A Derivative Discourse?* (London: Zed Books, 1986), chap. 5.

5. See Dhruv Raina and S. Irfan Habib, "The Unfolding of an Engagement: 'The Dawn' on Science, Technical Education and Industrialization: India, 1896–1912," *Studies in History*, n.s., 9:1 (1993), 87–117. Analyzing the writings in the journal *The Dawn* and writings of the nationalists organized around the national education movement, Raina and Habib show how these mounted a sharp critique of Western industrialism and projected the Indian artisan, whose indigenous art was to be supplemented by training in modern technology, as a counterpoint to the exploited and militant European industrial worker.

6. Jawharlal Nehru, *The Discovery of India* (New York, 1946; reprint, Delhi: Oxford University Press, 1989), 50. What follows, unless indicated otherwise, is based on pages 49–68, where Nehru explains his quest for India.

7. Ibid., 562–63.

8. Ibid., 392.

9. Ibid., 382.

10. Ibid., 520.

11. Ibid., 564.

12. Ibid., 565.

13. Ibid., 298–308 passim.

14. Ibid., 514.

15. Ibid., 508–09.

16. Ibid., 506.

17. Ibid., 554.

18. Ibid., 559.

19. Ibid., 520.

20. Etienne Balibar, "The Nation Form: History and Ideology," in *Race, Nation, Class: Ambiguous identities*, ed. Etienne Balibar and Immanuel Wallerstein (New York: Verso, 1991), 92.

21. Gandhi, *Hind Swaraj*, 47.

22. M. K. Gandhi, *Collected Works of Mahatma Gandhi* (Delhi: Publications Division, 1958–), vol. 25:251.

23. M. K. Gandhi, *Satyagraha in South Africa*, trans. Valji Govindji Desai (1928; reprint, Ahmedabad: Navjivan Publishing, 1972), 85.

24. Gandhi, *Hind Swaraj*, 38.

25. Ibid, 41. Gandhi wrote in a letter to Henry Polak: "It is not the British people who are ruling India, but it is modern civilisation, through its railways, telegraphs, telephones, and almost every invention which has been claimed to

be a triumph of civilisation. . . . If British rule was replaced tomorrow by Indian rule based on modern methods, India would be no better, except that she would be able then to retain some of the money that is drained away to England; but, then, India would become a second or fifth edition of India or America." Gandhi, *Collected Works*, 9:478–81.

26. Gandhi, *Hind Swaraj*, 93–94.

27. Ashis Nandy, "From outside the Imperium: Gandhi's Cultural Critique of the West," in *Traditions, Tyranny, and Utopias: Essays in the Politics of Awareness* (Delhi: Oxford University Press, 1987), 127–62.

28. Gandhi, *Collected Works*, 64:118.

29. Ibid., 25:251.

30. Gandhi, *Hind Swaraj*, 50–51, 53.

31. Bhikhu Parekh argues that "Gandhi's political thought thus more or less completely bypassed the characteristic nature and vocabulary of European nationalism, and conceptualised the Indian struggle for independence in a non-nationalist and non-national language." Bhikhu Parekh, *Gandhi's Political Philosophy: A Critical Examination* (London: Macmillan, 1989), 194. Gandhi, to be sure, did define India in the language of European nationalism, but to say that he viewed Indian independence in non-nationalist terms is to assume that the conception of India as a plural civilization consisting of different communities stood opposed to the idea of a people. In fact, Gandhi used both descriptions for India: a nation that was also a civilization; Indians were a people with a distinct (Hindu) civilizational ethos.

32. Cf. Partha Chatterjee, *Nationalist Thought and the Colonial World*, chap. 4.

33. Gandhi, *Hind Swaraj*, 30.

34. Gandhi, *Collected* Works, 68:265.

35. Ibid., 85:32–34.

36. This is how Chatterjee interprets Gandhi's appropriation by modern bourgeois nationalism. See his *Nationalist Thought and the Colonial World*, 101.

37. The interpretation that follows owes a great deal to discussions with Aamir Mufti.

38. Gandhi, *Hind Swaraj*, 46.

39. Gandhi, *Collected Works*, 81:319–21.

40. Jawaharlal Nehru, *Selected Works of Jawaharlal Nehru*, ed. S. Gopal (Delhi: Orient Longman, 1981), 14:554–57.

41. Gandhi, *Collected Works*, 82:71–72.

CHAPTER EIGHT
DIVIDED LOVE

1. Rabindranath Tagore, *Nationalism* (London, 1917; reprint, Calcutta: Rupa, 1992), 57–59.

2. Theodor Adorno, *Minima Moralia*, trans. E. F. N. Jephcott (London: NLB, 1974), 52.

3. Ibid., 52–53.

4. Friedrich Nietzsche, *The Use and Abuse of History*, trans. Adrian Collins, 2nd rev. ed. (Indianapolis: Bobbs-Merrill, 1957), 21.

Bibliography

UNPUBLISHED PRIMARY SOURCES

India Office Library and Records, London

Government of India. Department of Agriculture, Revenue and Commerce (Industrial Arts, Museums, Exhibitions) Proceedings.

Government of India. Department of Revenue and Agriculture (Museums and Exhibitions) Proceedings.

Government of India. Economic Department Proceedings.

Government of Bengal. Financial Department (Industry and Science) Proceedings.

Government of Bengal. Statistical Department (Industry and Science) Proceedings.

Mss.Eur.178. Diary of Monorama Bose.

National Archives of India, New Delhi

Government of India. Home (Public) Proceedings.

Nehru Memorial Museum and Library, New Delhi

M. N. Saha Private Papers.

St. Xavier's College Library, Calcutta

Annals of St. Xavier's College, Calcutta, 1835–1935. Typescript compiled by A. Verstreten.

PUBLISHED PRIMARY SOURCES

Official Publications

Bryden, James L. *Epidemic Cholera in the Bengal Presidency: A Report on the Cholera of 1866–68, and its relation to the Cholera of Previous Epidemics.* Calcutta: Superintendent of Government Printing, 1869.

Central Museum, Lahore. *Report on the Working of the Lahore Museum.* 1892–1935. Annual Series. Lahore: Government Printing.

Couchman, M. E. *Account of Plague Administration in the Bombay Presidency from September 1896 until May 1897.* Bombay: Government Central Press, 1897.

East India Industrial Commission. *Report of the Indian Industrial Commission, 1916–18.* London, HMSO, 1919.

Government of Bengal. *Indian Industrial and Agricultural Exhibition, 1906–07. Catalogue of Exhibits of the Bengal Agricultural Department.* Calcutta: Bengal Secretariat Press, 1907.

Government of Bengal. *Report on the Calcutta Medical Institutions.* 1871–1900. Annual series. Calcutta: Bengal Secretariat Press.

———. *Record of Cases Treated in the Mesmeric Hospital, From June to December 1847: With Reports of the Official Visitors.* Calcutta: Military Orphan Press, 1847.

———. *Report of the Commissioner Appointed under Section 28 of Act IV B.C. of 1876 to Enquire into Certain Matters connected with the Sanitation of the Town of Calcutta.* Calcutta: Bengal Secretariat Press, 1885.

———. *Report of the Smallpox Commissioners.* Calcutta: Military Orphan Press, 1850.

———. *Selections from the Records of the Bengal Government,* no. 22. Calcutta: Calcutta Gazette, 1855.

Government of Bombay. *Selections from the Records of the Bombay Government, new series, no. 83. Report on the Government Central Museum and on the Agricultural and Horticultural Society of Western India for 1863. With Appendices, being the History of the Establishment of the Victoria and Albert Museum and of the Victoria Gardens, Bombay.* Bombay: Education Society's Press, 1864.

———. *Supplement to the Account of Plague Administration in the Bombay Presidency from September 1896 till May 1897.* N.p., n.d.

Government of India. *The Conference of Orientalists including Museums and Archaeology Conference held at Simla, July 1911.* Simla: Government Central Branch Press, 1911.

———. *Minute by the Right Honourable the Governor-General* [Lord Auckland]. [Delhi]:n.p., 1840.

———. *Proceedings of the First All-India Sanitary Conference.* Calcutta: Government Printing, 1912.

———. *Report of the Commissioners appointed to Inquire into the Cholera Epidemic of 1861 in North India.* Calcutta: Government Printing, 1862.

———. *Report of the Nagpore Exhibition of Arts, Manufactures and Produce, December 1865.* Nagpore: Central Provinces Printing Press, n.d.

———. *Report on the Conference as regards Museums in India Held at Calcutta on Dec. 27th to 31st, 1907.* Calcutta: Superintendent, Government Printing, 1908.

Government of Madras. *Administration Report of the Government Central Museum,* 1890–1935. Annual Series. Madras: Government Press.

———. *Report of the Committee on Indigenous Systems of Medicine.* 2 vols. Madras: Office of the Committee on the Indigenous Systems of Medicine, 1923.

———. *Selections from the Records of the Madras Government, no. 32A. Report on the Agricultural Exhibition in the Provinces in the Year 1856.* Madras: Asylum Press, 1856.

————. *Selections from the Records of the Madras Government, no. 50. Report on the Agricultural Exhibition in the Provinces in the Year 1857.* Madras: Asylum Press, 1858.

————. *Selections from the Records of the Madras Government, no. 29. Report Upon the Government Central Museum and the Local Museums in the Provinces For the Year 1855–56 with Appendices.* Madras: Asylum Press, 1857.

————. *Selections from the Records of the Madras Government, no. 45. Report on the Agricultural Exhibitions in the Provinces in the Year 1856.* Madras: Fort St. George Gazette Press, 1858.

Great Britain. *Memorandum on Measures Adopted for Sanitary Improvements in India upto the end of 1867; together with Abstracts of the Sanitary Reports hitherto forwarded from Bengal, Madras, and Bombay.* London: HMSO, 1868.

————. *Report on Measures Adopted for Sanitary Improvements in India during the year 1868, and upto the month of June 1869; together with Abstracts of Sanitary Reports for 1867 forwarded from Bengal, Madras, and Bombay.* London: HMSO, 1869.

————. *Report on Measures Adopted for Sanitary Improvements in India, from June 1869 to June 1870; together with abstracts of Sanitary Reports for 1868 forwarded from Bengal, Madras, and Bombay.* London: HMSO, 1870.

Great Britain. House of Commons. "Correspondence Lately Received from India on Railway Undertaking in that Country." *Parliamentary Papers 1852–53*, Vol. 76, 481, paper 787.

————. "Report of the Commissioners Appointed to Inquire into the Sanitary State of the Army in India." *Parliamentary Papers, 1863.* Vol. 19, part 1.

Indian Irrigation Commission. *Report of the Indian Irrigation Commission 1901–03.* London: HMSO, 1903.

Lewis, T. R., and D. D. Cunningham, *Cholera in relation to Certain Physical Phenomena.* Calcutta: Superintendent of Government Printing, 1878.

Provincial Museum Committee, Lucknow. *Letter from the President, Provincial Museum Committee, Lucknow, dated 5th June, 1886.* N.p., n.d.

Snow, P. C. H. *Report on the Outbreak of Bubonic Plague in Bombay, 1896–97.* Bombay: Times of India, 1897.

Contemporary Books, Pamphlets, Reports

Multum in Parvo or Morality, Religion, Sociology and Science. Chingleput and Trichinopoly: Indian Press & South Indian Times, 1894.

————. *Vedanta—The Philosophy of Science.* Chittur: Victoria Jubilee Press, 1903.

————. *Godward Ho!* Tanjore: V. Govindan & Brothers, 1909.

————. *Religio-Scientific Philosophy or Religion of Science and Science of Religion.* Tanjore: Kalyansundaran Pown Press, 1910.

279

Aiya, N. K. Ramaswami. *The Strange Story of My Spiritual Evolution*. Madras: Theosophist Office, 1910.

Ali, Moulvi Arshad, ed. *A Report on Pagla Mian's Mela with Agricultural and Industrial Exhibition*. Feni, Noakhali: published by the editor, 1915.

Aligarh Scientific Society. *Proceedings of the Scientific Society*. Ghazeepore: printed at Syed Ahmud's private press, 1864.

Arya Pratinidhi Sabha. *The Rules and the Scheme of Studies of the Proposed Gurukula Sanctioned by the Arya Pratinidhi Sabha*. Lahore: Mufid-'i'- am Press, 1899.

Asiatic Society. *Proceedings of the Asiatic Society of Bengal, January to December, 1866*. Calcutta: Baptist Mission Press, 1867.

———. *Proceedings of the Asiatic Society of Bengal for November, 1867* (Calcutta: Baptist Mission Press, 1868), 157–62.

———. *Proceedings of the Asiatic Society of Bengal, January to December, 1868* (Calcutta: Baptist Mission Press, 1869), 29–31.

Baijnath, Rai Bahadur Lala. *The Plague in India: Its Causes, Prevention and Cure*. Meerut: Vaishya Hitkari Office, 1905.

Banerjea, Rev. K. M. *A Lecture Read Before the Bethune Society on February 13, 1868*. Calcutta: Thacker, Spink and Co., 1868.

Banerjea Manindranath. "On the Ancient Hindu Conception of Ether." *Proceedings of the Indian Association for the Cultivation of Science* 1 (1915): 53–62.

Behar Scientific Society. *Proceedings of the Behar Scientific Society*. Calcutta: Thacker, Spink, & Co., 1868–71.

Benaras Institute. *The Transactions of the Benaras Institute for the Session 1864–65*. Benaras: Medical Hall Press, 1865.

Bengal Social Science Asociation. *Transactions of the Bengal Social Science Association*. 6 vols. Calcutta: City Press, 1867–78.

Bethune Society. *Selections from the Bethune Society's Papers*. Calcutta: P. S. O'Rozario and Co., 1854.

———. *Selections from the Bethune Society Papers*. Calcutta: Stanhope Press, 1857.

———. *Minutes of Proceedings of the Bethune Society For the Session Ending April 21st 1870*. Calcutta: Stanhope Press, 1870.

Bhatt, Omkar. *Bhugolsār* [Hindi]. Agra: Agra School Book Society, 1841.

Bhishagratna, Kaviraj T. S. Ram. *In Defense of Ayurveda (An Answer to the Attack of Ayurveda by Dr. T. M. Nadir, M.D.)* Cachinnate: Manoranjini Press, 1909.

Biswas, B. B. *Half-Hour with Plague*. Calcutta: n.p., 1907.

Blavatsky, H. P. *The Secret Doctrine: The Synthesis of Science, Religion, and Philosophy*, 5th ed. 6 vols. Wheaton, Ill.: Theosophical Press, 1945.

———. *Occult or Exact Science*. H. P. Blavatsky Series, no. 19. Bangalore: Theosophical Company, 1984.

Bose, Jagadish Chandra. *Literature and Science: the Substance of the Presidential*

Address Given in Bengali by Prof. J. C. Bose to the Literary Conference at Mymensing, April 14, 1911. Calcutta: n.p., 1911.

British Indian Association. *The British Indian Association, Behar*. N.p., n.d..

Burra Bazar Family Literary Club. *The Seventeenth Anniversary Report of the Burra Bazar Family Literary Club, Established in 1857, with the Abstracts of Anniversary Address and other Lectures*. Calcutta: Calcutta Press, 1874.

Cautley, Colonel Sir Proby T. *Ganges Canal. A Valedictory Note to Major-General Sir Arthur Cotton, respecting the Ganges Canal*. London: printed for private circulation, 1864.

Chattopadhyaya, Bankimchandra. "Mill, Darwin, and Hinduism." In *Sociological Essays*. Trans. and ed. S. N. Mukherjee and Marian Maddern. Calcutta: Rddhi-India, 1986.

Chaudhary, Shaukat Rai. *Ayurveda Ka Vaigyanik Swaroop* [Hindi]. Kangri: Gurukul Yantralaya, 1918.

Cotton, Major-General Sir Arthur. *Reply, by Major-General Sir Arthur Cotton to Colonel Sir Proby T. Cautley's "Disquisition" on the Ganges Canal*. London: printed for private circulation, 1864.

———. *Reply to Sir Proby Cautley's Valedictory Note on the Ganges Canal*. London: printed for private circulation, 1865.

Cotton, Major-General Sir Arthur, and Colonel Sir Proby T. Cautley. *The Ganges Canal: A Discussion Regarding the Projection and Present State of the Ganges Canal*. London: printed for private circulation, 1864.

Cunningham, J. M. *A Sanitary Primer for Indian Schools*. Lahore: Arya Press, 1882.

Davidson, Edward. *The Railways of India: With an Account of their Rise, Progress, and Construction*. London: E & F. N. Spon, 1868.

Dev Samaj. *Religion of the Age*. Lahore: Dev Samaj, 1914.

Devi, Yashoda. *Grihini Kartayvashāstra, Ārogyashāstra arthāt Pākshāstra* [Hindi]. 3rd ed. Allahabad: Hitaishi Yantrālaya, 1924.

———. *Ārogya Vidhān: Vidyārthi Jīvan* [Hindi]. Allahabad: Stree Aushadhālaya Press, 1929.

Dey, Kanny Loll. *Hindu Social Laws and Habits viewed in Relation to Health*. Calcutta: R. C. Lepage & Co., 1866.

Dhingra, M. L. *The Science of Health for the Public in India showing how health may be preserved, disease prevented, and life prolonged*. Allahabad: The Pioneer Press, 1900.

Dhur, Gobind Chunder. *The Plague: Being a Reprint of Letters Published in the Indian Mirror for Allaying Popular Alarm and Conciliating the People to the Action of the Authorities*. Calcutta: Sanyal & Co., 1898.

Doss, Colly Coomar. *The Address Delivered before the meeting held at the School Society's School on 7th June, 1845 for the purpose of establishing the Calcutta Phrenological Society*. Calcutta: n.p., n.d.

Dutt, R. C. *The Economic History of India*. 2nd ed. 2 vols. London: Kegan Paul, Trench, Trübner & Co., 1906.

Esdaile, James. *Mesmerism in India and its Practical Application in Surgery and Medicine*. London: Longman, Brown, Green, and Longmans, 1846.

Ewart, Joseph. *A Digest of Vital Statistics of the European and Native Armies in India*. London: Smith, Elder and Co., 1859.

Gandhi, M. K. *Hind Swaraj or Indian Home Rule* Natal, South Africa: 1910. Reprint, Ahmedabad: Navjivan Publishing House, 1938.

———. *Satyagraha in South Africa*. Trans. Valji Govindji Desai. 1928. Reprint, Ahmedabad: Navjivan Publishing, 1972.

———. *A Guide to Health*. Trans. A. Rama Iyer. Madras: S. Ganesan, 1930.

———. *Self-Restraint Versus Self-Indulgence*. Navjivan: Ahmedabad, 1933.

———. *Collected Works of Mahatma Gandhi*. 90 vols. Delhi: Publications Division, 1958—.

———. *Autobiography: The Story of My Experiments with Truth*. Trans. Mahadev Desai. New York: Dover, 1983.

Ganguli, Jadu Nath. *A National System of Medicine for India*. Calcutta: Beni Madhav Ganguli, 1911.

Ghosh, Jogendra Chandra. *The Hindu Theocracy: How to Further its Ends*. Calcutta, S. K. Lahiri & Co., 1897.

Goode, S. W. *Municipal Calcutta: Its Institutions in their Origin and Growth*. Edinburgh: T. and A. Constable, 1916.

Indian Association for the Cultivation of Science. *Report of the Indian Association for the Cultivation of Science and Proceedings of the Science Convention for the year 1918*. Calcutta: Anglo-Sanskrit Press, 1920.

Indian Museum. *The Indian Museum 1814–1914*. Calcutta: Baptist Mission Press, 1914.

Jha, Pandit Jwala Prasad. *Chromopathy or the Science of Healing Diseases by Colours*. Madras: Theosophical Book-Depot, 1912.

Khan Bahadoor, Abdool Luteef. *A Discourse on the Nature, Objects, and Advantages of a Periodical Census, read at a meeting of the Bethune Society, held on the 5th of April, 1865*. Calcutta: Hurkaru Press, 1865.

———. *A Short Account of My Public Life*. Calcutta: W. Newman & Co., 1885.

Krishnamachari, U. P. *The Tribunal of Science Over Reformation Vs. Orthodoxy*. Benaras: published by the author, 1916.

Macgeorge, G. W. *Ways and Works in India: Being an Account of the Public Works in that Country from the Earliest Times up to the Present Day*. Westminster: Archibald Constable and Co., 1894.

Mahomedan Literary Society. *A Quarter Century of the Mahomedan Literary Society of Calcutta: A Resumé of its Work from 1863 to 1889 for the Jubilee of the Twenty-Fifth Year*. Calcutta: Stanhope Press, 1889.

Markham, S. F. and H. Hargreaves. *The Museums of India*. London: The Museums Association, 1936.

Martin, James Ranald. *Notes on the Medical Topography of Calcutta*. Calcutta: Huttman, 1837.

———. *The Influence of Tropical Climates on European Constitutions, Including Practical Observations on the Nature and Treatment of the Diseases of Europeans on their Return from Tropical Climates*. London: Churchill, 1856.

Mathur, Prem Bihari. *Plague-Panacea or a Pamphlet on Plague and its Remedies*. Agra: Damodar Printing Works, 1907.

Mitra, Kissory Chandra. *Hindu Medicine and Medical Education*. Calcutta: R. C. Lepage & Co., Metropolitan Press, 1865.

Mitra, Rajendralal. *A Scheme for the Rendering of European Scientific Terms in India*. Calcutta: Thacker, Spink & Co., 1877.

Mritak Śrāddha Khandan. Lahore: Virajanand Yantralaya, 1893.

Muir, Ramsay. *The Making of British India, 1756–1858*. Manchester: Manchester University Press, 1915.

Mukerji, Satya Chandra. *Allahabad in Pictures*. Allahabad: Indian Press, 1910.

Mukerji, U. N. *Medical Practice in Bengal*. Calcutta: S. Lahiri & Co., 1907.

Mulraj, M. A. *A Sanitary Primer: Being an Elementary Treatise on Personal Hygiene, For the use of Indian Schools and General Public*. Allahabad: Victoria Press, 1879.

Murti, G. Srinivasa. *Memorandum on "Science and the Art of Indian Medicine."* Delhi: Government of India, 1948.

Mutukumaraswami, V. *Symbolic Worship in India*. Rangoon: Mercantile Press, 1904.

National Planning Committee. *National Planning Committee: Being an Abstract of Proceedings and other particulars relating to the National Planning Committee*. Bombay: National Planning Committee, 1939.

Nehru, Jawaharlal. *The Discovery of India*. New York: 1946. Reprint, Delhi: Oxford University Press, 1989.

———. *Selected Works of Jawaharlal Nehru*. Vol. 14. Ed. S. Gopal. Delhi: Orient Longman, 1981.

———. *Jawaharlal Nehru on Science and Society: A Collection of His Writings and Speeches*. Ed. Baldev Singh. New Delhi: Nehru Memorial Museum and Library, 1988.

New Calcutta Directory, The. Calcutta: Military Orphan Press, 1856.

Olcott, Henry Steel. *Old Diary Leaves: The History of the Theosophical Society*. Vol. 2. 1900. Reprint, Madras: Theosophical Publishing House, 1974.

———. *Old Diary Leaves: The History of the Theosophical Society*. Vol. 6. 1935; Reprint, Madras: The Theosophical Publishing House, 1975.

Parkes, Edmund A. *A Manual of Practical Hygiene*. London: Churchill, 1864.

Prasad, Durga *A Triumph of Truth*. Lahore: Virajanand Press, 1889.

Ray, Binaybhushan. *Unnis Shataker Banglaya Vigyan Sadhana* [Bengali]. Calcutta: Subarnarekha, 1987.

Ray, P. C. *A History of Hindu Chemistry*. Rev. ed., 2 vols. Calcutta: Chuckervertty, Chatterjee & Co., 1904–25.

———. *Pursuit of Chemistry in Bengal* [Calcutta University Extension Lecture, delivered on 10th January 1916]. Calcutta: B. M. Gupta, 1916.

———. *Antiquity of Hindu Chemistry*. Calcutta: published by the printer, 1918.

———. *Pursuit of Chemistry in Ancient India*. Calcutta: published by the printer, 1918.

———. *Life and Experiences of a Bengali Chemist*. Calcutta: Chuckervertty, Chatterjee & Co., 1932.

Rogers, Leonard. *Small-Pox and Climate in India*. London: HMSO, 1926.

———. *The Incidence and Spread of Cholera in India; Forecasting and Control of Epidemics*. Calcutta: Thacker, Spink & Co., 1928.

Saha, M. N. *Annual Address to the National Institute of Sciences in India*. Calcutta: National Institute of Sciences, 1938.

Sahni, Lala Ruchi Ram. *Science and Religion: Being the Substance of a Lecture Given at the 32nd Anniversary of the Punjab Brahmo Samaj, Lahore*. Lahore: n.p., 1895.

Sandes, E. W. C. *The Military Engineer in India*. 2 vols. Chatham: Institution of Royal Engineers, 1935.

Sangit, Babulji Sadashiv. *An Essay in English read at the Pāthāre Prabhū Social Samaj Hall on Sunday 20th August 1905, Mr. Balaram Krishnanath Dhurandhar B.A., L.L.B., being in the chair*. Bombay: published by the author, 1906.

Sanyal, R. B. *Hours with Nature*. Calcutta: S. K. Lahiri & Co., 1896.

Sanyal, Ram Gopal. *Reminiscences and Anecdotes of Great Men of India*. Calcutta, 1894. Reprint, Calcutta: Riddhi-Indiia, 1984.

Sarasvati, Swami Dayananda. *Satyārth Prakāsh* [Hindi]. 1882, 2nd edition. Reprint, Delhi: Govindram Hasananda, 1963.

Seal, Brajendranath *The Positive Sciences of the Hindus*. London: 1915. Reprint, Delhi: Motilal Banarasidas, 1991.

Sen, Kaviraj Gananath. *Hindu Medicine: An Address Delivered at the Hindu University Foundation Ceremony at Benaras*. Madras: Ayurvedic Printing Works, 1916.

Sen, Nabin Chandra. *Āmār-Jāban* [Bengali] Vol. IV. Calcutta, 1912. Reprinted in *Nabin Chandra Rachnabali*, vol. 2, ed. Sajanikant Das, 428–37. Calcutta: Bangiya Sahitya Parishad, 1959.

Shah, K. T. ed. *Report. National Planning Committee*. Bombay: Vora & Co., 1949.

Śāstrārtha beech Ārya Samāj aur Pandit Ganesh Datta Śāstri [Hindi]. Lahore: Punjab Economical Press, 1896.

Singh, Shriman Amar. *The Advent of a Science-Grounded Religion for All Mankind.* Lahore: Dev Ashram, 1913.

Sircar, M. N. *Life of Peary Churn Sircar.* Calcutta: published by the author, 1914.

Sircar, Mahendralal. *On the Physiological Basis of Psychology.* Calcutta: Anglo-Sanskrit Press, 1870.

————. *A Sketch of the Treatment of Cholera.* Calcutta: Anglo-Sanskrit Press, 1870.

————. *The Projected Science Association for the Natives of India.* Calcutta: Anglo-Sanskrit Press, 1872.

Society for the Acquisition of General Knowledge. *Selection of Discourses Read at the Meetings of the Society for the Acquisition of General Knowledge.* 3 vols. Calcutta: Bishop's College Press, 1843.

Srivastava, Shaligram. *Prayāg Pradeep* [Hindi]. Allahabad: Hindustani Academy, 1937.

Swarg Men Subject Committee. Dinapore: Aryavarta Patra, 1895.

Tagore, Rabindranath. *Nationalism.* London, 1917. Reprint, Calcutta: Rupa, 1992.

Thornton, T. H. and J. L. Kipling. *Lahore.* Lahore: Government Civil Secretariat Press, 1876.

Thurston, Edgar. *Castes and Tribes of Southern India.* 7 vols. Madras: Government Press, 1909.

Turner, J. A. and B. K. Goldsmith. *Sanitation in India.* 2nd ed. Bombay: Times of India, 1917.

Vicajee, Framjee R. *Political and Social Effects of Railways in India.* London: R. Clay & Sons, 1875.

Vidyarthi, Guru Datta. *Wisdom of the Rishis or Complete Works of Pandita Guru Datta Vidyarthi.* Ed. Swami Vedananda Tirtha. Lahore: Arya Pustakalaya, n.d..

Visvesvaraya M., *Reconstructing India.* London: S. King & Son Ltd., 1920.

————. *Nation Building: A Five-Year Plan for the Provinces.* Bangalore: Bangalore Press, 1937.

Webb, Allan. *The Historical Relations of the Ancient Hindu with Greek Medicine in connection with the Study of Modern Medical Science in India: Being a General Introductory Lecture Delivered June 1850; at the Calcutta Medical College.* Calcutta: Military Orphan Press, 1850.

Contemporary Journals, Newspapers, Occasional Publications

Arogya-Jiwan [Hindi]
Arya Patrika
Asiatic Journal
Bengalee

Calcutta Monthly
Calcutta Review
Empress
Englishman
Friend of India
Hindi Pradeep [Hindi]
Hindoo Patriot
Kayastha Samachar
Nagari Pracharini Patrika [Hindi]
Pānchāl Panditā [Hindi and English]
Pioneer
Saraswati [Hindi]
Satya Prakash [Hindi]
Science and Culture
Vigyan [Hindi]

SECONDARY SOURCES

Adas, Michael. *Machines as the Measure of Men: Science, Technology, and Ideologies of Western Dominance*. Ithaca and London: Cornell University Press, 1989.

Adorno, Theodor. *Minima Moralia*. Trans. E. F. N. Jephcott. London: NLB, 1974.

Alter, Joseph S. "Celibacy, Sexuality, and the Transformation of Gender into Nationalism in North India." *Journal of Asian Studies* 53:1 (February 1994): 45–66.

Alvares, Claude. *Science, Development and Violence: The Twilight of Modernity*. Delhi: Oxford University Press, 1992.

Anderson, Benedict. *Imagined Communities*. London: Verso, 1983.

Anderson, Robert S. *Building Scientific Institutions in India: Saha and Bhabha*. Montreal: Centre for Developing Area Studies, McGill University, 1975.

Andrews, C. F. *Zaka Ullah of Delhi*. London, 1929. Reprint, Lahore: Universal Books, 1976.

Arnold, David. "Medical Priorities and Practice in Nineteenth-Century British India." *South Asia Research*, 5:2 (1985): 167–83.

———. *Colonizing the Body: State Medicine and Epidemic Disease in Nineteenth-Century India*. Delhi: Oxford University Press, 1993.

Arnold, Ken. "Cabinet for the Curious: Practicing Science in Early Modern English Museums." Ph.D. diss., Princeton University, 1991.

Bala, Poonam. *Imperialism and Medicine in Bengal*. New Delhi: Sage, 1991.

Balibar, Etienne. "The Nation Form: History and Ideology." In *Race, Nation, Class: Ambiguous Identities*, ed. Etienne Balibar and Immanuel Wallerstein, 86–106. New York: Verso, 1991.

Ballhatchet, Kenneth. *Race, Sex, and Class under the Raj: Imperial Attitudes and Policies and their Critics.* London: Weidenfield and Nicolson, 1980.

Basalla, George. "The Spread of Western Science." *Science* 156 (1967): 611–22.

Bayly, C. A. *The Local Roots of Indian Politics: Allahabad 1880–1920.* Cambridge: Cambridge University Press, 1975.

Benjamin, Walter. *Illuminations.* Ed. Hanna Arendt. New York: Schocken Books, 1969.

Bennett, Tony. "The Exhibitionary Complex." *New Formations* 4 (Spring 1988): 73–102.

Bhabha, Homi K. "DissemiNation: Time, Narrative, and the Margins of the Modern Nation." *Nation and Narration*, ed. Homi K. Bhabha, 291–322. London and New York: Routledge, 1990.

———. "Of Mimicry and Man: The Ambivalence of Colonial Discourse." In *The Location of Culture*, 85–92. London and New York: Routledge, 1994.

———. "Signs Taken for Wonders: Questions of Ambivalence and Authority under a Tree outside Delhi, May 1817." In *The Location of Culture*, 102–22. London and New York: Routledge, 1994.

Bose, Nemai Sadhan. *The Indian Awakening and Bengal.* Calcutta: Firma K. L. Mukhopadhyaya, 1969.

Brass, P. "The Politics of Ayurvedic Education in India." In *Education and Politics in India* ed. S. H. Rudolph and L. I. Rudolph, 356–67. Cambridge, Mass.: Harvard University Press, 1972.

Breckenridge, Carol. "The Aesthetics and Politics of Colonial Collecting: India at World Fairs." *Comparative Studies in Society and History* 32:2 (1989), 195–215.

Bynum, W. F. *Science and the Practice of Medicine in the Nineteenth Century.* Cambridge: Cambridge University Press, 1994.

Catanach, I. J. "Plague and the Tensions of Empire: India, 1896–1918." In *Imperial Medicine and Indigenous Societies*, ed. David Arnold, 149–71. Delhi: Oxford University Press, 1989.

Chandra, Bipan. *The Rise and Growth of Economic Nationalism in India.* Delhi: People's Publishing House, 1966.

Chatterjee, Partha. *Nationalist Thought and the Colonial World—A Derivative Discourse?* London: Zed Books, 1986.

———. *The Nation and its Fragments: Colonial and Postcolonial Histories.* Princeton: Princeton University Press, 1993.

———. "The Disciplines of Colonial Bengal." In *Texts of Power: Emerging Disciplines in Colonial Bengal*, ed. Partha Chatterjee, 1–29. Minneapolis and London: University of Minnesota Press, 1995.

———. "Two Poets and Death: On Civil and Political Society in the Non-Christian World." In *Questions of Modernity*, ed. Timothy Mitchell. Minneapolis: University of Minnesota Press, forthcoming.

Chatterjee, Santimay and Enakshi Chatterjee. "Mahendra Lal Sircar: Darkness before Dawn." In *The Urban Experience: Calcutta*, ed. Pradip Sinha, 122–33, Calcutta: Riddhi-India, 1987.

———. *Meghnath Saha*. Delhi: National Book Trust, 1984.

Chattopadhyaya, Debiprasad. *Indian Philosophy: A Popular Introduction*. Delhi: People's Publishing House, 1964.

———. *Lokayata: A Study in Ancient Indian Materialism*. Delhi: People's Publishing House, 1968.

Cohn, Bernard. "Notes on the History of the Study of Indian Society and Culture." In *Structure and Change in Indian Society*, ed. Milton Singer and Bernard Cohn, 3–28. Chicago: Aldine, 1968.

Conrad, Joseph. *The Heart of Darkness*. 3rd ed. New York: W. W. Norton, 1988.

De S. K. *Bengali Literature in the Nineteenth Century, 1757–1857*. 2nd rev. ed. Calcutta: Firma K. L. Mukhopadhyaya, 1962.

Derbyshire, Ian. "The Building of India's Railways: The Application of Western Technology in the Colonial Periphery, 1850–1920." In *Technology and the Raj: Western Technology and Technical Transfers to India*, ed. Roy Macleod and Deepak Kumar, 177–215. Delhi and London: Sage, 1995.

Derrida, Jacques. *Of Grammatology*. Trans. Gayatri Chakravorty Spivak. Baltimore and London: Johns Hopkins University Press, 1976.

———. "Declarations of Independence." *New Political Science* 15 (Summer 1986): 7–15.

Dumont, Louis. "The 'village community' from Munro to Maine." *Contributions to Indian Sociology* 9 (1965): 67–89.

Eliot, T. S. *Four Quartets*. London: Faber and Faber, 1944.

Eyler, John M. *Victorian Social Medicine: The Ideas and Methods of William Farr*. Baltimore and London: Johns Hopkins Press, 1979.

Farquhar, J. N. *Modern Religious Movements in India*. New York: Macmillan, 1915.

Forbes, Geraldine. *Positivism in Bengal: A Case Study in the Transmission and Assimilation of an Ideology*. Calcutta: Minerva, 1975.

Foucault, Michel. *The Order of Things*. New York: Vintage, 1973.

———. *The History of Sexuality. Volume I: An Introduction*. Trans. Robert Hurley. New York: Vintage, 1980.

———. "Governmentality." In *The Foucault Effect: Studies in Governmentality*, ed. Graham Burchell et. al., 87–104. Chicago: University of Chicago Press, 1991.

Franco, Eli. *Perception, Knowledge and Disbelief: A Study of Jayarāśi's Scepticism*. Weisbaden: Steiner, 1987.

Gallagher, John, Gordon Johnson, and Anil Seal, ed. *Locality, Province and Nation: Essays on Indian Politics*. Cambridge: Cambridge University Press, 1973.

Ghose, Saroj. "Commercial Needs and Military Necessities: The Telegraph in India." In *Technology and the Raj*, ed. Roy Macleod and Deepak Kumar, 153–176. Delhi and London: Sage, 1995.

Gilmartin, David. "Scientific Empire and Imperial Science: Colonialism and Irrigation Technology in the Indus Basin." *Journal of Asian Studies* 53:4 (November 1994), 1127–49.

Greenhalgh, Paul. *Ephemeral Vistas: The Expositions Universelles, Great Exhibitions, and World's Fairs, 1851–1939*. Manchester: Manchester University Press, 1988.

Guha, Ranajit. "Dominance without Hegemony and Its Historiography." In *Subaltern Studies VI*, ed. Ranajit Guha, 210–309. Delhi: Oxford University Press, 1989.

Gupta Atulchandra, ed. *Studies in the Bengal Renaissance*. Jadavpur: The National Council of Education, Bengal, 1958.

Gupta, B. "Indigenous Medicine in Nineteenth-Century and Twentieth-Century Bengal." In *Asian Medical Systems: A Comparative Study*, ed. C. Leslie, 368–78. Berkeley and London: University of California Press, 1976.

Gupta, Bela Dutt. *Sociology in India*. Calcutta: Centre for Sociological Research, 1972.

Habib, S. Irfan. "Institutional Efforts: Popularization of Science in the Mid 19th Century." *Fundamenta Scientiae* 6:4 (1985): 299–312.

Habib S. Irfan and Dhruv Raina. "The Introduction of Scientific Rationality into India: A Study of Master Ramchandra—Urdu Journalist, Mathematician and Educationalist." *Annals of Science* 46 (1989): 597–610.

Hacking, Ian. *The Taming of Chance*. Cambridge: Cambridge University Press, 1990.

Hare, E. H. "Masturbatory Insanity: The History of an Idea." *The Journal of Mental Science* 108:452 (January 1962), 2–25.

Harrison, J. B. "Allahabad: A Sanitary History." In *The City in South Asia: Pre-Modern and Modern*, ed. Kenneth Ballhatchet and John Harrison, 167–95. London: Curzon Press, 1980.

Harrison, Mark. *Public Health in British India: Anglo-Indian Preventive Medicine 1859–1914*. Cambridge: Cambridge University Press, 1994.

Headrick, Daniel R. *The Tentacles of Progress: Technology Transfer in the Age of Imperialism, 1850–1940*. New York: Oxford University Press, 1988.

Heidegger, Martin. "The Question Concerning Technology." In *Martin Heidegger: Basic Writings*, ed. David Farrell Krell, 311–41. New York: Harper, 1993.

Hooper-Greenhill, Eilean, *Museums and the Shaping of Knowledge*. London: Routledge, 1992.

Horkheimer, Max, and Theodor Adorno. *Dialectic of Enlightenment*. Trans. John Cumming. New York: Herder and Herder, 1972.

289

Hurd, John. "Railways." In *The Cambridge Economic History of India*. Vol 2., ed. Dharma Kumar, 737–61. Cambridge: Cambridge University Press, 1982.

Jones, Kenneth W. *Arya Dharm: Hindu Consciousness in 19th-Century Punjab*. Berkeley and Los Angeles: University of California Press, 1976.

Jones, Kenneth W. *Socio-Religious Reform Movements in India*. Vol. 3, part 1 of *The New Cambridge History of India*. Cambridge: Cambridge University Press, 1989.

Jordens, J. F. T. *Dayananda Sarasvati: His Life and Ideas*. Delhi: Oxford University Press, 1978.

Kaviraj, Sudipta. *The Unhappy Consciousness: Bankimchandra Chattopadhyaya and the Formation of Nationalist Discourse in India*. Delhi: Oxford University Press, 1996.

Kejariwal, O. P. *The Asiatic Society of Bengal and the Discovery of India's Past 1784–1838*. Delhi: Oxford University Press, 1988.

Kerr, Ian J. *Building the Railways of the Raj, 1850–1900*. Delhi: Oxford University Press, 1995.

Kipling, Rudyard. "The Bridge Builders." In *The Day's Work*, 3–47. New York: Doubleday & McClure, 1898.

———. *Kim*. London, 1901. Reprint, Harmondsworth: Puffin Classics, 1987.

Klein, Ira. "Death in India." *Journal of Asian Studies* 32 (1973): 632–59.

———. "Urban Development and Death: Bombay City, 1870–1914." *Modern Asian Studies*, 20 (1986): 725–54.

Kopf, David. *British Orientalism and the Bengal Renaissance: The Dynamics of Indian Modernization, 1773–1835*. Berkeley: University of California Press, 1969.

———. *The Brahmo Samaj and the Shaping of the Modern Indian Mind*. Princeton: Princeton University Press, 1988.

Kumar, Deepak. *Science and the Raj, 1857–1905*. Delhi: Oxford University Press, 1995.

Kumar, Dharma ed. *The Cambridge Economic History of India*, Vol. 2. Cambridge: Cambridge University Press, 1982.

Latour, Bruno. *We Have Never Been Modern*. Cambridge, Mass.: Harvard University Press, 1993.

Lelyveld, David. *Aligarh's First Generation*. Princeton: Princeton University Press, 1978.

Leslie, C. "The Professionalization of Indigenous Medicine." In *Entrepreneurship and Modernization of Occupational Cultures in South Asia*, 216–42. Durham: DUPCSSA, 1973.

Lindberg, David C. *The Beginnings of Western Science: The European Scientific Tradition in Philosophical, Religious, and Institutional Context, 600 B.C. to A.D. 1450*. Chicago and London: University of Chicago Press, 1992.

Macleod, Roy M. "Scientific Advice for British India: Imperial Perceptions and Administrative Goals, 1898–1923." *Modern Asian Studies* 9:3 (1975): 343–84.

Macleod, Roy M. and Deepak Kumar, ed. *Technology and the Raj: Western Technology and Technical Transfers to India.* Delhi and London: Sage, 1995.

Madhava, Acharya. *Sarva-Darśana-Saṃgraha.* Trans. E. B. Cowell and A. E. Gough. London: K. Paul, Trench, Trubner, 1914.

Mcgregor, R. S. *Hindi Literature of the Nineteenth and Early Twentieth Centuries.* Wiesbaden: Otto Harrassowitz, 1974.

Mill, John Stuart. *On Liberty.* London, 1859. Reprint, Northbrook, Ill.: AHM Publishing, 1947.

Minault, Gail. "Sayyid Ahmad Dehlavi and the 'Delhi Renaissance'." In *Delhi through the Ages*, ed. Robert E. Frykenberg, 287–98, Delhi: Oxford University Press, 1986.

Misra, B. B. *The Indian Middle Classes.* London: Oxford University Press, 1961.

Mullaney, Steven. "Strange Things, Gross Terms, Curious Customs: The Rehearsal of Cultures in the Late Renaissance." In *Representing the English Renaissance*, ed. Stephen Greenblatt, 65–92. Berkeley: University of California Press, 1988.

Nandy, Ashis. *The Intimate Enemy: Loss and Recovery of Self under Colonialism.* Delhi: Oxford University Press, 1983.

———. "From outside the Imperium: Gandhi's Cultural Critique of the West." In *Traditions, Tyranny, and Utopias: Essays in the Politics of Awareness*, 127–62. Delhi: Oxford University Press, 1987.

———. "Introduction: Science as a Reason of State." In *Science, Hegemony and Violence: A Requiem for Modernity*, ed. Ashis Nandy, 1–23. Delhi: Oxford University Press, 1988.

Naraindas, Harish, "Poisons, Putrescence and the Weather: A Genealogy of the Advent of Tropical Medicine." *Contributions to Indian Sociology* n.s., 30:1 (1996): 1–35.

Nietzsche, Friedrich. *The Use and Abuse of History.* Trans. Adrian Collins 2nd rev. ed. Indianapolis: Bobbs-Merrill, 1957.

Oldenberg, Veena. *The Making of Colonial Lucknow.* Princeton: Princeton University Press, 1984.

Parekh, Bhikhu. *Colonialism, Tradition and Reform: An Analysis of Gandhi's Political Discourse.* New Delhi: Sage, 1989.

———. *Gandhi's Political Philosophy: A Critical Examination.* London: Macmillan, 1989.

Patairiya, Manoj Kumar. *Hindi Vigyan Patrakarita* [Hindi]. Delhi: Takshila Prakashan, 1990.

Pelling, Margaret. *Cholera, Fever and English Medicine 1825–1865.* Oxford: Oxford University Press, 1978.

Poddar, Arabinda. *Renaissance in Bengal: Quests and Confrontations*. Simla: Indian Institute of Advanced Study, 1970.

Pollock, Sheldon. "The Theory of Practice and the Practice of Theory in Indian Intellectual History." *Journal of the American Oriental Society* 105:3 (1985): 499–519.

Pollock, Sheldon. "From Discourse of Ritual to Discourse of Power in Sanskrit Culture." *Journal of Ritual Studies* 4:2 (Summer 1990): 317–45.

Prior, Katherine. "The Angry *Pandas:* Hindu Priests and the Colonial Government in the Dispersal of the Hardwar Mela in 1892." *South Asia* 16:1 (1993): 25–52.

Raina, Dhruv. "The Early Years of P. C. Ray: The Inauguration of the School of Chemistry and the Social History of Science (1885–1907)." Mss.

Raina, Dhruv. and S. Irfan Habib, "The Unfolding of an Engagement: 'The Dawn' on Science, Technical Education and Industrialization: India, 1896–1912." *Studies in History*, n.s. 9:1 (1993): 87–117.

Ramasubban, Radhika. "Imperial Health in British India, 1857–1900." In *Disease, Medicine, and Empire: Perspectives on Western Medicine and the Experience of European Expansion*, ed. Roy Macleod and Milton Lewis, 38–60. London and New York: Routledge, 1988.

Ray, Binaybhushan. *Unnis Shataker Banglaya Bigyan Sadhana* [Bengali]. Calcutta: Subarnarekha, 1987.

Raychaudhuri, Tapan. *Europe Reconsidered: Perceptions of the West in Nineteenth Century Bengal*. Delhi: Oxford University Press, 1988.

Roseselli, John. "The Self-Image of Effeteness: Physical Education and Nationalism in Nineteenth-Century Bengal." *Past and Present* 86 (February 1980): 121–48.

Rydell, R. W. *All the World's a Fair*. Chicago: University of Chicago Press, 1988.

Said, Edward. *Culture and Imperialism*. New York: Alfred A. Knopf, 1993.

Sanyal, Rajat. *Voluntary Associations and the Urban Public Life in Bengal 1815–1876*. Calcutta: Rddhi-India, 1980.

Sardar, Ziauddin, ed. *The Revenge of Athena: Science, Exploitation and the Third World*. London and New York: Mansell Publishing, 1988.

Sarkar, Sumit. "Rammohun Roy and the Break with the Past." In *Rammohun Roy and the Process of Modernization in India*, ed. V. C. Joshi, 46–68. Delhi: Vikas, 1975.

———. "Calcutta and the 'Bengal Renaissance'." In *Calcutta: The Living City*, Vol. 1, ed. Sukanta Chaudhuri, 95–105. Calcutta: Oxford University Press, 1990.

Scott, David. "Colonial Governmentality." *Social Text* 43 (Fall 1995) 191–220.

Sen, S. N. "Survey of Studies in European Languages. " In *History of Astronomy in India*, ed. S. N. Sen and K. S. Shukla, 50–67. New Delhi: Indian National Science Academy, 1985.

Sinha, P. *Nineteenth Century Bengal: Aspects of Social History.* Calcutta: Firma K. L. Mukhopadhyaya, 1965.

Smith, Brian K. *Reflections on Resemblance, Ritual, and Religion.* New York: Oxford University Press, 1989.

Dr. G. Srinivasamurti Foundation. "Dr. G. Srinivasamurti —A Memoir." In *The Doctor G. Srinivasamurti Birth Centenary,* 2–4. Madras and Bangalore: Dr. G. Srinivasamurti Foundation, 1987.

Srivastava, Premchandra, *Amrit Jayanti Samaroh Smarika.* Prayag: Vigyan Parishad, 1988.

Stille, Alexander. "The Ganges' Next Life." *The New Yorker,* January 19, 1998, 58–67.

Stoler, Ann Laura. *Race and the Education of Desire: Foucault's* "History of Sexuality" *and the Colonial Order of Things.* Durham: Duke University Press, 1995.

Stone, Ian. *Canal Irrigation in India: Perspectives on Technological Change in a Peasant Economy.* Cambridge: Cambridge University Press, 1984.

Suleri, Sara. *The Rhetoric of English India.* Chicago: University of Chicago Press, 1992.

Suntharalingam, R. *Politics and Nationalist Awakening in South India, 1852–1891.* Tucson: University of Arizona Press, 1974.

Tinker, H. R. *The Foundations of Local Self-Government in India, Pakistan and Burma.* London: The Athlone Press, 1954.

Visvanathan, Shiv. *Organizing for Science: The Making of an Industrial Research Laboratory in India.* Delhi: Oxford University Press, 1985.

Wakankar, Milind. "Body, Crowd, Identity: Genealogy of a Hindu Nationalist Ascetics." *Social Text* 45 (Winter 1995): 45–73.

Washbrook, D. A. *The Emergence of Provincial Politics: The Madras Presidency 1870–1920.* Cambridge: Cambridge University Press, 1976.

Whitcombe, Elizabeth. "Irrigation." In *The Cambridge Economic History of India,* ed. Dharma Kumar, 2:677–737. Cambridge: Cambridge University Press, 1982.

Winner, Langdon. *Autonomous Technology: Technics-out-of-Control as a Theme in Political Thought.* Cambridge, Mass.: MIT Press, 1977.

———. "Do Artifacts Have Politics?" *Daedalus* 109:1 (Winter 1980), 121–36.

Index

aborigines, 27–30
Adorno, Theodor, 5, 227
Advaita Vedantic philosophy, 252n.85
Agnihotri, Pandit Shiv Narayan, 76–77
agriculture, 188–90
Aiya, N. K. Ramaswami, 79–80, 252n.85
Ajaib-Gher. *See* Lahore Central Museum
Ali, Moulvi Arshad, 244n.59
Ali, Sayyid Imdad, 60, 248n.31
Aligarh Scientific Society, 61
Alipur Agricultural Exhibition, 25, 44
Allahabad Exhibition (1910–11), 23, 33
Allahabad University, 192, 197
All India Ayurvedic Conference, 256n.37
All India Board of Ayurvedic Education, 256n.37
Allopathy, 117, 147
ancestor worship, 86–87
Anderson, Benedict, 88, 201, 254n.8
anthropometry, 22, 45, 241n.12
anticolonialism, 179–83, 201–3, 224–26
Arnold, David, 126, 137–40, 145, 259n.2, 260n.12–14, 16, 262n.31, 263n.45, 264n.49, 53–54, 58, 265n.66
Arogya-Jiwan, 256n.38
Ârogya Vidhân: Vidyârthi Jîvan (Devi), 152
Arthur Road Hospital, 264n.58
Arya Samaj, 76–77, 80, 113, 255n.19; and religious reform, 86–87, 92, 106–9; and social reform, 95–96, 147–48
Asiatic Society. *See* Royal Asiatic Society of Bengal
astrology, 80, 108–9
astronomy, 65–69, 72–73
atman, 80–81, 83
Awakener of India, The, 79
ayurveda, 99–100, 102–5, 116–17, 129, 146–49, 152, 158, 256n.37, 257n.52, 266n.71

Baconian philosophy, 59
Baden-Powell, Baden Henry, 184
Balibar, Etienne, 213
Banerjea, K. M., 74
Bangadarshan, 57
Basalla, George, 245n.76
Behar Scientific Society, 60–61, 248n.31
Benaras Debating club, 60
Bengal Chemical and Pharmaceutical Works, 101, 116
Bengalee, 39
Bengal renaissance, 52–70
Bengal Social Science Association, 58
Benjamin, Walter, 49, 51, 254n.8
Bennett, Tony, 245n.74
Bentham, Jeremy, 125
Bernier, François, 189
Besant, Annie, 79, 252n.85
Bethune, John Drinkwater, 55
Bethune Society, 54–56, 74–75, 144
Bhabha, Homi K., 71, 258n.60
bhadralok, 53–60, 74, 80, 84, 99, 144, 248n.30
Bhâgvat, 65, 68
Bhargava, Saligram, 63
Bhaskaracharya, 65–68, 84
Bhatt, Omkar, 65–66, 68
Bhishagratna, Kaviraj T. S. Ram., 257n.52
Bhore Ghat, 167
Bhugolsâr (Bhatt), 64–69, 72–73, 75
Bible, 92, 229
biopower, 125, 157
black towns, 133
Blavatsky, Helena Petrovna, 77–78, 251n.72
"Blessings of Science, The," 49
Board of Scientific Advice (BSA), 172–75, 177
Bose, J. C., 80, 117, 191, 229
Bose, Monorama, 37–38